HEALTH INFORMATION
IN A CHANGING WORLD

HEALTH INFORMATION IN A CHANGING WORLD

Practical Approaches for Teachers, Schools, and School Librarians

W. Bernard Lukenbill and
Barbara Froling Immroth

AN IMPRINT OF ABC-CLIO, LLC
Santa Barbara, California • Denver, Colorado • Oxford, England

Library of Congress Cataloging-in-Publication Data

Lukenbill, W. Bernard.
Health information in a changing world : practical approaches for teachers, schools, and school librarians /
W. Bernard Lukenbill and Barbara Froling Immroth.
        p. cm.
    Includes bibliographical references and index.
    ISBN 978–1–59884–398–9 (acid-free paper) — ISBN 978–1–59884–399–6 (ebook)
1. Health education (Elementary) 2. Health education (Secondary) 3. Health education—Curricula.
4. Health education—Curricula—United States. 5. School librarian participation in curriculum planning.
6. Children—Health and hygiene—Information services. 7. Youth—Health and hygiene—Information
services. I. Immroth, Barbara Froling. II. Title.
LB1587.A3L85   2010
372.37—dc22   2010007505

ISBN: 978–1–59884–398–9
EISBN: 978–1–59884–399–6

14 13 12 11 10   1 2 3 4 5

This book is also available on the World Wide Web as an eBook.
Visit www.abc-clio.com for details.

Libraries Unlimited
An Imprint of ABC-CLIO, LLC

ABC-CLIO, LLC
130 Cremona Drive, P.O. Box 1911
Santa Barbara, California 93116-1911

This book is printed on acid-free paper ∞

Manufactured in the United States of America

This book is dedicated to our children and grandchildren and to all the children at the M. D. Anderson Hospital in Houston, Texas, who inspired this book.

Contents

List of Illustrations   xvii

Acknowledgments   xix

Introduction and Guide   xxi

1. Schools, Libraries, and Health Education   1
   The Role of Schools in Health Education   1
   Information and Health Literacy   3
   Defining Health Literacy   3
   What Is Skills-Based Health Education?   4
   Health Information and Education across the Curriculum   4
   Good Health through Curriculum Empowerment   5
     Skill-Based Learning and Curriculum Empowerment of Students   5
   How Can Skill-Based Concepts and Themes Be Introduced across   6
     the Curriculum?
     Teachable Health Concepts for Youth   6
     Teachable Health Themes   7
   Public Health and Education   7
   How Government Helps in Health: Health Care Information and Curriculum   8
     Development
   Help from the Nongovernmental Section   9
   Help from Hospitals and Clinics   10
   Help from For-Profit Companies   10
   Helpful Professional Guides to Health Information   10
     Reference and Background Sources   11

      Health Literacy and Information Skills   12
   Reflections   12
   Notes   12

2. Health Curriculum and Instruction   15
   Models for Curriculum and Instruction   15
   Major Curriculum Ideas and the Implications for Health School Libraries   15
      The Liberal Educator Curriculum: Education Is Transmission   16
      The Scientific Curriculum: Education Produces a Product   16
      The Developmental Curriculum: Learning Is Process   17
      The Social/Moral Curriculum: Education Is Social Change   17
   Curriculum, Collaboration, and Teamwork   18
   Instruction and Strategies: Theory and Design   19
      Instructional Design in Providing Health Information   19
      Instructional Design and Instructional Approaches   20
   Instructional Strategies for Health   20
      Demonstration Programs   20
      Home and Community Demonstrations and Extension Programs   20
      School Demonstrations   21
      Health Demonstrations   23
      Standard Lectures and Questioning as Instruction   23
      Types of Questions and Educational Reasons for Questioning   25
      Audiovisuals and Interactive Technology   25
      Field Trips and Visits   26
      The Virtual Field Trip   26
      Speaker Programs and Speaker Opportunities   27
      Distance, Online, and Audio-Visual Transmission   27
      Commercial, Community, and Cable Network Television and Radio   28
   Reflections   28
   Notes   29

3. Teaching and Holistic Health Information Literacy   31
   Teachers and School Librarians as Holistic Health Educators   32
   Major Issues in Holistic Health Education and Literacy   32
   Standards, Outcome Measures, and Assessments for Health Instruction   35
      Standards   35
      Assessments   35
      Approaches to Assessments   35
      Outcome Measures   36
      Examples of Outcome Measures in a Unit Entitled "Stereotype & Bias"   38
      Teaching with Textbooks   39
   Using Textbooks Effectively in Collaboration and Collection Development   40
   Instructional Centered Materials and Teacher-Librarian Collaboration   40

School Library Standards and Collaboration   41

Suggestions for Health Instructional Units   42

Helpful Resources   43

The For-Profit Consultant and Publisher   44

The Link between School Librarians and Health Literacy   45

Standards and Guidelines: Basic Elements in Planning Health Instruction   45

Integrating National Curriculum Standards into Health Instruction   48

  Music   48

  Art   48

  English and Foreign Language Arts   48

  Mathematics   49

  Science   49

  National Social Studies and History   49

  Physical Education and Health   49

  Technology and Information Literacy Standards (NETS)   49

  Business and Commerce   50

A Review of Basic Instructional Unit Design   50

Reflections   52

Notes   52

4. Searching for Health Information and Developing Library Use Skills   57

Basic Approaches to Searching   57

Health Information Needs   58

Information Literacy Strategies for Youth   59

Major Sources for Health Information   60

Accessing Information   61

  The Library Catalog   61

  The Web Page   62

Structure of Information in Databases for Online Searches   62

  Fields and Records   62

  Boolean Logic and Operations   63

  Venn Diagrams   63

  Truncations and Wildcards   63

  Phrase and Proximity Searching   63

  Controlled and Natural Language   64

  Subject Heading Lists and Thesauruses   64

  Field Searching   65

The Process of Searching   66

Collection Development Considerations for Health Databases   67

TexShare Guidelines and Principles for Access and Review   67

  Rationale for Selection of Materials   67

  Rationale for Challenged Materials   68

Health Databases   68

Selected Free Access Databases Available on the Internet   68
Selected Commercial Consumer Health Information   70
Library Accessible Databases   70
Health Literacy: Challenges to Holistic Health Information   71
Holistic Health Information Instructional Plan   72
Learning Outcomes   72
Questions and/or Activities (Adjust According to Age and Abilities) 73
Reference Materials for Health Information   76
Resources   76
Reflections   76
Notes   77

5. Materials for Health Instruction and Information   81
Making Good Selections   81
Criteria for Good Selection   83
Ensuring Information Quality   84
E-Health: Electronic Health Information for Youth and Their Caregivers 84
Selection Aids and Sources: Offering Access to Health Information 90
Health Books in Series and Films   94
Sources of Pamphlets and Brochures   96
Materials in Other Languages and Cultural Contexts   96
Resources for the Special Child and Parent Needs   96
Reflections   97
Notes   97

6. Literature, the Arts, Performance Activities, and Languages   99
A Brief Review and a Look Ahead   99
Building Health Units and Resources throughout the Curriculum   100
Part 1. Literature, Music, Drama, Biography   100
Literature and Drama   101
Literary Criticism Using Medical Fiction   101
Definitions and Approaches to Literary Criticism   101
Learning Outcomes   103
Questions and/or Activities (Adjust for Age and Abilities)   103
Response to Reading Medical Fiction   104
Literary Biography and Drama   105
Learning Outcomes   105
Questions and/or Activities (Adjust for Ages and Abilities)   106
Part 2. Performance Activities and Health: Music, Dance, Athletics 106
Classical Musicians and Their Health Challenges   107
Learning Outcomes   107
Questions and/or Activities (Adjust for Age and Abilities)   107

Musicians (Classical), Health, and Their Music   108
   Learning Outcomes   108
   Questions and/or Activities (Adjust for Age and Abilities)   108
Popular Music and Musical Theater   110
   Learning Outcomes   110
   Questions and/or Activities (Adjust for Age and Abilities)   110
Health Relationships and Issues Shared by Musicians, Athletes, and Dancers   111
   Learning Outcomes   111
   Questions and/or Activities (Adjust for Age and Abilities)   112
Musicians: Health Issues Affecting the Voice and Hearing   112
   Learning Outcomes   112
   Questions and/or Activities (Adjust for Age and Abilities)   112
Health Issues Affecting Dancers and Athletes   113
Biographies of Dancers and Athletes   113
   Learning Outcomes   113
   Questions and/or Activities (Adjust for Age and Abilities)   114
Part 3. Art and Health   114
Biographies of Artists   114
Art in Health Care and Evidence-Based Research   115
The Society for the Arts in Health Care   115
Using Art to Promote Health Awareness and Literacy   116
   Learning Outcomes   116
   Questions and/or Activities (Adjust for Age and Abilities)   117
Foreign Languages and Health Information   118
   Learning Outcomes (For All Language Levels)   118
   Questions and/or Activities (Adjust for Age and Abilities) (For All Language Levels)   119
Resources   128
Reflections   128
Notes   128

7. Connections to Good Health: Social and Behavioral Sciences, and Languages   131
   What Are the Connections to Health?   131
   Instructional Themes, Skill Sets, and Learning Outcomes in the   131
   Social Sciences
      Theme 1. Living Together and Social Dependency   131
      Theme 2. Living in, Preserving, and Protecting the Environment   132
      Theme 3. Rights and Duties of Citizenship   132
      Theme 4. Responsibility to Respect Diversity and Those in Adversity   132
      Theme 5. Health in a Social and Cultural Context   132
      Useful Skill Set   133
   The Social Base for Foreign Languages and Health Education: A Rationale   134
   Role of Government in Health   134
   Thematic and Holistic Health Instruction   135

Learning Outcomes 135
Learning Activities and/or Questions (Adjust for Age and Abilities) 136
Social and Historical Aspects of Illness 137
For Older Students (Grades 5–12) 137
For Younger Students (K–4) 141
Resources 142
Reflections 142
Notes 143

8. Connections: Health, Physical Education, Science, and Mathematics 145
What Is the Connection? 145
Overview of Physical Education History 145
Comprehensive Physical Education and Health Programs: An Introduction 146
The Values of Comprehensive Physical Education 147
Science and Mathematics: Providing Directions for Physical and Health Education 148
Basic Concept for All Students: Scientific Reasoning, Skill Sets, and Relationships 149
Science and Health 149
Scientific Reasoning and Skill Sets 149
Mathematics, Statistics and Health: A Brief Overview 151
Learning Outcomes (Adjust for Age and Abilities) 153
Questions and/or Activities (Adjust for Age and Abilities) 153
Textbooks in Physical Education and Health: A Rationale 155
Review of Health and Physical Education Lessons Plans 157
Resources 159
Reflections 159
Notes 159

9. Globalization, Instruction, and Youth Health 163
What Is Globalization? 163
Youth in a Globalized World 164
Teaching Globalization and Health: A Fundamental Relationship 164
Globalization Themes 165
Theme 1: Food and Water 165
Theme 2. Climate and Weather Changes 165
Theme 3. Ecological Changes 165
Theme 4. Populations and Migrations 166
Theme 5. Diseases 166
Theme 6. Medical Care, Interventions, and Public Health 166
Theme 7. Information and Communication Technology 166
Theme 8. Travel and Transportation 166
Theme 9. Justice and Litigation Systems 166

Theme 10. Labor and Work   166
Theme 11. Governments and Health Policies   167
Theme 12. Market Demands   168
Globalization, Health Information, and Instruction: Some Examples   168
Technology Education   168
Agriculture Education   168
Economics Education   168
Human Ecology (Home Economics)   169
Selected Instructional Thematic Procedures   169
Themes and Procedures   170
Resources   189
Reflections   189
Notes   189

10. Outreach, Health, and the School Community   191
Defining the School Health Community   191
Community Development: Concepts and School Health Information   192
  Literacy
School Programs   193
Help to Parents   193
Help to Staff   193
Help for Students   193
Outreach to the Community   193
Reaching the Wider School Community with Health Information   194
Basic Guides to Planning and Managing Health Fairs and Conferences   196
Developing Objectives and Activities   197
Coordinated School Health Program Conference: GetHIP   198
Activities for Health Fairs, Workshops, and Conferences   200
Taking Care of Details   201
Implementation   201
Housekeeping and Hospitality   202
Reflections   202
Notes   203

11. Into the Future: Health, Curriculum, and Librarians   205
The Science of Predicting the Future   205
Participatory Medical Approaches   206
Information Technology and Communication   206
Networking and Collaboration   207
Facilities: The School Library as Place   207
School Librarian as Mentor   207
Collection Development   207

Reflections   208
Notes   208

Appendix A: Resources   209
  Chapter 4. Searching for Health Information and Developing   209
    Library Use Skills
    For Older Students   209
    For Younger Students   209
    For Librarians and Teachers   210
  Chapter 5. Materials for Health Instruction and Information   210
  Chapter 6. Literature, the Arts, Performance Activities, and Languages   210
    Suggested Resources: Drama and Fiction   210
  Biographical Materials   212
    Extraordinary People and Experiences   212
    Biographies of Artists   212
    Biographies of Athletes   213
    Biographies of Dancers   213
    Biographies of Musicians   214
    Hearing and Health   214
    Dance and Athletic Health   214
    Art and Health   216
    Foreign Languages   216
  Chapter 7. Connections to Good Health: Social and Behavioral Sciences,   218
    and Languages
    Sociology of Health (Living Together and Social Responsibilities)   218
    History and Geography of Health and Medical Discoveries   219
    Psychological and Developmental Health   221
    Governments and Health   222
  Chapter 8. Connections: Health, Physical Education, Science,   223
    and Mathematics
    Mathematics and Health   223
    Science and Health   224
  Chapter 9. Globalization, Instruction, and Youth Health   224
    For School Librarians and Teachers   224
    Resources for Students   225
    Food and Water   225
    Climate and Weather Changes   225
    Ecological Changes   225
    Populations and Migrations   225
    Medical Care and Interventions (Public Health)   225
    Information and Communication Technology   226
    Travel and Transportation   226
    Justice and Litigation Systems   227
    Labor and Work   228

Governments and Health Policies 228
Market Demands 229
Appendix B: A Selected List of Health and Physical Education Textbooks 231
Used in North American Schools
American Textbooks 231
Health and Fitness 231
Anatomy and Physiology 232
Health Occupations 232
Terminology 233
Ontario Ministry of Education Textbooks 233

Index 235

List of Illustrations

Figure 1.1. Commentary United States postage stamp honoring health workers, 1881–1931   1

Figure 1.2. The UNESCO Guidelines   5

Figure 1.3. Toothbrush drill in a New York City public school, ca. 1913   7

Figure 1.4. From left to right, the emblems of the U.S. Federal Drug Administration, the National Library of Medicine, and the Centers for Disease Control and Prevention   8

Figure 1.5. Emblem of the United States Department of Agriculture   9

Figure 2.1. Collaborative school health model, CDC   18

Figure 2.2. U.S. Army poster designed to fight sexually transmitted diseases after World War I   21

Figure 2.3. Domestic education, Travis County (Texas) Negro Extension Service, ca. 1950   22

Figure 2.4. School Health Day Rally, California School Health Centers   23

Figure 2.5. Community health demonstration by students of the South Texas Independent School District   24

Figure 3.1. Problems inhibiting good instruction, including health instruction   32

Figure 3.2. Principles of assessment promoted by the *National Health Education Standards*   35

Figure 3.3. Examples of health assessment criteria at four levels of obtainment based on evidence   37

Figure 3.4. Teachers involved with the teacher enrichment initiatives   38

Figure 3.5. Examples of levels of assessments   39

Figure 4.1. Venn Diagram: Searching for apples AND oranges,   64
            but NOT pineapples

Figure 4.2. *Library of Congress List of Subject Headings*   65

Figure 4.3. Elements in basic and advanced research approaches   67

Figure 5.1. Attractive and useable collections of health information 82
            are necessary for good health

Figure 6.1. Reading and literature are fundamental in society.   101
            Drawing of a woman reading to children

Figure 6.2. Research shows that landscape art and other pleasing   116
            images help promote healing

Figure 7.1. Social message from the United States during World   132
            War I—"Uncle Sam Says 'Garden to Cut Food Cost' "

Figure 7.2. Crippled children playing on roof. Henry Street,   133
            New York City, ca. 1909

Figure 7.3. Government school lunch programs   135

Figure 8.1. A coeducation physical exercise class, ca. 1909,   146
            Washington, D.C.

Figure 8.2. Joseph J. Kinyoun's Zeiss microscope used to discover 149
            the organism that causes cholera in his Laboratory of Hygiene,
            United States Marine Hospital Service

Figure 8.3. "Make Healthy Choices." Observational skills and informed 152
            decisions about food choices is fundamental to good health

Figure 8.4. "How Much Is Too Much Salt?" Good nutrition requires   154
            the ability to observe and measure

Figure 8.5. Textbook and microscope in use in a military biology class 155

Figure 9.1. Health is a worldwide concern in times of change   165

Figure 9.2. Public health information campaign on preventing diseases, 167
            United States Agency for International Development,
            South Pacific Commission, New Caledonia, 1987

Figure 9.3. Government warnings in Spanish about the dangers of smoking 167

Figure 9.4. Emblem of the U.S. Environmental Protection Agency   185

Figure 10.1. Library service, Kelly Field Library, ca. 1920 (l).   194
            WPA Bookmobile Services (r)

Figure 10.2. Conference attendees at the GetHIP health conference, 195
            San Antonio, Texas

Figure 10.3. Logo designed for the conference on health information for 200
            librarians and school health professionals serving K–12 students

Figure 11.1. A simple planning diagram for the future. Based on a concept 206
            by Vijay Govindarajan

Acknowledgments

We thank all the people and institutions that have helped us in the preparation of this book. Dean Dillon and the faculty and staff at the School of Information at the University of Texas at Austin who have provided welcome assistance and support when needed; Richard Hendler, artist and illustrator, for his contributions; Lucy Hansen, lead librarian of the Biblioteca Las Americas, and her staff have been most gracious and generous in sharing their experiences with us; and Keith W. Cogdill, Ph.D., AHIP, the director of South Texas Regional Information Services.

The University of Texas's Health Science Center San Antonio Libraries and the GetHIP San Antonio committee members with whom we planned and presented a wonderful multidisciplinary seminar for educators were all generous and creative colleagues from whom we learned more about the topics presented.

Karen Vargas, the Consumer Health Outreach Coordinator at the National Network of Libraries of Medicine, South Central Region, Houston, has been an enthusiastic supporter from the time she heard us speak and saw our last book to the present.

We thank our friends and colleagues who have supported us throughout this project. We appreciate the encouragement of Ron Maas, editor, of Libraries Unlimited and Blanche Woolls, our editor and longtime friend, for their continuing advice and critiques to improve our work. Most of all, to our families, thank you for being there whenever we need you.

Introduction and Guide

Health is one of the most important social and cultural issues in modern-day society. Health care and information is expensive and raises many questions about access, affordability, and quality of services. In many societies, it raises political and philosophical concerns that pull at the fabric of social life.

We know that health information must be technical and scientific for various types of health practitioners, but health information must also be understandable to the general public as consumers of health care and as managers of their own health. This applies to all elements in society, including youth in and out of school.

THE ROLE OF SCHOOLS IN HEALTH EDUCATION

Schools exist in various forms in almost all societies. Traditionally, schools—with their access to mass populations of youth and their caregivers—have served as avenues for the control of infectious diseases and providing information about basic hygiene. In recent decades, international as well as national health agencies have focused more on the role of schools in providing health care information. These include the WHO (the World Health Organization), UNESCO, and the European Union, among others.

For example, in the United States, the federal government funds and operates Healthy Youth! Coordinated School Health Program (CSHP) through its Centers for Disease Control (CDC). CSHP's guidelines are issued by the Division of Adolescent and School Health and promote health as a unified and coordinated effort that involves all elements of society. Listed below are CSHP's essential elements for this coordinated effort to provide for better health care for youth:

- Family and community involvement
- Health promotion for staff
- Healthy school environment
- Counseling, psychological, and social services
- Nutrition services

- Health services
- Physical education

Teachers of subject areas and school administrators are mentioned as important elements in most of these components, but school librarians are never mentioned. This serious omission offers school librarians the opportunity to assert themselves into this dialogue and, in so doing, help improve the health of youth.

Although not directed specifically at schools, in March, 2010 FAIFE (Committee on the Free Access to Information and Freedom of Expression) and its parent body, IFLA (International Federation of Library Associations), announced the availability of a set of learning materials designed to help libraries provide better health information to people around the world (www.ifla.org/en/taxonomy/term/443). In announcing this, the committee stated "[l]ibraries of all kinds need to make clear their commitment to the welfare and concerns of their users by strong commitment to key issues such as health" (www.ifla.org/en/publications/learning-materials-for-workshops-on-public -access-to-health-information-through-librari).

This book addresses major issues, most of which are reflected in various governmental directives concerning how school librarians can play active and collaborative roles with classroom teachers and other health authorities in their communities in providing better health information to students and their caregivers in grades K–12.

HOLISTIC EDUCATIONAL PRINCIPLES

We follow a general holistic approach to health education. Holistic approaches hold that no part is greater than the whole. The word holistic comes from the Greek word "holoe" and embraces a number of ideas, such as entire, total, heal, health, holy, whole, etc.[1,2] Holistic Education Inc. notes that the following elements define a holistic approach to teaching and learning:

The purpose of holistic education is to prepare students to meet the challenges of living as well as academics. Holistic education believes it is important for young people to learn:

- About themselves
- About healthy relationships and pro-social behavior
- Social development
- Emotional development
- Resilience
- To see beauty, have awe, experience transcendence, and appreciate some sense of truths[3]

Health education embraces many if not all of these principles

INTEGRATED HEALTH CURRICULA

To be effective, health education must be integrated throughout the curriculum. We address these holistic principles by considering these major issues:

- The role of schools and instruction in health education
- The use of information technologies to find health information

- The selection of appropriate materials for health education
- Curriculum and subject integration and approaches
- School and community coordination and collaboration in providing health information
- The future of libraries as sources of health information

The topics are diverse but yet holistically focused on providing better health information across the curriculum, K–12. Major concepts addressed in this book include:

- **Role of Schools in Health Education**. The role of schools in health education and how schools and their staffs have played and continue to play in health education introduces the book's framework and direction. This theme defines and addresses issues of skills-based health education as well as how schools can interact with other health agencies in fostering better health care information among students and their caregivers.
- **Curriculum and Instructional Concepts and Implications for the School**. The various concepts of curriculum design and theory are presented with this theme. Significant implications that these various curriculum concepts have for school librarians in their roles as designers, presenters, and collaborators in health education are emphasized here. Practical definitions and suggestions about instructional methods are also provided (e.g., demonstrations, field trips, speaker programs, online distance education).
- **Teaching and Promoting Health Education**. New developments in how to teach and how to assess teaching effectiveness through outcome measures are discussed in detail here. Outcome measures for learning and guidelines for assessing student achievement based on the National Cancer Society's *National Health Education Standards* are discussed in detail. UNESCO's suggestions for including health information across the curriculum are presented in relationship to information literacy concepts from AASL's *The 21st Century Learner*.
- **Health Information across the Curriculum**. Here, we describe in considerable detail how subjects taught in schools around the world can be used to teach and promote good health information concepts. Subjects include these broad fields:

• Art	• History
• Agriculture	• Human ecology
• Business and commerce	• Literature (and biography)
• Drama	• Music
• Economics	• Physiology and human development
• Foreign language and culture	• Psychology
• Geography	• Sociology and social policy
• Health and physical education	• Technology education

In our discussion, these areas are integrated into broad curriculum areas in relation to how they support health instruction. Suggested lesson plans include background information, procedures, activities, and resources, and age and grade-level designations are provided.

As stated, we do not attempt to address all subject areas separately but instead use a holistic approach, believing that no part of the curriculum can be seen in isolation from health education. We describe with considerable detail how subjects taught in schools around the world can be used to teach and promote good health information concepts. Subjects and their relationships to health include these broad subject content areas:

- **Humanities:**
Fictional literature, biography, drama, music, and art
- **Social science and social life:**
History, geography, foreign language and culture, business and industry, sociology and social policy, globalization, psychology, physiology and human development, human ecology, physical education, community and family life, and sexual health, human economy, government and civics, and technology education
- **Mathematics and science:**
Measurements, experimental design, and applications of scientific principles to health information, medical sociology, and anthropology
- **Health and physical education:**
Because health and physical education curricula are well-developed and widely available, a best practice overview is provided that highlights some of the outstanding units and resources. Major health textbooks used in North American schools are reviewed, especially as they highlight current issues and trends in health instruction.
- **Globalization:**
Globalization and its impact on health and health education are discussed. Globalization is broad-based and includes such topics as medical anthropology, sociology, medical demographics, open borders and health issues, trade agreements and their impacts of health, economics, and business practices and values, technology education, and human ecology. Additionally, the need for international agreements and cooperation in health policies are examples of issues discussed that youth of all ages need to be made aware of as consequences of globalization.
- **Outreach and community instructional programs for schools and school libraries:**
Outreach to the school as well as communities beyond the school are important in a comprehensive health information program. To meet this need, we provide examples of instructional and informational programs that can be undertaken by school librarians in cooperating with others. Among others, these include health fairs, demonstrations, guide speaker programs, and virtual tours of health facilities in the community.
- **Future directions, health curriculum, and school libraries:**
The final chapter of this book looks at the future of health education in relation to the patient as participant and the need for better health literacy, the place of new communication, and the role of "library as place." Included here are assessments of the role that school librarians will assume as mentors bringing better health information to youth.

We also include:

- **Databases and the uses of databases in health education:**
Electronic resources are important to health education. We include instruction on how to help students acquire good search techniques in health and how to develop their skills as independent evaluators of health information contents. Electronic resources that school librarians can use, such as MedlinePlus, and commercial resources are considered along with how to introduce and use these with students.
- **Resources:**
The appendixes provide annotated resource suggestions for all the areas discussed, including textbooks in health and physical education. Although our book devotes considerable attention to instructions and resources, its major aim is to address issues that will help the school librarian in collaboration with teachers bring health information literacy to all areas of the modern school curriculum. It is important that we address these issues now not only because of their importance

in promoting better health knowledge, attitudes, and behaviors in students but also because health education and literacy will play a huge role in national and international policies and debates in years to come. The school librarian and teachers must be a part of this dialogue, and this book is planned and designed to help advance this goal.

Bill Lukenbill, Professor, School of Information
University of Texas at Austin
Barbara Immroth, Professor, School of Information
University of Texas at Austin

NOTES

1. Gaia Holistic Circle. www.gaiahh.com. Accessed Dec. 14, 2009.

2. SteadyHealth.com: Holistic Healing." www.steadyhealth.com/holistic_healing _t110358.html. Accessed Dec. 14, 2009.

3. Holistic Education, Inc. "Purpose of Holistic Education." www.holistic -education.net/visitors.htm. Accessed Dec. 14, 2009.

I

Schools, Libraries, and Health Education

THE ROLE OF SCHOOLS IN HEALTH EDUCATION

Health care is a major social force in today's world. Most countries have honored health care-workers and even health itself in various ways. A common method is to issue postage stamps, as shown in Figure 1.1.

Since the beginning of the public health movement in the nineteenth century, schools—in their position as social agencies—have played significant roles in the control and prevention of diseases. This responsibility has almost always included a strong emphasis on educating the school-age public and their caregivers in disease prevention and health management.

Figure 1.1.
Commentary United States postage stamp honoring health workers, 1881–1931. Courtesy of the U.S. Postal Service.

The relationship of school libraries and health information becomes even more important in relation to Coordinated School Health Program (CSHP) guidelines, "Healthy Youth!" These guidelines, issued by the Division of Adolescent and School Health of the Centers for Disease Control and Prevention (CDC), list eight guideline components. These include:

- family community involvement
- health promotion for staff
- healthy school environment
- counseling, psychological, and social services
- nutrition services
- health services
- physical education
- health education

The guidelines acknowledge that schools must have the help of other community agents to meet these directives. Teachers and school administrators are mentioned as important elements in most of these components, but librarians are never mentioned. One may overlook this in developing countries, but this is a serious omission in the United States, where school libraries are fundamentally a part of school structures. School libraries are incorporated into instruction and curriculum. Librarians directly instruct students in a variety of subjects including information literacy, technology, and cultural studies. Librarians provide reference services to the school community, including parents, and school librarians consult directly with teachers in developing resources and teaching strategies. This omission presents the opportunity for school librarians to assert themselves into this dialogue, allowing them to help improve the health of the nation's youth.

Health issues are not limited to only a few nations; they are worldwide problems facing all nations. For years, the United Nations Educational, Scientific and Cultural Organization (UNESCO) has recognized the importance of health care for children and youth as well as the necessary role that schools play in improving health care for young people.[1]

UNESCO has identified these youth-related global issues that must be seriously addressed in the twentieth-first century:

- Hunger
- Micronutrient deficiencies and malnutrition
- Intestinal infections
- HIV infections and other sexually transmitted diseases
- Malaria
- Violence
- Drug and alcohol abuse

UNESCO believes that solving and reducing health problems allows children and youth to have the sound psychological support that can enable them to learn and develop. UNESCO asserts that health improvement can be promoted by "skills-based health education, good health policies developed for individual schools, and on-site school health care."[2]

INFORMATION AND HEALTH LITERACY

Closely related to both CDC and UNESCO guidelines are information literacy and its definition by the American Association of School Librarians (AASL) in their new standards. Information literacy and health information literacy have much in common; they both stress the importance of information and how to evaluate it and apply it when needed. *Standards for the 21st-Century Learner* by the AASL (2007) outlines four major elements of information literacy. Learners use information skills, resources, and tools for these purposes:[3]

- Inquire, think critically, and gain knowledge
- Draw conclusions, make informed decisions, apply knowledge to new situations, and create new knowledge
- Share knowledge and participate ethically and productively as members of our democratic society
- Pursue personal and aesthetic growth

The standards state that a definition of information literacy has become more complex as resources and technologies have changed. Multiple literacies are now required, including digital, visual, textual, and technology skills.[4] We can add that information literacy crosses disciplines and is closely tied to the context in which the need arises and its purpose. The 2009 *Standards for the 21st-Century Learner in Action* continues this discussion by presenting action points on how to ensure that learning takes place. The emphasis is on learning strands, skills, actions, responsibilities, and self-assessment, which are supported by concrete statements on how all these combine into a holistic relationship.[5]

DEFINING HEALTH LITERACY

Health writers Gloria Mayer and Michael Villaire define health literacy as using a broad array of literacy skills in the context of health care. For example, health care literacy requires understanding basic medical terms used in conservation with health providers; understanding abbreviations on charts and prescriptions; and reading and understanding technical medical texts.[6] These writers provide research evidence that health information literacy skills are low among citizens. This lack of health information literacy often leads to poor health, a deficiency of good medical care management and care, more hospitalization, and a poor understanding of treatments and treatment options. Persons with poor health information skills are less likely to follow medical directions.[7]

These remarks underscore the need for adequate health information for youth. Training and education programs must ensure that the knowledge and skills provided will sustain health. Generally agreed criteria for overall health information literacy programs in schools include:[8]

- Well-defined staff roles
- Access to nutrition, water, and sanitation on the premises
- Health education
- Curriculum content
- Stress management
- Gender mainstreaming

- Nonviolent conflict resolution
- Accessibility to counseling
- Assessment and outcome measures

These all lead into a skills-based health education program.

WHAT IS SKILLS-BASED HEALTH EDUCATION?

As mentioned earlier, UNESCO promotes skill-based health education programs as a part of health literacy. It is basically a "how to do" approach that encourages behavior changes. It is based on promoting and developing knowledge, attitudes, values, and skills that are necessary to make good, positive, and lifelong decisions about health.

Changes in social behaviors are most important in skill-based health programs. Health is seen in a variety of social contexts and goes well beyond health instruction and information. Skills-based instruction includes the usual health issues, but its added value is how it extends across the curriculum. Skills-based health education embraces such social problems as gender equality, peer relationships and pressures, and the psychology and sociology of disease and health. It also finds a place in social sciences through understanding social policy and implementation.

In history and literature classes, students can discuss health issues as well as how diseases and health have influenced historical development. Of course, health education finds a natural place in science and mathematics through the study of disease recognition and measurement.[9] With the rise of globalization, business and commercial curricula also benefit from health issues and health-based discussions.

HEALTH INFORMATION AND EDUCATION ACROSS THE CURRICULUM

Figure 1.2 presents UNESCO's suggestions on how to integrate health as well as health skills throughout the curriculum. Later chapters in this book will develop these concepts as applied to actual instructional units.[10]

HEALTH AND SCIENCE
    Encourages students to:
        Observe and record
        Measure and make comparisons
        Ask questions, hypothesize, and predict
        Make experiments and interpret the results

MATHEMATICS
    Promotes in students:
        Use of numbers
        Weights and measurements
        Estimating and recording data
        General applications to healthy living (e.g., medication measurements and timeframes for medicine use, body and weight monitoring, water and sanitation, nutrition and food intake calculations)

SOCIAL STUDIES

Develops in student analytical skills related to ideas about social living and cooperating

Living together and social and group dependency

Health and environment and responsibility to preserve a healthy environment

Rights and duties of citizens to encourage healthy living

Responsibility to respect differences in health conditions

Developing skills to understand the geography and history of health

Studying the health of a community through demographic surveys and other basic research methods

Sharing information and promoting understanding of various views about lifestyles

Sharing information and customs regarding food as well as food practices

Developing empathy for others who suffer health problems

Considering one's immediate environments (e.g., home safety driving and driving responsibilities)

LANGUAGE AND INFORMATION LITERACY

Promote health and health information through communication and understanding by:

Using the language correctly, through grammar and correct usage

Listening, speaking, reading, and writing effectively

Using language as a tool for thinking and doing: finding, interpreting, and working with information and ideas

Writing used in observing, describing, and recording

Promoting information literacy skills in finding, understanding, and using information

Figure 1.2.
The UNESCO Guidelines.

GOOD HEALTH THROUGH CURRICULUM EMPOWERMENT

A solid health curriculum is practical and based on skills. Skills offer psychological support for students as well as provide them with useful information about health.

Skill-Based Learning and Curriculum Empowerment of Students

Some of the hallmarks of empowerment in instructing youth about health include:

- Accepting the rights of young people to make informed decisions about their health
- Helping youth understand and discover factors that might harm their health
- Helping youth understand how to identify factors that they need to face regarding their own health
- Helping youth understand how they can best address those factors
- Encouraging youth to debate and examine their own health as well as others' and to form an informed opinion that can lead to good decision-making
- Encouraging youth to see health issues in a holistic way and not isolated to single circumstances or issues
- Helping youth discover ways that they can participate and interact with health promotion
- Encouraging youth to take leaderships roles in health promotion

From an education perceptive, we need to recognize that students should carefully consider empowerment and the social, political, legal, and ethical issues that impact health care. Does government law and policy permit youth to make certain decisions (e.g., sexual information)? How well do peer involvements work? What kinds of training must occur to ensure that peers can be good leaders? Ethically, do educators have the right to promote health issues that might conflict with values in the community or at home? All these questions simply mean that each teacher, librarian, and policymaker must "judge for themselves how to empower their practices."[11] In the case of school librarians, they can often frame these issues with information literacy standards endorsed by the AASL as well as other organizations that see information as an important empowering agent in young people's lives. Beyond that, state and local curriculum guides will offer direction.

HOW CAN SKILL-BASED CONCEPTS AND THEMES BE INTRODUCED ACROSS THE CURRICULUM?

Instructors can introduce skill-based concepts as well as other health concepts into instructional settings, with many of these being dictated by age and developmental appropriateness.[12] We present only a few examples here; we consider other concepts and skills in later chapters.

Teachable Health Concepts for Youth

- **Concept: Developing Healthy Children and Youth in Society**
  How healthy are you? What conditions and behaviors promote good health? What rights do you have in managing your health? What makes you vulnerable to poor health? How can you protect yourself from poor health conditions? How can parents help in making you healthy? How can teachers help in making you healthy? What do you need to be taught to be healthy? Who should be your teachers and leaders in promoting good health? What do you want to know today?
- **Concept: Health and Social Services**
  What kinds of health services are available in your community and in your neighborhood? Do you know how to reach them? Do you know how to report a health emergency? What does "social services" mean? What kinds of help do social services provide? How do you make contact with social services? Do you know what you can expect from social services? How would you ask your parents to contact social services? How might clubs and other memberships help in improving the health of children and youth in your community and neighborhood?
- **Concept: Responsibility for Others—Homeless Children and Youth**
  How can you help children and teens who have no home? How can schools and clubs help homeless children and youth? How can your city help homeless children and youth? What are the conditions that homeless children and teens face that might make them less healthy than you and your friends?
- **Concept: Understanding Mental Health**
  What is good mental health? How can you recognize a mental health problem in you or your friends? How can you seek help for yourself, your friends, or your family?
- **Concept: Gender Relationships**
  What does it mean to be male or female? What are stereotypes? How are males and females often stereotyped? What are gender roles? Who determines gender roles? What health issues are associated with gender and gender roles?

- **Concept: Understanding Others—Health and Minority Groups, Including Gay, Lesbian, and Transgendered Communities**
    What are minority groups? Who determines who is a minority (e.g., government policy, community, religion). What health issues are associated with minority communities? What is the role of society in providing health care for minority groups?

Teachable Health Themes

- **Theme: Understanding and Personalizing the Vocabulary of Health**
    Basic themes: Information literacy skills: inquiry, thinking critically, gaining knowledge, drawing conclusions, sharing knowledge, and using effective language and communication skills
- **Theme: Understanding How Health and Diseases Affect Social Life**
    Basic themes: Information literacy skills: Critical thinking, drawing conclusions, applying new knowledge, sharing knowledge, creating new knowledge, and understanding how health affects history and social life
- **Theme: Understanding the Vocabulary of Health in Science and Math**
    Basic themes: Information literacy skills: critical thinking, decision-making, applying new knowledge, pursuing personal growth, and using the vocabulary of science and mathematics in personal health management

We expand on many of these ideas and questions in later chapters.

PUBLIC HEALTH AND EDUCATION

In designing health information services and programs, school librarians owe a great deal of thanks to the public health development in almost all western countries. Public health has a long and respected history, and its association with schools is

Figure 1.3.
Toothbrush drill in a New York City public school, ca. 1913. Courtesy of the U.S. National Medical Library.

well-founded. Historically, both in North America and in Europe, public health focused on preventing the spread of diseases. The developing school systems in the West allowed for health information to be distributed to a mass of children and their parents and/or caregivers. Along with these came informational programs, demonstration programs, parent information, hygiene, and nutrition information (Figure 1.3).[13] Although librarians of the time were not (as far as historical records show) directly involved in these programs, public librarians were certainly involved in outreach into the communities, both rural and urban, with books and reading programs designed to increase literacy and generally improve the life of children and their parents.[14] State and provincial libraries often involved themselves in outreach programs to rural communities.[15] Although not directly associated, both library and public health outreach helped in expanding the progressive philosophy of the time and helped improve general society.

HOW GOVERNMENT HELPS IN HEALTH: HEALTH CARE INFORMATION AND CURRICULUM DEVELOPMENT

A number of government agencies can offer support for teachers and school librarians in curriculum development, instruction, and reference. In the United States, these include the Centers for Disease Control (CDC); the Federal Drug Administration (FDA); the Department of Agriculture (USDA); and the National Library of Medicine (NLM) (Figures 1.4 and 1.5).

In 1946, the U.S. federal government established the CDC to prevent and contain the spread of malaria in the southern states during World War II. Historically, its many programs have included publishing national guidelines for various types of health conditions and offering mass vaccinations, especially those for polio and smallpox. Its current programs range from education to disease surveillance and prevention to statistic gathering and reporting.[16]

The FDA dates from 1863, when it was an office under the purview of the U.S. Department of Agriculture (USDA). Its duties and administration further enlarged and changed with the 1906 Food and Drug Act. "Agency scientists evaluate applications for new human drugs and biologics, complex medical devices, food and color additives, infant formulas, and animal drugs."[17] The "For Kids" page," hosted by the FDA, should be of special interest to librarians and teachers of younger children.[18]

Established by President Lincoln, the USDA has existed as an independent cabinet-level department since 1862. Health is among its many activities associated with agricultural development and life as well as the scientific management of agriculture. Over

Figure 1.4.
From left to right, the emblems of the U.S. Federal Drug Administration, the National Library of Medicine, and the Centers for Disease Control and Prevention. Courtesy of the U.S. government.

Figure 1.5.
Emblem of the United States Department of Agriculture, established in 1862 to help advance a scientific base for agriculture. Courtesy of the U.S. government.

the years, the department has offered guidance in food preparation and management, nutrition programs for children and youth, healthy living, food safety, diet and health, and weight management. Its programs for rural youth in earlier years included demonstration programs. Today, its 4-H clubs are particularly extensive.[19]

The United Kingdom has the National Health Service (NHS), and Canada has Health Canada. The NHS is composed of the four public health components servicing England, Scotland, Wales, and Northern Ireland. Its services are widespread, and its Web site (www.nhs.uk) offers guidance in health management as well as how to better access the services available through NHS.[20]

The BBC offers considerable amounts of curriculum-related material supporting the national mandated in United Kingdom schools. Its Web site (www.bbc.co.uk) serves parents, teachers, and students. Much of its curriculum supports information literacy by including critical thinking, decision making, and the informed application of information.[21]

Health Canada, overseen by the Canadian Ministry of Health, offers health information and statistics on health management and government directives and policies. Its Web site (www.hc-sc.gc.ca) is attractive, but its attention to youth is largely directed at teachers and other adult leaders who have responsibility for delivering health information to youth. Awareness of its existence allows you to share many of its ideas to help build and guide curriculum development in various areas.[22]

HELP FROM THE NONGOVERNMENTAL SECTION

Associations have played significant roles in advancing health care and health information throughout modern times. They do this in several ways. Among these are:

- Supporting research and development
- Offering grants for service programs
- Facilitating information dissemination
- Providing emotional support

For example, almost all the following associations have resources intended for multi-audiences:

- The National Youth Mental Health Foundation in Australia seeks "to change the way that mental health services for young people are delivered" by encouraging youth to understand that there are ways to solve emotional problems. Its Web site is www.headspace.org.au.

- The Institute for Science and Health, founded in 2001, is a worldwide organization devoted to promoting research on youth. Its site offers an abundance of information of value about youth health. Its Web site is www.ifsh.org.
- The Paso del Norte Health Foundation (PdNHF), located on the U.S.-Mexico border, seeks to "improve the health and promote the wellness of the people living in western Texas, southern New Mexico, and Ciudad Juárez, Mexico through education and prevention." Its Web site is www.pdnhf.org/who.asp.
- Sierra Health Foundation is a private foundation that promotes improved health and quality of life for the people in 26 counties in northern California through programs that include grants, conferences, and health leadership; the REACH Youth Program; Grizzly Creek Ranch Camp and Conference Center; and the brightSMILES Dental Partnership. Its Web site is www .sierrahealth.org.
- The Gates Foundation works with and supports organizations throughout the world to fight serious diseases and other problems that affect health. The program includes research to help develop vaccines and medicines and to provide health solutions to those who are most in need. Through its grant programs, the Gates Foundation targets "diseases and health conditions that cause the greatest illness and death in developing countries, yet receive little attention and resources." Its Web site (www.gatesfoundation.org) provides reports and statistical information about its grant programs.

HELP FROM HOSPITALS AND CLINICS

Most hospitals and large clinics offer health information through their Web sites and publication programs. Children's Hospitals (www.childrenshospitals.net) is a large advocacy organization that offers a wide range of information regarding hospitals for children, including location information.[23] The following are well-known hospitals that offer health services as well as patient and health care information for families and children:

- Arkansas Children's Hospital (www.archildrens.org)
- Children's Hospital Boston (www.childrenshospital.org)
- ULC Institute of Child Health, London (www.ich.ucl.ac.uk)
- Hospital for Sick Children (www.sickkids.ca)
- Sydney Children's Hospital (www.sch.edu.au)

HELP FROM FOR-PROFIT COMPANIES

In their role as developers and marketers of drugs and medical treatments, for-profit companies often engage in public relations and marketing programs that offer medical and health information. Generally, this information is closely associated with their own products, but some—such as the Pfizer drug company—offer information for patients and caregivers through a "medicine safety education" program.[24] Other companies have similar promotions, but the better sources for information and guidance include foundations, associations, and medical hospitals for children and youth.

HELPFUL PROFESSIONAL GUIDES TO HEALTH INFORMATION

Health care and health information are vast and complicated. Here are some recently published guides that might prove helpful to school librarians in building collections and health information programs:

Reference and Background Sources

- Marie Bartlett. *The Frontier Nursing Service: America's First Rural Nurse-Midwife Service and School.* Jefferson, N.C.: McFarland: 2008. ISBN 978-0-786-43342-1.
  Recounts how the "Frontier Nursing Service, opened in 1925 in Leslie County, Kentucky, set out to meet the health needs of women and infants."
- *Black's Medical Dictionary.* Harvey Marcovitch, ed. 41st ed. Lanham, Md.: Scarecrow Press, 2006. 768 pp. ISBN: 978-0-810-85713-1.
  "[P]rovides over 5,000 definitions and descriptions of medical terms and concepts, along with over 100 diagrams and drawings including several pages of color illustrations."
- Jo Anne Boorkman, Jeffrey T. Huber, and Jean Blackwell. *Introduction to Reference Sources in the Health Sciences,* 5th ed. New York: Neil-Schuman, 2008. 392 pp. ISBN: 978-1-555-70636-4.
  A "standard guide to health sciences sources is essential for students, librarians, and health professionals. Prepared with the Medical Library Association. . . . "
- Terry Ann Jankowski. *The MLA Essential Guide to Becoming an Expert Searcher.* New York: Neil-Schuman, 2008. 150 pp. ISBN: 978-1-555-70622-7.
  Provides a guide to "skills, resources, and techniques" that expert searchers use when looking up health information.
- Beatrice Levin. *Women and Medicine.* 3rd. ed. Lanham, Md.: Scarecrow Press, 2002. 232 pp. ISBN: 978-0-810-84238-0.
  "[P]rovides a comprehensive and definitive history, from early riots in medical schools when women tried to enroll, to women finally overcoming obstacles, making medical breakthroughs and enjoying brilliant medical careers."
- *Living Under the Sword: Psychosocial Aspects of Recurrent and Progressive Life-Threatening Illness.* Co-published with the American Institute of Life-Threatening Illness and Loss. Harold B. Haley, Austin H. Kutscher, and the American Institute of Life-Threatening Illness and Loss, eds. Lanham, Md.: Scarecrow Press, 2004. 200 pp. ISBN: 978-0-810-83487-3.
  "[C]ollection of essays by a renowned set of doctors, nurses, and caregivers examines the recurrence of disease as it relates to a host of mental and physical illnesses, including Alzheimer's, hemophilia, AIDS, cancer, amyotrophic lateral sclerosis, choriocarcinoma, Tay-Sachs, Huntington's disease, and suicide."
- W. Bernard Lukenbill and Barbara Froling Immroth. *Health Information for Youth: The Public Library and School Library Media Center Role.* Westport, Conn.: Libraries Unlimited. 2007. 219 pp. ISBN: 978-1-591-58508-4.
  "Covers the general status of youth healthcare, the issues and concerns providing a model of health delivery and their relationship to the school and public library."
- Kerry Segrave. *Women and Smoking in America, 1880–1950.* Jefferson, N.C.: McFarland, 2005. 241 pp. ISBN: 978-0-786-42212-8.
  "This social history traces the evolution of women's smoking in the United States from 1880 to 1950."
- Bonnie Snow. *Drug Information: A Guide to Current Resources,* 3rd. ed. New York: Neil-Schuman, 2008. ISBN: 978-1-555-70616-6. 800 pp.
  "Third edition of the most comprehensive compilation of drug information resources available."
- Michele Spats. *Answering Consumer Health Questions.* New York: Neil-Schuman. 2008. 150 pp. ISBN: 978-1-555-70632-6.
  "Outlines the most common inquiries and behaviors of health information searchers and the most useful go-to resources."

- Laura Townsend Kane, Rozalynd P. McConnaughy, and Steven Patrick Wilson. With David L. Townsend, M.D. *Answers to the Health Questions People Ask in Libraries*. New York: Neil-Schuman, 2008. 247 pp. ISBN: 978-1-555-70642-5.

  "A ... consumer-focused, handy reference volume [that provides library staff with] reliable authoritative resource to suggest when patrons [ask] health questions."

- Jacqueline Noll Zimmerman. *People Like Ourselves: Portrayals of Mental Illness in the Movies* Series: Studies in Film Genres #3. Lanham, Md.: Scarecrow Press, 2003. 184 pp. ISBN: 978-0-810-84876-4.

  "Considers mental illness in such films as *The Snake Pit* and *Now, Voyager* and including such contemporary successes as *A Beautiful Mind* and *As Good As It Gets* and films by legendary directors Billy Wilder, William Wyler, Alfred Hitchcock, Stanley Kubrick, Oliver Stone."

Health Literacy and Information Skills

- Frances K. Groen. *Access to Medical Knowledge Libraries, Digitization, and the Public Good*. Lanham, Md.: Scarecrow Press. 2006. 298 pp. ISBN: 978-0-810-85272-3.

  Explains the role of medical libraries: "providing access to information, preserving the accumulated knowledge of the past, and helping the public to understand how to help themselves to this information."

- Marge Kars, Lynda M. Baker, and Feleta Wilson, eds. *The MLA Guide to Health Literacy at the Library*. New York: Neil-Schuman, 2008. ISBN: 978-1-555-70625-8.

  "Offers help in understanding the vital role that medical, hospital, public, and health libraries ... play in improving health literacy ... [and] in providing health information."

REFLECTIONS

Health is integrated into all segments of all societies and cultures. In fact, health is often a strong indicator of how a nation or groups of people will survive within human history and culture. Education is one of the prime weapons we have against disease and unhealthy living conditions. This chapter has discussed some of the major issues that must be faced by school librarians, teachers, and teacher-librarians as we seek to play an important role in health care information delivery now and in the future.

School librarians are especially equipped to support and engage in meaningful health information programs. We are experts at knowing resources and understanding how to find answers. As effective teachers and collaborators with other teachers, we can help empower youth and their caregivers through innovative and age-appropriate health information instruction.

NOTES

1. UNESCO. "Focusing Resources for Effective School Health." portal.unesco.org/es/ev.php-URL_ID=22054&URL_DO=DO_TOPIC&URL_SECTION=201.html. Accessed Oct. 6, 2008.

2. UNESCO.

3. American Association of School Librarians. *Standards for the 21st-Century Learner*. Chicago: American Library Association, 2008. www.ala.org/ala/mgrps/divs/

aasl/aaslproftools/learningstandards/AASL_LearningStandards.pdf. Accessed Oct. 6, 2008.

    4. American Association of School Librarians.

    5. American Association of School Librarians. *Standards for the 21st-Century Learner in Action*. Chicago: American Library Association, 2009.

    6. Mayer, Gloria G. and Michael Villaire. *Health Literacy in Primary Care: A Clinician's Guide*. New York: Springer Publishing Co., 2007, pp. 2–3.

    7. Mayer and Villaire, pp. 413.

    8. Barnekow, Vivian and others. *Health-Promoting Schools: A Resource for Developing Indications*. Accessed March 6, 2010. http://www.schoolsforhealth.eu/upload/pubs/Healthpromotingschoolsaresourcefordevelopingindicators.pdf.

    9. UNESCO. "Education for All by 2015." unesdoc.unesco.org/images/0015/001548/154820e.pdf. Accessed Sept. 26, 2008.

    10. UNESCO. "Focusing Resources for Effective School Health."

    11. Graham, Grainne. "Youth Health Promotion in the Community." In Joanne Kerr, ed., *Community Health Promotion: Challenges for Practice*, pp. 125–154. London: Baillière Tindall, 2000.

    12. Kerr, Joanne, ed. *Community Health Promotion: Challenges for Practice*. London: Baillière Tindall, 2000.

    13. Fee, Elizabeth. "Public Health and the State: The United States." In *The History of Public Health and the Modern States*, Dorothy Parker, ed. (Amsterdam: Editions Rodopi B.V., 1994), pp. 233–235; Graham Moody, "Education and Mothering," Lecture 5. www.nlm.nih.gov/hmd/collections/digital/syllabi/mooney2.pdf. Accessed Oct. 11, 2008.

    14. DuMont, Rosemary. *Reform and Reaction: The Big City Library Public Library in American Life*. Westport, Conn.: Greenwood Press, 1977.

    15. DeGruyter, Lisa. "The History and Development of Rural Public Libraries," *Library Trends*, Spring 1980. https://www.ideals.illinois.edu/bitstream/handle/2142/7108/librarytrendsv28i4d_opt.pdf. Accessed Oct. 7, 2008; Libraries Today. "The Electronic History File: Canadian Library Biographies and Histories www.uoguelph.ca/~lbruce/history.shtml#public. Accessed Oct. 7, 2008.

    16. Centers for Disease Control and Prevention. www.cdc.gov. Accessed March 6, 2010.

    17. FDA. www.fda.gov. Accessed Oct. 6, 2008.

    18. FDA, "For Kids." www.fda.gov/ForConsumers/ByAudience/ForKids/default.htm. Accessed Oct. 5, 2008.

    19. USDA. www.usda.gov/wps/portal/usdahome. Accessed Oct. 5, 2008.

    20. "Insurance." en.wikipedia.org/wiki/History_of_the_National_Health_Service. Accessed Oct. 4, 2008.

    21. BBC. "Curriculum Relevance." http://news.bbc.co.uk/2/hi/school_report/5283094.stm. Accessed Oct. 4, 2008.

    22. Health Canada. www.hc-sc.gc.ca/index-eng.php. Accessed Oct. 3, 2008.

    23. Children's Hospitals. www.childrenshospitals.net/AM/Template.cfm?Section=About_Us6. Accessed Oct. 3, 2008

    24. Pfizer. www.pfizer.com/home. Accessed Oct. 3, 2008.

2

Health Curriculum and Instruction

MODELS FOR CURRICULUM AND INSTRUCTION

As we discussed in Chapter 1, schools have long been involved in public health largely thorough their contact with large groups of children and their parents or caregivers. When children are sent to school, it carries an understanding that the school will be a safe haven from accident or illness and that if a child is hurt or becomes ill, that the child will be sent home. While parents may have less of an understanding that their children will learn about health, it is a part of the school's curriculum in varying degrees at every level. What parents and caregivers may not consider is that the school has a certain responsibility to help them learn about health issues. In this chapter, we will consider the meaning of curricula, its base in theory, and how it and instruction are related in the goal to provide a full-service health learning agenda.

Curriculum has several practical bases, all of which have influenced how we as educators and school librarians think about our goals and missions. In a broad sense, curriculum is defined as "All the learning which is planned and guided by the school, whether it is carried on in groups or individually, inside or outside the school."[1]

The first part of this chapter will briefly outline the four major models that have and continue to influence how educators, including school librarians and teachers, plan and deliver instruction and provide reliable health information to students and their caregivers. The second part will outline some useful instructional models and concepts.

MAJOR CURRICULUM IDEAS AND THE IMPLICATIONS FOR HEALTH SCHOOL LIBRARIES

Mark Smith's synthesis[2] of some of the major curriculum theories and ideas are given in this section. These include the education curriculum: Education is transmission; the scientific curriculum: Education produces a product; the developmental curriculum: Learning is process; and the social/moral curriculum: Education is social change.

On the surface, these may seem in conflict with each other, but when looked at carefully, they provide our background for providing health information to youth. Each of these curriculum models is explained with the implications for school librarians.

The Liberal Educator Curriculum: Education Is Transmission

The liberal educator theory, sometimes referred to as "mental disciplinarian," promotes "reason" as the hallmark of western culture. Curricula that follow this theory are developed in systematic ways that promote critical thinking and reasoning skills. At the core, the assumption is that there exists a core of knowledge that must be carefully taught and passed on to younger generations. This theory does not necessarily promote social reform, but it assumes that critical and analytical thinking will lead to a better society.

Implications for the School Library

The current focus of school librarians on teaching critical thinking skills and the critical use of information reflects much of this concept. School librarians assume that when students have critical thinking and critical analytical skills, they as individuals and society as a whole will be better served. This seems especially useful when learners can locate relevant information and then make well-informed decisions regarding their health issues.

Because of this theory's emphasis on a central core of culture and knowledge that must be codified and taught, critics often claim that it is too western-centered, racist, and classist. We argue that the emphasis that it gives to critical thinking skills and its adherence to systematically presenting knowledge and information well serves the premise that health information and its provision through the school library should be a goal of the school librarian.

The Scientific Curriculum: Education Produces a Product

The scientific curriculum supports the performance of activities that lead to specific goals that can be measured as to how well-identified performances are achieved. Following a scientific management approach, educators must present curricula and systems that are carefully constructed so that specific learning objectives are obtained efficiently. It also includes testing to see that the objectives have been met.

Implications for the School Library

Behavioral objectives and testing to see how well learning objectives have been met thorough efficient and systematic instruction have been a part of a school librarian's education and training for decades. This approach now plays major roles in North America, Great Britain, and other countries. The No Child Left Behind Act is a good example of how this theory has assumed power in educational policy and operations in the United States.[3]

In Great Britain, the national curriculum places emphasis on student achievement through the measurement of performance based on clear objectives.[4] Canada also measures its students' performance through testing.[5] It is easy to see how health information instruction adheres to this scientific approach based on outcome measures. Health information providers, including school librarians, often use observational data as well as tests to measure how students act on the information that they are given. A student may be able to make a perfect score on a true and false test about health issues but may not retain that information beyond the day of the test. Observing how children display their knowledge of health issues beyond the paper and pencil test seems a better "test."

The Developmental Curriculum: Learning Is Process

Developmentalists hold that education must be based on the natural order of how students develop. They contend that science has provided ample evidence that educational procedures and instruction can and should fit into age-appropriate curriculum for youth. Harmony must be attained between students' development, interests, needs, and how they learn.

Implications for the School Library

School librarians have certainly been influenced by this theory. We see this in curricula that carefully take into account the age and maturity of students when planning both group and individualized instruction. Age and developmental appropriateness play significant roles in how health information and instruction are offered to youth, and it can be problematic.

Many parents have a different concept of when it is appropriate to offer some kinds of health instruction to students or even if the school should be providing it at all. Yet, children today are maturing at ever younger ages, and what might have been considered not age-appropriate 20 years ago seems critical today. Any discussion of smoking and drug-related problems should begin at a very early age. This could challenge Piaget's child development theories.

Based on Piaget's line of reasoning, health information should move from the concrete to the more abstract in well-defined age progressions. The criticism of this theory is that it might be too simplistic, ignoring other factors in the child's environment, such as family and cultural influences.

The Social/Moral Curriculum: Education Is Social Change

The social/moral theory holds that education is a means of promoting social change and improvement. Schools play a fundament role in this process. Therefore, the primary goal is to educate younger generations to fight social injustice and to improve society. This theory holds that curricula must be designed to focus on abuses related to such problems as racial and gender discrimination the misuse of political, social, and economic power. The outcomes based on this approach are hard to measure and are often not immediate because this type of education is one that must be measured over time, and success or failure is usually not immediately discernible. The high school student who volunteers in a soup kitchen over a holiday may be exhibiting the inclination to fight social injustice and to improve society, but it will take a review of this person's activities for the next 20 years to determine if that graduate stopped doing anything at all, continued to serve in a soup kitchen once a year, or if he or she moved into an active life fighting social injustice.

Implications for the School Library

Progressive education advocated by John Dewey stressed the relationship of a child's life to the social, constructive, expressive, and artistic needs and manifestations. These have undoubtedly played a role in how school librarians have built collections and designed programs. Their relationships with health information are evident. Providing good health information can bring about changes in the behavior of people in society.

As discussed in Chapter 1, schools as government agents have played important roles in promoting good health behavior—first by attempting to prevent the spread of disease and later by seeking to promote better health management among youth. For example, schools and their libraries have played significant roles in helping to reduce smoking and alcohol use among youth. Because Social Change theory is culturally based, many of the ills that it seeks to address are controversial, including sex education discussions regarding condoms, abortion, birth control, teenage pregnancy, and other societal values related to health, include dieting and recreational activities that might be harmful to youth.

CURRICULUM, COLLABORATION, AND TEAMWORK

All these concepts involve the interaction of students, teachers, school librarians, community, and health. Curriculum occurs in the classroom, the school library media center, and the community. Figure 2.1 effectively demonstrates the Centers for Disease Control's (CDC) ideas for this broad-based collaborative model.

Figure 2.1.
Collaborative school health model, CDC. Courtesy of the U.S. government.

In our concepts of providing health information, teachers and school librarians interact in the preparation and evaluation of both how and where this information is to be presented and also in determining how effective the information is acquired and applied. The basic premise of this book is that health information can be a part of every curriculum being taught and placed in with other information to make it seem an integral part of a student's education.

These processes—no matter what the concept or which unit of instruction—involve constant interaction and collaboration. Teachers and school librarians must think critically as well as promote critical thinking in students. They must understand their roles and the roles that others have assigned to them as social agents in promoting better health behaviors. This role also becomes one of making sure the community is aware of health issues.

In the case of school librarians and health information, defining their roles to others in better, more concrete ways is both a challenge and a necessity. This understanding is important because both the talents and resources brought by both teachers and school librarians working as a team to create curriculum and produce effective learning outcomes can come only through their collaborative instructional efforts. Working together, health information and learning can be woven into the curriculum across ability, age, and grade levels.

INSTRUCTION AND STRATEGIES: THEORY AND DESIGN

These four theories have many meanings and applications. Theories help explain phenomena. Definitions of theory include philosophical statements, abstract thoughts, beliefs, policy statements, procedures based on ideas, assumptions, and hypotheses.[6] Scientific theory holds that theories are based on known facts that best explain what is occurring within observed situations. Instructional design theory favors the scientific theory model.

Instructional Design in Providing Health Information

Instructional design theory can be applied to health information and how it is presented to youth because it is based on how to arrange materials so that learning can occur. It draws heavily on behaviorism and cognitive ideas about how youth learn. Classic behaviorism supports the idea that learning comes entirely from external stimuli as well as trial and error. If you are allergic to poison ivy and you come in contact with it, you will have a reaction. Your skin will become red and itchy. If you continue to walk through poison ivy, your skin will continue to be irritated. So, you learn to avoid poison ivy.

Cognitive theory supports the notion that people learn by how they process information and facts. This includes how they come to understand facts as well as diagnose and solve problems that concern themselves as individuals as well as how they come to make sense out of their social and cultural world, including social relationships. Cognition becomes a bridge between external stimuli and the mental processes that help make sense out of these many and complex external stimuli. The mental process provides structures, rules, and insights that help solve problems and the acquiring of new information.[7] Instructional design attempts to put these two together.

Instructional Design and Instructional Approaches

As an instructor in a literary discipline, Morgan used instructional design to help inform her colleagues of its value. In doing this, she relied on standard authorities such as Spector (1996) and Ely (1996) in defining instructional design.[8] In defense of instructional design, Spector argued that instructional design is a structuring of the learning environment for the purpose of facilitating learning or improving learning effectiveness. Ely maintains that the term is directly applied to "direct applications of technology in teaching and learning." Both of these definitions are valid in how we provide health information experiences for youth.

Instructional design and instruction have rather long associations with health information. Perhaps the earlier serious application of this relationship came during World War I when the United States had to train many military personnel in a very short time. This training not only included the use of military hardware and fighting techniques but also health management. This was particularly true of hygiene and the prevention of sexually transmitted diseases. To do this, the military used an educational film, thus ensuring that it became one of the first large scale uses of electronic-based educational technology applications in history.[9] Films were also used in conjunction with a variety of print materials, including posters. Figure 2.2 illustrates the fact that this problem concerned the army even after the war ended.

INSTRUCTIONAL STRATEGIES FOR HEALTH

The Ely definition stresses the importance that instructional theory gives to practical application. Providing and teaching health information can rely on many of these applications for guidance. Here are some brief discussions of selected applications that have been and are presently used in the promotion of health care and health care information both in the community and in context of the school.

Demonstration Programs

Demonstrations programs have a long and respected history of use in health care and health care information. Historically, governments around the world have used demonstrations conducted by experts to teach vital skills to their people. Early in the twentieth century, the United States and England initiated public health programs to improve health. These programs were often established in connection with urban neighborhood health clinics that were staffed with health providers who gave out information and offered demonstrations in health management.[10]

Home and Community Demonstrations and Extension Programs

The U.S. Department of Agriculture as well as many state departments used demonstrations and extension services to teach household management and basic health care to rural populations. For example, extension and demonstrations services began in North Carolina in 1909, in Oklahoma in 1910, and in Texas in 1912 with the girls' tomato clubs in Milam County.[11]

By the 1940s, these programs were engaged in the war effort by emphasizing the value of proper canning techniques to prevent food contamination along with food

Figure 2.2.
U.S. Army poster designed to fight sexually transmitted diseases after World War I.
Courtesy of the U.S. government.

production and Victory Gardens. Among others, the emphasis continues today with food preparation, food safety and nutrition, healthy lifestyles, home and work environment and safety, and relationship and parenting skills (Figure 2.3).[12]

School Demonstrations

In 1947, the Minneapolis public schools system introduced a two-year health demonstration project in two of its schools. These demonstrations featured health services,

Figure 2.3.
Domestic education, Travis County (Texas) Negro Extension Service, ca. 1950. Austin Public Library History Center Collection. AR.2000.025. Published by permission of the Austin History Center, Austin Public Library.

healthful living, necessary equipment, and curriculum initiatives. The curriculum emphasized basic skills and health information needed in the schools based on the observed health needs of students, such as dental care and hygiene. Instructional procedures were developed along with testing guides. Each school developed its own program based on its documented needs. In-service training for staff was also included. Basically, each school centered its activities on health information, health guidance for individuals, mental and physical health environments, resources needed for good health, and recreation and physical education. The projects were generally considered a success based on outcome measures obtained from student records and observations of students' improved health behaviors and attitudes.[13]

Today, some of these elements exist in the modern school-based health clinics. The Center for Health and Health Care in Schools located at the George Washington University School of Public Health and Health Services advocates for better health care services through schools. It is particular concerned with helping educators and health professionals collaborate through school-based programs and services. The center views health information as essential in this effort to improve the health of youth.[14]

California has a very active school-based health clinic program. The California School Health Center Association reports that California has 153 clinics and describes them as much like any health clinic where low-cost primary health care, mental health, health education, and dental care services are provided (Figure 2.4).

For example, Santa Clara County operates six clinics located in elementary, middle, and high schools throughout the county. The ages served include children from birth to age 18. The basic goals of the clinics are:[15]

Deliver comprehensive care
Advance health promotion activities
Provide leadership in adolescent and child health care
Involve students and their families in their health care
Support the schools and the community

Health Demonstrations

Health demonstrations share much in common with those of the home demonstration projects and school-based clinics just mentioned. These demonstrations use standard instructional techniques, including lectures, questioning, and the use of both visuals and printed materials along with hands-on experiences to provided needed health information and techniques. In recent years, the U.S. government has encouraged the use of home health demonstrations to reduce the cost of hospital and emergency care. For similar reasons, UNESCO also promotes health demonstrations in various part of the world.

Special magnet schools, such as Med High (South Texas High School for Health Professions) in the South Texas Independent School District in the lower Rio Grande Valley of Texas, have extensive outreach programs where students go out into the community and other schools and present various types of health demonstrations. These demonstrations have proved effective in teaching students how to present health care information, and have benefited the community by providing quality health care information (Figure 2.5).

Standard Lectures and Questioning as Instruction

Standard lectures and the use of questions by instructors have been hallmarks of teaching since ancient times. Lecturers are useful in that they can provide information to groups of people in a short and organized space of time. The essentials of good lectures are to focus on a well-defined topic, understand the needs and backgrounds of audience members, and to provide organized information, engage the audience, and pay attention to time. Generally, a good lecture should be no more than 20 to 25 minutes and should be interactive as appropriate to the audience and to the topic. In an informal setting, interaction can include group discussions and questioning.

Figure 2.4.
School Health Day Rally, California School Health Centers. Published with permission of the California School Health Centers Association.

Figure 2.5.
Community health demonstration by students of the South Texas Independent School District. Published with permission of Lucy Hansen, photographer.

Larger audiences can benefit from the use of audiovisual presentations, demonstrations, integrative technology, handouts, and opportunities to question and interact with the presenter(s) and audience members. Whatever the size of the audience, always provide additional references and resources that will promote future study. Be enthusiastic and show interest in the audience and the topic.

Questioning as Instruction

Although questioning has many applications, this brief discussion centers on how to use questioning in an instructional context. Good questioning of the audience requires a background in the topic and the ability to phrase the question in terms of the topic and the vocabulary of the information. ChangingMinds.org suggests that we use instructional questioning in several different ways. With some modification, in presenting health information, you or the teachers might use questioning to:

Check what they know. What do you know about how to treat minor burns?

Test the audience about what they know and how well they are following the lecture. What is the best way to remove a bandage?

Involve the audience, retain their interest, and offer encouragement. How many of you have faced a situation where you have to make a quick decision about helping a friend who has just burned his or her finger on a stove?

Help the audience to think and discover things for themselves. If you are faced with an emergency and there is no 911 to call, what might you do?

Start a conversation or dialogue. How many of you have wondered about how to calm a person who has just experienced a trauma?

Gather information about the audience. How many of you have been to a minor emergency clinic?

Ascertain basic ideas and beliefs of the audience (via rhetorical questions). What would you want young people like you to know about health in the next 20 years?

Types of Questions and Educational Reasons for Questioning

B. F. Bloom's taxonomy of learning and his Taxonomy of Thinking Skills help us formulate useful questions and questioning strategies, applicable in presenting health information. Factual questions draw out factual answers, check recall, or recognize critical information. Comprehension questions help the learner translate information, extrapolate ideas, or interpret information. This encourages independent thinking. Application questions frame problems that approximate real-life situations. This helps learners practice the principles as they encounter them. Analytic questions encourage learners to become conscious about what is being learned and to accept necessary "rules and principles that provide the foundation to reach a valid conclusion." Synthesis questions help students become creative and original thinkers. Evaluative questions help the instructor determine whether the information had been acquired and understood. Through evaluative questions, learners can appraise and "defend their understanding during all levels of learning."[16] All these types of questions play important roles in presenting health information to all kinds of audiences.

Questioning within an instructional and learning environment offers many avenues for engagement. Questions can:[17]

Arouse curiosity
Stimulate interest in the topic
Clarify concepts
Emphasize key points
Enhance problem-solving ability
Encourage students to think at higher cognitive levels
Motivate student to search for new information
Ascertain students' knowledge level to aid in modifying instruction

Audiovisuals and Interactive Technology

Audiovisuals and information technology (not including printed materials) that employs sight and sound to present information are instructional. Among others, such technologies include audiotapes, videocassettes, CDs and DVDs, slides and slide tape presentations, radio, and television, and emerging digitized media. Audiovisual technology has played a huge role in providing health information to various publics throughout the decades. Although newer technologies, including digitization, are now primary means of visual instruction, advantages learned from previous experiences with audiovisual technologies can still offer us guidance. Digitization in various formats can:[18]

Enhance understanding of ideals and information
Add authenticity to information presentation
Add variety to instruction
Promote lasting impact of information
Enhance retention of information

Promote persuasion toward healthy lifestyles
Help the presenter in planning and organizing information
Help in illustrating complex health concepts

Field Trips and Visits

Field visits have enjoyed a long-established place in educational strategies. They involve a trip or journey to places away from one's normal educational environment. The major aim of the field trip is to provide opportunities for observation, allowing students to have experiences outside of their usual classrooms. Various sciences have used field trips extensively, as have health curricula. Field trips in health often include visits to offices, hospitals, clinics, and laboratories. Research exercises can be included in field trips where students make observations and collect data and/or samples.

Most schools have field trip policies that protect both the student and school personnel. Civic responsibilities are closely aligned with good health behaviors, and these principles often underlie many health information concepts. In the United States, Close Up—a nonprofit organization—promotes American democratic government through field trips to places of civic importance in the Washington, D.C., area[19] Promoting American minority students' interest in the health professions is another of its programs. The Hispanic-Serving Health Professions Schools (HSHPS) also offers field trip opportunities.[20] The U.S. National Institutes of Health (NIH) encourages visits to its facilities, which include the National Library of Medicine. Visit its Web site at www.nih.gov/about/visitor/index.htm.

The Virtual Field Trip

With the advent of the computer and online delivery systems, the virtual field trip offers alternatives to actual field visits. The Teacher Education Center in the College of Education at Illinois State University provides two definitions of the virtual field trip:[21]

Conceptual Definition: "A digitally vicarious experience that allows the participant to travel through space and time free of the constraints of real-world travel, including places, people and events that occur naturally throughout human and natural history."

Working Definition: "A topical collection of Web sites that help students to build upon their existing understanding of a subject or concept by vicarious experience."

A wealth of virtual field trip experiences in a variety of subjects exist on the Internet, many of them free for public use. These trips range from trips to art, scientific, and natural history museums to visits to sites that provide specific health information, such as the Centers for Disease Control and Prevention, the Smithsonian Institution's Global Health Odyssey Museum, and the Franklin Institute's The Human Heart.[22]

Hospitals and other types of health clinics also offer virtual tours. These are often designed to display their facilities and services and to prepare patients who are about to enter the hospital or clinic for treatment. Some examples include Children's Hospital of Wisconsin, the Methodist Children's Hospital of South Texas, and the McLean Hospital of Belmont, Massachusetts, and its Hall-Mercer Children and Adolescents program.[23]

Speaker Programs and Speaker Opportunities

Speakers in classrooms offer much to the classroom teacher in providing good health information. At the local level, many health providers will be glad to speak to classes. These include physicians, physicians' assistants, nurses, and nurse assistants, government health employees, health care administration, and others in the broad field of health care. Often, personal acquaintance will provide avenues for contacts and invitations. Good community networking will make it possible to make contact through local health care associations for well-informed speakers. Local associations often maintain ways of contacting community health care providers. Educational institutions, such as nursing schools, can also offer contact information. Medical associations at the state and local levels customarily have special committees that have expertise in special areas of health, and these committee lists are generally available to the public, offering contact information.

Well-informed and community-based school librarians can bring to the school knowledge of health professionals who are willing to provide presentations at the school or perhaps through video transmission. These persons could let their presentations be archived for later use. It is one of the most effective ways to get an expert to address health issues. If the person is a member of the community, it helps keep the presentation in the local context.

National, state, and local health care agencies generally provide speakers bureaus. For example, CDC lists on its Web site ways to acquire its employees as speakers. Similarly, speaker bureaus are offered by state and local governmental departments of health states. The South Carolina Department of Mental Health, a part of the Department of Public Health, provides a speaker's bureau that lists topics of importance to children and adolescent health, as does the Henderson County (North Carolina) Department of Health. Local hospitals and service groups are especially active in providing speakers within their communities. Some examples of hospitals that offer speaker services include St. John Health in southeast Michigan and Northside Hospital serving the Atlanta area.[24] Commercial agents and speaker bureaus also provide means to acquire speakers under contract based on fee and price structures.

Distance, Online, and Audio-Visual Transmission

Distance learning has become widespread in education in the last few decades. It is often defined in different ways. One prevailing definition of distant learning is:

A type of education, typically college-level, where students work on their own at home or at the office and communicate with faculty and other students via e-mail, electronic forums, videoconferencing, chat rooms, bulletin boards, instant messaging and other forms of computer-based communication.[25]

Another form of distance learning involves interactive television and/or radio. Often, educational service centers and educational television stations will offer interactive television as a means of bringing curriculums to schools that may not have resources to offer a broad-based curriculum. Iowa Learning Online is a product of the Iowa Department of Education. Using both audio-visual transmissions and the Internet, it offers both high school and college course credit to schools throughout Iowa. Among its offerings is Skills for Health, presented through the Internet.[26] Education Service Center 20 in San Antonio offers ways for students K–12 to receive educational experiences through videoconferencing. Generally, it offers contact-to-provider sites that offer appropriate videoconference experiences. For example, one of its providers, Cook Children's Medical Center—located in Ft. Worth, Texas—describes its videoconference services this way:

Cook Children's videoconferencing services include helping to prepare classmates for a patient's return to school, organizing virtual visits with friends and family (especially for patients experiencing extended hospital stays), and providing a variety of videoconference programs to help educate students and educators about many health-related issues.[27]

Commercial, Community, and Cable Network Television and Radio

Over the years, television in its many formats has offered health-related programming to the public. These include public access channels, educational television and radio broadcasting, and hospital-produced films for public presentation. Among others, these include the University of San Diego Medical Center, Redland Community Hospital (California), and the Sutter Health TV serving northern California. Cable Network television is particularly active in offering health commercial television. For example, Discovery Channel produces *Discovery Health*. Some of the *Discovery Health* programs require a certain level of maturity, but for the most part, secondary students can learn a great deal from them.[28]

Radio has been used for decades to promote health and healthy lifestyles. This is especially true in developing countries. UNICEF Radio is a worldwide service that promotes "health, education, equality and protection of children." It presents news and in-depth accounts of health situations around the world. Its technology "includes streaming audio for listeners everywhere, and high quality MP3s available for broadcasters to download free of charge."[29] Other important radio health services include those offered by the BBC[30] in Great Britain and NPR in the United States.[31] Access to most of these programs is available through the Internet and local listings. Yahoo! provides a directory of health-related sites, such as radio and television listings, as well as health education of various types.[32] School librarians can use these listings to alert both teachers and students about upcoming and continuing health programs.

Good health information programs depend on well-understood concepts regarding curricula development and the influences that help shape them. These influences certainly include cultural, social, and educational factors. Instructional strategies naturally follow from this understanding. Health traditionally relies on a number of instructional strategies—notably, demonstrations, small group work, audiovisual methods, and, more recently, electronic transmission through the Internet and audiovisual transmissions. This chapter has briefly discussed these and attempted to place them into the context of how librarians working with youth can use them with understanding and success.

REFLECTIONS

The amount of health information available to the public is enormous. School librarians have the experience and know-how to help their clientele access, understand, question, evaluate, and use this information. Both traditional and newly emerging technologies are available that help make this important task successful.

NOTES

1. Smith, Mark K. "Curriculum Theory and Practice." www.infed.org/biblio/b-curric.htm. Accessed Sept. 19, 2008.

2. Smith.

3. Darling-Hammond, Linda. "Evaluating 'No Child Left Behind.' " *The Nation*, May 21, 2007. www.thenation.com/doc/20070521/darling-hammond. Accessed Sept. 22, 2008.

4. Nutall, Desmond L. and Gordon Stobart. "National Curriculum Assessment in the U.K." *Educational Measurement: Issues and Practice*, 13 (Summer, 1994): 24–27, 39.

5. Volante, Louis and Sonia Ben Jaafar. "Educational Assessment in Canada." *Assessment in Education: Principles, Policy & Practice*, 15 (July 2008): 201–210.

6. Theory. www.merriam-webster.com/dictionary/theory. Accessed Sept. 23, 2008.

7. Cognitive Learning Theory. teachnet.edb.utexas.edu/~lynda_abbott/Cognitive.html. Accessed Sept. 23, 2008.

8. Morgan, Sylvia. "What Is Instructional Design Theory?" http://www.oescher.net/~george/Class/2001Fall/EDCI4993603/Design/WhatIsDesign.html. Accessed March 5, 2010. Citing Ely, D. P. (1996), Instructional Technology: Contemporary and Spector, M. (1996), A Reclamation Project. *Instructional Technology Forum*.

9. Saettler, Paul. *The Evolution of American Educational Technology*. Englewood, Colo.: Libraries Unlimited, 1990, pp. 184–194.

10. Rosen, George. *A History of Public Health*. Expanded ed. Baltimore: Johns Hopkins University Press, 1993.

11. North Carolina State University, D. H. Hill Library, "Green 'N' Growing—The History of Home Demonstration and 4-H Youth Development on North Carolina." www.lib.ncsu.edu/specialcollections/greenngrowing. Accessed Sept. 16, 2008; Cottrell, Debbie Mauldin. "Home Demonstration." *Handbook of Texas Online*. www.tshaonline.org/handbook/online/articles/HH/aah1.html. Accessed Sept. 16, 2008; Wilson, Linda. "Home Demonstration Clubs." *Encyclopedia of Oklahoma History & Culture*. digital.library.okstate.edu/encyclopedia/entries/H/HO020.html. Accessed Sept. 16, 2008; Austin Public Library, Austin History Center, "Travis County Negro Extension Service Photograph Collection, 1940–1964: An Inventory of the Collection at the Austin History Center." www.lib.utexas.edu/taro/aushc/00012/ahc-00012.html. Accessed Sept. 16, 2008.

12. National Extension Association of Family & Consumer Sciences. "About Extension." www.neafcs.org/content.asp?pageID=2. Accessed Sept. 16, 2008.

13. Starr, Helen M. "Health Demonstrations in Two Minneapolis Schools." *American Journal of Public Health*, 29 (Sept. 29, 1949): 1156–1162.

14. The Center for Health and Health Care in Schools, George Washington University School of Public Health and Services. www.healthinschools.org/en/About-Us.aspx. Accessed Sept. 18, 2008.

15. "School Health Clinics of Santa Clara County." www.schoolhealthclinics.org. Accessed Sept. 17, 2008.

16. "Effective Questioning." www.uab.edu/uasomume/cdm/questioning.htm. Accessed Sept. 23, 2008.

17. Effective Questioning.

18. Shelton, Michael W. "Workplace to Workplace—Training Health Educators in the Use of Audiovisual Aids." Paper presented at the annual meeting of the Southern States Communication Association, New Orleans, April 5–9, 1995. Citing Osborn, Michael and Osborn, Susanne. *Public Speaking*. Dallas, Houghton Mifflin, 1992. ERIC reproduction no. ED 384 919.

19. Close Up. www.closeup.org/About/AboutUs.aspx. Accessed Sept. 22, 2008.

20. HSHPS. www.hshps.org/scorner-centers.html#. Accessed Sept. 22, 2008.

21. ETP Ed Tech Immersion Plus. www.coe.ilstu.edu/etip/activities/virtualtrips .shtml. Accessed Sept. 22, 2008.

22. "Global Health Odyssey Museum. www.cdc.gov/gcc/exhibit; Franklin Institute's "The Human Heart." www.fi.edu/learn/heart. Accessed March 5, 2010.

23. Children's Hospital of Wisconsin. www.chw.org/display/PPF/DocID/25763/ router.asp; the Methodist Children's Hospital of South Texas. tour.mhschildrens.com; McLean Hospital of Belmont, Massachusetts, and its Hall-Mercer Children and Adolescents program. www.mclean.harvard.edu/about/virtual. Accessed Sept. 22, 2008.

24. Internet contact information: CDC. www.cdc.gov/od/speakers/index.htm; South Carolina Department of Mental Health. www.state.sc.us/dmh/speakers.htm; Henderson County (North Carolina) Department of Public Health. www.henderson.lib.nc.us/ county/health/web%20pages/speakersbureauhealtheducation.html); St. John Health, southeast Michigan. www.stjohn.org/SpeakersBureau; Marquette General Health System, Marquette, Michigan. www.mgh.org/education/bureau/speaker.html; and Northside Hospital (Atlanta area). www.northside.com/classes_events/speaker_bureau.aspx. All sites accessed Sept. 20, 2008.

25. Distance Learning definition. www.webopedia.com/TERM/D/distance _learning.html. Accessed Sept. 24, 2008.

26. Iowa Learning Online. www.iowalearningonline.org/about.cfm. Accessed Sept. 22, 2008.

27. Cook Children's Medical Center. www.cookchildrens.org/Pages/default.aspx. Accessed Sept. 22, 2008.

28. San Diego Medical Center. http://health.ucsd.edu/index.aspx; Redlands. www.redlandshospital.org; Sutter Health. www.sutterhealth.org. Accessed March 5, 2019; Discovery Channel, *Discovery Health*. health.discovery.com. Accessed Sept. 19, 2008.

29. UNICEF Radio. www.unicef.org/videoaudio/video_radio.html. Accessed Sept. 24, 2008.

30. BBC. www.bbc.co.uk/worldservice/programmes/health_check.shtml. Accessed Sept. 24, 2008.

31. NPR. www.npr.org/templates/story/story.php?storyId=1007. Accessed Sept. 25, 2008.

32. Yahoo! Health Directory. dir.yahoo.com/Health. Accessed Sept. 24, 2008.

3

Teaching and Holistic Health Information Literacy

In this chapter, we discuss how to provide good health instruction. Problems that affect good health instruction are diverse. Some of these are not connected directly to schools but nevertheless significantly influence instruction and environment in the school. Figure 3.1 outlines these.

Poor Physical Health of Students
- Lead poisoning
- Asthma
- Diabetes
- Cancer
- Epilepsy
- Low birthrate
- Chronic illnesses affect between 5 and 15 percent of youth
- Lack of food nourishment
- Mental and emotional well-being

Dysfunctional Family Life
- Marital instability
- Family relocations
- Violence in the home
- Homelessness
- Achievement difficulties
- Abusive family life
- Poverty

Community Risks
- Economically deprived communities
- Culturally and socially disorganized communities

- ○ Lack of employment opportunities
- ○ Lack of youth support structures
- ○ Community violence
- ○ Unsupervised out-of-school time

School and School Environments

- ○ Poor teacher attitudes and support
- ○ Unsatisfactory school values (e.g., undue competition)
- ○ Unsafe environments (emotional and physical safety)
- ○ Lack of opportunities for school involvement (students and family)
- ○ Poor and/or destructive peer culture[1]

Figure 3.1.

Problems inhibiting good instruction, including health instruction.

Nevertheless, advocating good health instruction addresses the causes of these issues and their remedies. Helping teachers cooperate in teaching health issues will raise their awareness caused by these problems, and it may prepare them to be more aware and helpful with students who have these problems.

TEACHERS AND SCHOOL LIBRARIANS AS HOLISTIC HEALTH EDUCATORS

A standard dictionary definition of holistic is "emphasizing the organic or functional relation between parts and the whole" (wordnetweb.princeton.edu/perl/webwn ?s=holistic). In medicine, the word holistic means "a philosophy of medical care that views physical and mental and spiritual aspects of life as closely interconnected and equally important approaches to treatment" (en.wikipedia.org/wiki/Holistic_medicine). In a theoretical sense

Holistic education is concerned with connections in human experience between mind and body, between linear thinking and intuitive ways of knowing, between academic disciplines, between individual and community, and between the personal self and the transpersonal self that all spiritual traditions believe exist beyond the ego.[2]

In this book, we offer a pragmatic view, believing that the holistic curriculum unites and blends all subject areas together to provide good, reliable, and understandable health information. In order for us as teachers and school librarians to become holistic health educators, we must remind ourselves of the major issues included not only in providing good instruction, but we must learn and accept the important connection between holistic health education and literacy. We must always keep in mind that holistic health literacy assumes an important role in advancing comprehensive information literacy.

MAJOR ISSUES IN HOLISTIC HEALTH EDUCATION AND LITERACY

Simply put, health instruction and health literacy is a central part of information literacy. In the words of the *National Health Education Standards* (2nd ed.), health instruction promotes critical thinking and problem solving, and it contributes to developing responsible, productive citizens.[3] In concert with information literacy, health education encourages self-directed learning and effective communication.

Research suggests that health instruction has an immediate effect on learning. Research in the 1980s indicated that: "Students receiving health instruction had higher knowledge scores than students with no health instruction, with the greatest differences seen in knowledge of substance use and abuse."[4] Even minimum exposure (e.g., 50 hours per school year) to health instruction increased students' health knowledge, indicating that more hours spent on health instruction would increase health knowledge significantly.[5]

Non-Health health specialists, such as teachers and school librarians, are fast emerging as necessary and important components of health education, but this poses challenges. Youth at all ages face unhealthy situations. Smoking, drinking, driving habits, drug use, sexual behavior, and dangers found in home environments are examples of behaviors and situations that place youth at risk. Unfortunately, just providing health information does not appear to impact how students internalize and apply this information. A variety of teaching skills are needed to reinforce health information and to help students apply it to their lives.

To reinforce health information are skills and techniques that nonhealth specialist teachers already have. For example, communication skills, decision-making, and refusal skills are essential for youth in handling and understanding their health situations, and most of these techniques and skills are found in all curriculum areas. A systematic, all-curriculum approach to health also influences better academic achievement. Health-aware students appear to transfer to a healthier life with added academic confidence. In some ways, teachers may have more influence on health attitudes and behaviors of students because of actually spending more time with them than do their parents.[6]

Of course, teachers have significant demands on their time. These include classroom management, use of technology, multicultural education, and preparing mandated content. The increasing use of standardized testing to measure educational attainment also prevents many teachers from spending time on any non-test-related curriculum, such as health and physical education, music, and art. Health education often includes sensitive subjects, such as sexuality, anatomy, and drug abuse. Teachers sometimes find these difficult to teach and feel that their pre-professional education has not properly equipped them for this type of instruction.[7]

To overcome some of these limitations, health educator Summerfield recommends that schools and teachers rely on the *National Health Education Standards* (2007). Included in these standards are basic behaviors that student should learn. According to these standards, students are able to:

- Understand how to prevent disease
- Access health information accurately
- Demonstrate good health behaviors and skills
- Understand, analyze, and influence and improve cultural and social health and risk situations
- Use technology and media for good health information
- Implement good international communication in improving health
- To set and follow-through on goal setting and decision-making for better health
- Become advocates for better health in home, school, and community

Within these objectives are suggestions for subject content that will help students better acquire these behaviors:

- Community health
- Consumer health
- Environmental health
- Personal health and fitness
- Family life education
- Nutrition and healthy eating
- Disease prevention and control
- Safety and injury prevention
- Substance use and abuse prevention
- Growth and development[8]

The hallmark of all these suggestions is that they should and must be implemented within all areas of the curriculum. As mentioned, at a minimum, broad-based health instruction should provide at least 50 hours per year of health instruction. School librarians working with the faculty and staff can play important roles in health curriculum and instruction and increase time devoted to health instruction beyond the limits of 50 hours. In terms of curriculum integration, these guidelines work well with those of UNESCO outlined in Chapter 1.

Authorities have considered the confidence level of teachers to teach health subjects across the curriculum. A study of newly credentialed teachers in the United Kingdom focused on the importance of all English teachers to be involved in teaching health. This study noted that English teachers have unique skills needed to teach health topics but that they do not recognize these skills and have not been trained to employ them within health education. In fact, the study noted that because of the lack of pre-service training, external health education sources are often better at presenting health information to students. Such presentations are often not effective because they generally focus on large groups of students.[9]

Situations often require that classroom teachers provide health information that is very specific and goes far beyond general health information. These demands often come from government mandates that require nonhealth educators to become proficient at providing health instruction. Teachers are often not confident to do this. They feel that they lack the preparation to offer this level of instruction, and they have not been trained to engage students in meaningful ways based on these specific mandates. While it would take in-service and staff development sessions to update veteran teachers, university education programs could provide such instruction for pre-service teachers.

Pre-service education institutions are now beginning to offer health training for nonhealth specialist educators as well as others interested in the health of youth. At the University of Texas at Austin, several courses from many academic areas are offered for the general undergraduate population. Among others, these include Child and Adolescent Health; Family Violence; Introduction to Early Childhood Intervention Social Work in Health Care; Service to Abused/Neglected Children; Nutrition Through the Life Cycle; Family Policy Issues; and Socioeconomic Problems of the Family.

The values contained in such courses are becoming clear, especially in building teachers' confidence about teaching health concepts and facts. After completing a course called Drug and Health Issues for Educators, pre-service education students at Montana State University discussed with confidence such health topics as mental health, fitness, nutrition, sexuality, tobacco, alcohol, drugs, and social relationships. Additionally, they described the health profile of Montana's youth K–12 and identified students who were likely to be a risk for health-related situations. Most importantly, they applied health concepts to their areas of teaching concentrations and suggested appropriate health information for students. These students also felt more comfortable in defending and presenting their views regarding controversial health issues.[10]

As standards are generated for teaching specific subjects, teachers learn to teach to the standards. Standards are available for health instruction.

STANDARDS, OUTCOME MEASURES, AND ASSESSMENTS FOR HEALTH INSTRUCTION

Standards

The National Health Education Standards are based on education that provides clear identification of what students are expected "to know and be able to do." To accomplish this, teaching and instruction must be aimed at specific skills, attitudes, and behaviors. Standards must focus on student learning in terms of assessment, curriculum, and instruction.[11]

Assessments

In 1999, the National Center for Research on Evaluation, Standards, and Student Testing defined assessment as: "The process of gathering, describing, or quantifying information about performance."[12] Figure 3.2 outlines the essentials of assessment.

Approaches to Assessments

Assessment approaches are varied and include examinations and performance tasks. Structured response assessment examinations often provide for multiple choice, matching, and true and false questions. Constructed response assessment examinations

---

- Promotion of student learning
- Alignments of standards, assessment, curriculum, and instruction
- Use of a variety of equitable, valid, and reliable assessments that ensure flexibility to meet the needs of a diverse student body
- Provision to students of clear information about performance criteria
- Provision to students of multiple opportunities to apply and master health-related concepts and skills and ongoing feedback to enhance their learning of these concepts and skills
- Provision to students and family members of information regarding student achievement
- Ongoing review and improvement of assessments and assessment systems

---

Figure 3.2.
Principles of assessment promoted by the *National Health Education Standards*.

Source: Joint Committee on National Health Standards. *National Health Education Standard: Achieving Excellence.* 2nd ed. Atlanta, Ga.: National Cancer Society, p. 88.

incorporate short answer and essay questions. Performances and displays can include developing posters, performing skits, role-playing, preparing public service announcements, preparing and conducting surveys, developing personal and family health plans, keeping journals of readings and observations, preparing and publishing brochures, and writing letters to the editors of local, regional, and national newspapers and magazines.[13] Higher-level performances can have students involved in community activities, such as helping plan and execute health fairs and conferences, teaching younger students about health issues, performing demonstrations at public venues, enrolling in practicum and internships, and undertaking service learning projects.

Service-learning projects are systematic learning experiences that are designed to help students learn tasks, but they go beyond that in that they help students focus on social and psychological understandings that come for service-learning experiences. Service-learning is further explained as:

[A] method of teaching, learning and reflecting that combines academic classroom curriculum with meaningful service, frequently youth service, throughout the community. As a teaching methodology, it falls under the philosophy of experiential education. More specifically, it integrates meaningful community service with instruction and reflection to enrich the learning experience, teach civic responsibility, encourage lifelong civic engagement, and strengthen communities for the common good.[14]

Health instruction at higher levels of the curriculum can certainly benefit from service-learning activities. An example worth noting is the award-winning Y-RISE (Youth Replicating Innovative Strategies and Excellence in HIV/AIDS prevention) of the National Youth Leadership Council (NYLC). It is a multilevel "effort to mobilize young people in the fight against AIDS." Students conduct research, and they are given appropriate training that helps connect knowledge and behavior.[15]

Service-learning has the support of the U.S. government through the National and Community Service Act of 1990 and amended in 1999. Grants for service-learning projects based in schools are available through this act.[16]

Outcome Measures

Outcome measures for assessing teaching effectiveness are essential in health education. Outcome measures in teaching are not teaching objectives; rather, these outcomes are what we as teachers and instructors can measure as a result of our instruction. In other words, course outcomes are very specific statements that describe exactly what a student will be able to do in some measurable way after completing the course.[17] Observation scales are necessary for outcome measures. These are specific performances of students that include desired skills and behaviors. These may include assessing the developmental progress of students as they move toward meeting desired outcomes and standards.[18]

Health outcome measures are straightforward. For example, skilled-based learning describes a skill and states exactly what a student is to learn and how he or she can demonstrate the skill.

Health Rubric

Level 4

In this response, evidence shows that the student has a full and complete understanding of the question or problem.

Pertinent and complete supporting details demonstrate an integration of ideas.

The use of accurate scientific terminology enhances the response.

An effective application of the concept to a practical problem or real-world situation reveals an insight into health principles.

The response reflects a complete synthesis of information.

Level 3

In this response, evidence shows that the student has a good understanding of the question or problem.

The supporting details are generally complete.

The use of accurate scientific terminology strengthens the response.

The concept has been applied to a practical problem or real-world situation.

The response reflects some synthesis of information.

Level 2

In this response, evidence shows that the student has a basic understanding of the question or problem.

The supporting details are adequate.

The use of accurate scientific terminology may be present in the response.

The application of the concept to a practical problem or real-world situation is inadequate.

The response provides little or no synthesis of information.

Level 1

In this response, evidence shows that the student has some understanding of the question or problem.

The supporting details are only minimally effective.

The use of accurate scientific terminology is not present in the response.

The application, if attempted, is irrelevant.

The response addresses the question.

Level 0

In this response, evidence shows that the student has no understanding of the question or problem.

The response is completely incorrect or irrelevant or there is no response.

Figure 3.3.

Examples of health assessment criteria at four levels of obtainment based on evidence.

Source: Maryland State Department of Education (MSDE) form of the high school assessment (mdk12.org/assessments/high_school/look_like/index.html).

As we see from examples in Figure 3.3, learning outcomes are based on exact statements of what a student will demonstrate as a result of having been taught within a well-defined unit of study. Demonstrated outcomes are based on the expected level of learning and expected skills and information gained that can be measured and assessed.[19]

Examples of Outcome Measures in a Unit Entitled "Stereotype & Bias"

"Stereotype & Bias" is one of several health units developed by The Teacher Enrichment Initiatives.[20] This is an organization of San Antonio, Texas, area teachers, health professionals, and researchers from the University of Texas Health Science Center at San Antonio (UTHSCSA) (Figure 3.4). All the instructional units are designed to help teachers teach important concepts of health and health awareness.

The particular section under review here is within the "Stereotype & Bias" unit called "Old as I See It." Students first share their views of aging based on reviewing images of aging in the media and being exposed to the diversity among aged individuals. Students after instruction are again asked to depict their image of old age. Rather than draw a picture, collages are made that incorporate their own illustrations, pictures from magazines, and written descriptions. Students then compare and contrast their collages with the pictures developed for a previous unit called "Help the N.I.A." (National Institute of Aging), where they drew a picture of a typical old person. This exercise brings out the students' images of what they consider to be the characteristic appearance, dress, and habits of older persons. Learning outcomes at the end of the instructional unit state that students will be able to:

- Examine their own preconceived views of older people.
- Draw and describe an older person.
- Evaluate the portrayal of older people in the media.
- Develop a concept of "how old is old."

For each of the behaviors, students are measured against established criteria for performance and attainments.

The National Health Standards provide some examples of acceptable attainment levels, ranging from "not reach standards" to "sophisticated demonstration (exceeds

Figure 3.4.
Teachers involved with the teacher enrichment initiatives. Published with permission of University of Texas Health Science Center Library.

Levels of Standards Assessments for Students
    Level 1. Attempted demonstration. Does not meet standards.
      Response form is incomplete or completed with significant errors
    Level 2. Partial demonstration. Partially meets standards.
      Student accurately completes most of the response form, but some evidence may be
        missing
    Level 3. Proficient demonstration (meets standards)
      Student accurately completes response form with clear examples and explains evidence to
        support validity for 4–5 products and services
    Level 4. Sophisticated demonstration (exceed standards)
      Student accurately completes response form and "clearly explains evidence and a rationale
        that verifies reliability for each product and service."

Figure 3.5.
Examples of levels of assessments.

Source: "Performance Assessment. Tobacco Free Is the Way to Be." *National Health Education Standards,*
2nd ed., pp. 104–106.

standards)" in a unit entitled "Tobacco Free Is the Way to Be." One of the outcomes expected in this unit for grades 9–12 students is: "Students will know how to acquire valid information about health issues, services, and products." Students are asked to list two products and three services that can help tobacco users quit. On a worksheet, they are asked to list the products and services and then to provide evidence and a rationale for the validity of the products and services.[21] Figure 3.5 illustrates levels of assessments.

Teaching with Textbooks

Textbooks have played an important part in education for centuries. The use of the modern textbook in North America and especially in the United States begins in the mid-nineteenth century with the widespread use of the *McGuffey Readers* and Noah Webster's *Blue Back Speller.* Textbooks still flourish for several good reasons. Simply put, they do the following:

- Help to maintain a standard uniformity in instruction
- Attempt to ensure a consistent level of national identity and values
- Help with teacher's day-to-day preparation and delivery of instruction
- Help to overcome lack of teacher training
- Offer needed resources for instruction

The California Department of Education says this about textbooks:

Adoptions [of textbooks] in the core subject areas are a powerful leverage point for educational reform and improvement in student achievement. The impact of instructional materials on classroom learning is significant and has been shown to be an essential tool for teachers in today's classrooms. Recent research underscores the educational importance of textbooks and instructional materials, not only as the primary mode of access for California's students to State Content Standards and the knowledge and skills they must master, but also as an indispensable platform for fostering teacher learning and a key component of ongoing professional development.[22]

The department reminds us that countless days and hours go into making textbook selection decisions. While no one disputes that, textbook publishing is a huge industry. Texas alone is believed to spend approximately $500 million annually on textbooks.

USING TEXTBOOKS EFFECTIVELY IN COLLABORATION AND COLLECTION DEVELOPMENT

Textbooks are useful in developing library as well as classroom collections, although they should never be the mainstay of collections. Most textbooks list books and other resources. Consider these points in collection development:

- Examine appropriate bibliographies and lists contained in textbooks. Note their publication date and, in consultation with the subject teacher, decide if these or others titles need to be purchased to supplement the text and current instructional strategies. Often, textbook lists are dated, and an updating of new material will be helpful. Sometimes, textbooks will list items that do not find their ways into standard selection tools used by librarians and consequentially are not added to the collection. Examine texts for such items and, in consultation with instructors, determine items that need to be acquired that will add depth to an existing health collection.
- Online and other digitized instructional items are now an integral part of materials produced and supplied by textbook publishers to aid instruction based on their textbooks. Sometimes, these are available either online or on request from the publisher after purchase of a textbook for use. Librarians can collaborate with instructors to make sure that these are available to students and to teachers as needed.
- The Mississippi state textbook list offers information on many of these online and audiovisual resources.[23] For example:
  o Harcourt School Publishers, *Health*, Grade K–5 provides teaching transparencies, posters, interactive teaching transparencies CD-ROM, Be-Active Music for Daily Physical Activity CD, and All-in One CD-ROM for Planning.
  o The Macmillan/McGraw-Hill, *Health and Wellness*, K–5, offers an impressive array of support materials including CDs and the videos *Your Body Video: All About Boys* and *Your Body Video: All About Girls*, provides "School to Home Connection" component.

Chapter 8 discusses in more detail the use of textbooks within health and physical education and instruction.

INSTRUCTIONAL CENTERED MATERIALS AND TEACHER-LIBRARIAN COLLABORATION

Collaboration is discussed in many areas of instruction, and much of the literature and research surrounding this topic recognizes that this is not an easy task. Textbooks have a role to play in collaboration. Many variables enhance collaboration and/or discourage it depending on circumstances. For example, collaboration involves the willingness to recognize and share useful expertise and knowledge with others. Collaboration requires teachers and school librarians to know when territoriality and authority require respect and to know when they become a hindrance to collaboration. Social and personal rewards are important in all collaboration undertakings, as they bring a sense of professional and personal achievement. All collaborative situations have social and administrative characteristics that must be recognized, used, and/or altered to advance positive collaboration. On a larger scale, cultural and political considerations will play a role in how collaboration develops.[24] Understanding textbooks and classroom-centered materials and the role they play in a teacher's planning can only help the school librarian engage in better collaboration efforts.

SCHOOL LIBRARY STANDARDS AND COLLABORATION

Like textbooks, the school librarian who understands professional standards in all curriculum areas is better equipped to engage the teacher in collaboration. *Standards for the 21st-Century Learner in Action* developed by the American Association of School Librarians (AASL) offers a detailed plan that librarians can use to collaborate with physical education and health teachers. The basic AASL standards followed in this guide clearly match those of classroom health and physical education as well as *National Standards for Health Education*. The AASL standards (discussed elsewhere in this book) are:

1. Inquire, think critically, and gain knowledge.
2. Draw conclusions, make informed decisions, apply knowledge to new situations, and create new knowledge.
3. Share knowledge and participate ethically and productively as members of our democratic society.
4. Pursue personal and aesthetic growth.[25]

We discuss a selected list of national subject area standards later in this chapter. Lesson plans suggestions in Chapter 6 provide ideas about how teachers and librarians can collaborate through the use of literature (fiction, poetry, and drama), biography, sports, dance, music and other forms of artistic expression and performances, and foreign languages. Comments and teaching suggestions are found in Chapters 7 and 8, and Chapter 9 continues these ideas associated with social and behavioral sciences and mathematics. Chapter 9 also considers how standards for economics, agriculture, technology education (formerly industrial arts), and human ecology (also known as home economics) play important roles in health education.

In terms of collaboration, AASL specifically notes how librarians and teachers can collaborate. Furthermore, the following suggestions are based on AASL's suggestions, with modifications to fit health and physical education instructions.[26]

- **Grade K. Community and Community Helpers.** Identify community helpers (including health providers) and learn how to seek help in emergencies.
- **Grade 1. Science.** Investigate insects and know how to identify harmful insects to be avoided.
- **Grade 2. History and Cultural Diversity.** Introduce students to health concepts in history through biography and contributions of minorities e.g., African-American contributions, such as Charles Drew and the development of blood plasma).
- **Grade 3. Political Science/Civics.** Introduce students to the role of governments in health and health services. Introduce some of the major government health agencies at the state, provincial, and national levels.
- **Grade 4. Science/Technology.** Consider the food supply chain and the major technologies used in food delivery (e.g., farm to market delivery, trucking, rail, air, refrigeration needs).

- **Grade 5. Health.** Introduce the healthy diet and ask students to consider the effects of consumption of junk food on their activities and health.
- **Grade 6. Science.** Develop the concept of energy sources (e.g., dependency on fossil fuels) and resulting environment effects on health.
- **Grade 7. Social Studies/Language Arts/Technology.** Introduce selected medical terms and show students how to use general and specialized dictionaries to better understand medical terms. Help students appreciate language history and how to use dictionaries to understand how words develop (etymology). Consider community history, and help students see how health providers played a role in community history (e.g., early hospitals, doctors, nurses, county health agencies).
- **Grade 8. Science/Math/Language Arts.** Introduce the concept of climate change and health. How will climate change affect persons with chronic illnesses, such as breathing difficulties and diabetes. Consider how climate change is measured scientifically. Discuss how the mass media reports on climate change. What is the tone of the language or arguments used? Ask students to consider if the mass media are more concerned with health issues or political issues? Ask students to consider if the need for profit in the mass media industry influences reporting about health?
- **Grade 9. English/Technology.** Introduce students to authors that write on health issues for the popular adult reader as well as young adult readers. Introduce information technologies and search strategies that will help students identify these authors.
- **Grade 10. Math/Comparing Data.** Introduce students to the concept of health demographics and to health data that are widely available on the Internet. Introduce students to Inspire Data software[27] and how data can be imported into this software. Have students select a recent time period and trace (analyze) the increase or decline of selected diseases over given times based on the data they import.
- **Grades 11–12. English/Language Arts.** Encourage students to consider health in cultural contexts. How is health expressed in the arts? Discuss the worldwide use of alternative medicines, non-western medical traditions, and the folklore of health and cures.

No matter what the grade, all these suggestions can be supported by appropriate grade-level information literacy instruction, research techniques, and information technologies. Ideas about health instruction and helpful sources for instruction are needed, and an abundance of sources and ideas do exist. Likewise, standards from many curriculum areas lend support for integrating health topics in instruction.

SUGGESTIONS FOR HEALTH INSTRUCTIONAL UNITS

As just stated, opportunities are available throughout a school's curriculum to develop topics that focus on health information. For example, these include:[28]

Science: Studying the effects of tobacco and smoking on the body
Math: Analyzing survey data on attitudes of students regarding smoking and tobacco use
Language Arts: Writing and producing anti-smoking and anti-tobacco use materials
Social Sciences and History: Studying and analyzing the economic factors involved for the individuals who smoke and use tobacco as well as its impact on communities where tobacco is grown and processed

Business and Commerce: Analysis of economic impact of tobacco use in terms of health care and health management and commercial profitability

As stated, curriculum standards developed to support learning objectives in several important subject areas are discussed further in this chapter; and additional ideas and procedures for introducing health in a variety of curriculum areas are presented in more detail in later chapters.

HELPFUL RESOURCES

Many helpful sources for curriculum and instruction support already exist. Some of these offer step-by-step guides to health literary instruction, while other provide resource support. The following is only a small example of what is available.

Educator's Reference Desk (a service of ERIC): Provides "high-quality resources and services to the education community." This includes Information Institute of Syracuse's AskERIC, Gateway to Educational Materials, and the Virtual Reference Desk. The Educator's Reference (www.eduref.org) offers more than 2,000 lesson plans and 3,000 links to online education information as well as a question responses archive. Health units include:

- Health
- Body systems and senses
- Chronic conditions
- Consumer health
- Environmental health
- Family life
- Human sexuality
- Mental health
- Nutrition
- Process skills
- Safety
- Substance abuse prevention

Health Teacher: Designed to help health teachers build health literacy among students (www.healthteacher.com). The curriculum ideas presented are based on the nine core topics identified in the *National Health Education Standards*. Health Teacher is a for- profit company. Samples of its curriculum units are available on its Web site.

Curriculum and Instructional Materials Collection (CIMC): "The CIMC is a specialized collection of resources for preschool through high school educators. Its primary mission is to assist education majors in the development of instructional activities by providing access to state-of-the-art instructional resources and technologies." It offers over 580 pages of 2,100 selected links to resources for K–12 instruction. A great deal of detail is provided for each link that it recommends. A search engine will take you right to health topics and resources (library.uncc.edu/display/?dept=reference&format=open&page=674).

KidsHealth in the Classroom: An online resource for educators (kidshealth.org/classroom). It offers free health curriculum materials for grades K–12 in various subject areas. The teachers' guides provide "discussion questions, activities, and reproducible handouts and quizzes— all aligned to recently updated national health education standards."

National Library of Medicine (US): Offers access and recommendations to a tremendous variety of health information that is useful to teachers, students, and the general public (www.nlm.nih.gov). Among these are:

- **BlackHealthcare (blackhealthcare.com).** "A culturally oriented and ethically focused comprehensive Internet-based health and medical information provider dedicated to addressing the special health problems of African-Americans."
- **Consumer Health Information in Many Languages (nnlm.gov/outreach/consumer/multi.html).** "A wealth of Internet sites that contain health information in several languages." The Spanish language section is the largest section.
- **Exhibition Program: K–12 Resources on the Web (NLM) (www.nlm.nih.gov/hmd/about/exhibition/index.html).** Exhibitions provide "primary sources and interdisciplinary topics that can engage young students visually and intellectually."
- **Genetics Home Reference (ghr.nlm.nih.gov).** "Provides summaries of genetic conditions and their molecular basic in straightforward, easy-to-understand language."
- **Healthfinder (www.healthfinder.gov).** "A free gateway to reliable consumer health and human services information." Available in Spanish at www.healthfinder.gov/espanol).
- **MedlinePlus (medlineplus.gov).** "A free, comprehensive, authoritative, up-to-date health information Web site." Designed for the consumer. Available in Spanish at medlineplus.gov/Spanish.
- **PubMed (www.ncbi.nlm.nih.gov/pubmed).** "The U.S. National Library of Medicine's premier search system for professional and technical health information."
- **Toxnet (toxnet.nlm.nih.gov).** Access to "databases on hazardous chemicals environmental health and toxic releases."
- **TocMystery (toxmystery.nlm.nih.gov and toxmystery.nlm.nih.gov/espanol.html).** An interactive children's game designed for children ages 7 to 10 . . . teaching important lessons about potential environmental health hazards,

In addition to these sources, NLM promotes Resources for Science Teachers that highlight NLM's resources available through their various Web sites in biology, chemistry, genetics, and Spanish-language resources, careers in science and health, and general health topics.

EthnoMed (ethnomed.org). Contains information about cultural beliefs, medical issues, and other related health issues of recent immigrants to the United States

The National Alliance for Hispanic Health (www.hispanichealth.org). "Health facts on numerous topics are available in English and Spanish."

National Center for Farmworker Health (www.ncfh.org) and Bilingual Patient Education Materials (www.ncfh.org/?pid=154). "The NCFH mission is to improve the health status of farmworker families through human, technical and informational services."

Noah New York Online Access to Health (www.noah-health.org). "Provides access to high quality full-text consumer health information in English and Spanish"

Spiral: Selected Patient Information Resources in Asian Languages (www.library.tufts.edu/hsl/spiral). "Provides increased access to Asian Language electronic resources for consumers and healthcare providers"

THE FOR-PROFIT CONSULTANT AND PUBLISHER

Commercial companies produce and publish health information instructional units. This includes companies like Health Teacher.[29] In addition, for-profit firms also provide instructors and consultants to help in delivering instruction; planning conferences and workshops; and developing other types of instructional presentations. One such service is the Health & Education Communication Consultants (HECC) firm located in California. Its activities include developing materials and publishing, social marketing, and offering training and technical assistance to its clients. A 2003 project included "On Your Own: Explorations in Nutrition and Physical Activity." For this project, HECC developed and field-tested a "high school nutrition/physical activity multimedia program with funding from the National Institute of Diabetes and Digestive and Kidney Diseases. The final curriculum is published by Glencoe/McGraw Hill."[30]

Too numerous to name in detail, many publishers offer both print and nonprint health information items for sale. For example, Salem Press offers Salem Health, a "new online resource that is free to libraries and schools purchasing the printed versions of Salem's healthcare reference." Gale Research offers online health-related databases designed for the general user. PBS offers a fine line of DVDs related to health issues. Some of these products provide downloadable resources for instruction. Library and information science publishers, such as Libraries Unlimited, McFarland, and Neal-Schuman, offer professional resources helping in collection development and program and service planning.

THE LINK BETWEEN SCHOOL LIBRARIANS AND HEALTH LITERACY

AASL's *Standards for the 21st Century*, outlined in Chapter 1, provide school librarians and teachers guidance as we face the complex issues of the twenty-first century. A review of these standards shows AASL's close relationship to the *National Health Education Standards* (2nd ed. 2007).[31]

School librarians not only have an opportunity but also an obligation to form close, collaborative relationships with teachers across the curriculum in promoting both information literacy and importantly health information literacy so youth can live productive personal and comfortable lives well into the future.

STANDARDS AND GUIDELINES: BASIC ELEMENTS IN PLANNING HEALTH INSTRUCTION

One of the basic assumptions we make in this book is that health information and health information literacy do not exist only in health units or in physical education but that they are integrated in all areas across the modern curriculum. As discussed earlier, this concept underpins the health education initiatives of both CDC and UNESCO.

Planning a basic instruction unit lies at the heart of good health information delivery and better health behaviors on the part of all people. All governments play roles in promoting viable health instruction through directives, guides, and standards. Professional groups also add to this dialogue by likewise publishing and/or promoting standards and teaching guides.

As we have seen, the second edition of the *National Health Education Standards* (NHES) reinforces the idea that health is found everywhere in the curriculum through its insistence that health education must be a coordinated component of school health programs. This approach must be reinforced by health education designed to promote positive health behaviors. All these standards are fundamental, as they all focus on changing poor health behaviors and reinforce already existing good health behaviors. NHES Standards 2 and 3 are particularly important for school library media specialists and teachers who teach outside the traditional areas of health and physical education. The rationale for Standard 2 follows:[32]

Health is affected by a variety of positive and negative influences within society. This standard focuses on identifying and understanding the diverse internal and external factors that influence health practices and behaviors among youth, including personal values, beliefs, and perceived norms.

Standard 2 reads: "Students will analyze the influence of family, peers, culture, media, technology, and other factors on health behaviors"[33] and makes these specific proposals:[34]

Pre-K–Grade 2. Students will:

• Identify how the family influences personal health practices and behaviors.
• Identify what the school can do to support personal health practices and behaviors.
• Describe how the media can influence health behaviors.

Grades 3–5. Students will:

• Describe how the family influences personal health practices and behaviors.
• Identify the influence of culture on health practices and behaviors.
• Identify how peers can influence healthy and unhealthy behaviors.
• Describe how the school and community can support personal health practices and behaviors.
• Explain how media influences thoughts, feelings, and health behaviors
• Describe ways that technology can influence personal health.

Grades 6–8. Students will:

• Examine how the family influences the health of adolescents.
• Describe the influence of culture on health beliefs, practices, and behaviors.
• Describe how peers influence healthy and unhealthy behaviors.
• Analyze how the school and community can affect personal health practices and behaviors.
• Analyze how messages from media influence health behaviors.
• Analyze the influence of technology on personal and family health.
• Explain how the perceptions of norms influence healthy and unhealthy behaviors.
• Explain the influence of personal values and beliefs on individual health practices and behaviors.
• Describe how some health risk behaviors can influence the likelihood of engaging in unhealthy behaviors.

Grades 9–12. Students will:

• Explain how school and public health policies can influence health promotion and disease prevention.
• Analyze how the family influences the health of individuals.
• Analyze how the culture supports and challenges health beliefs, practices, and behaviors.

- Analyze how peers influence healthy and unhealthy behaviors.
- Evaluate how the school and community can affect personal health practice and behaviors.
- Evaluate the effect of media on personal and family health.
- Evaluate the impact of technology on personal, family, and community health.
- Analyze how the perceptions of norms influence healthy and unhealthy behaviors.
- Analyze the influence of personal values and beliefs on individual health practices and behaviors.
- Analyze how some health risk behaviors can influence the likelihood of engaging in unhealthy behaviors.
- Analyze how public health policies and government regulations can influence health promotion and disease prevention.

The rational for Standard 3 is:[35]

Access to valid health information and health-promoting products and services is critical in the prevention, early detection, and treatment of health problems. This standard focuses on how to identity and access valid health resources and to reject unproven sources. Application of the skills of analysis, comparison, and evaluation of health resources empowers students to achieve health literacy.

Standard 3 offers particular value to school -librarians. It reads: "Students will demonstrate the ability to access valid information and products and services to enhance health."[36] Standard 3 makes these specific recommendations:[37]
   Pre-K–Grade 2. Students will:

- Identify trusted adults and professionals who can help promote health.
- Identify ways to locate school and community health helpers.

   Grade 3–5. Students will:

- Identify characteristics of valid health information, products, and services.
- Locate resources from home, school, and community that provide valid health information.

   Grade 6–8. Students will:

- Analyze the validity of health information, products, and services.
- Access valid health information from home, school, and community.
- Determine the accessibility of products that enhance health.
- Describe situations that may require professional health services.
- Locate valid and reliable health products and services.

   Grades 9–12. Students will:

- Evaluate the validity of health information, products, and services.
- Use resources from home, school, and community that provide valid health information.
- Determine the accessibility of products and services that enhance health.
- Determine when professional health services may be required.
- Access valid and reliable health products and services.

INTEGRATING NATIONAL CURRICULUM STANDARDS INTO HEALTH INSTRUCTION

Other important national standards from many areas of the curriculum reinforce the relationships between health education and health information literacy. Most of the elements in these standards can be integrated into well-planned health-based instructional units. Examples of such units are provided in Chapters 6, 7, and 9 as well as other chapters. The following statements are brief annotations of selected standards that illustrate major achievement concepts. Good, across-the-curriculum integrative health curriculum and instructional planning always begins with a clear understanding of national standards for subject areas. In later chapters, many of these standards are placed within health-based instructional units.

Music

National Standards for Music Education are developed by the National Association of Music Educators. These standards promote:

Singing, alone and with others, a varied repertoire of music
Performing on instruments, alone and with others, a varied repertoire of music
Improvising melodies, variations, and accompaniments
Composing and arranging music within specified guidelines
Reading and notating music
Listening to, analyzing, and describing music
Evaluating music and music performances
Understanding relationships between music, the other arts, and disciplines outside the arts
Understanding music in relation to history and culture[38]

Music standards are also provided by the Consortium of National Arts Education Associations. These standards are similar to those offered by the music educators for grades 9–12:[39]

Art

The National Art Standards, developed by the Consortium of National Arts Education Associations, outline basic art learning outcome for grade K–12. These standards include music, dance, theater, and visual arts.[40]

English and Foreign Language Arts

National Standards for Language Arts include Standards for the English Language Arts promoted by the National Council of Teachers of English (NCTE). Standards for the Foreign Language Arts come from the American Council on the Teaching of Foreign Languages. The NCTE standards promote literacy, reading, writing, and associating spoken words with graphics representation. The foreign language standards emphasize the linguistic and cultural importance of foreign language in a pluralistic society.[41]

Mathematics

Standards for mathematics for grades K–12 are formulated by the National Council of Teachers of Mathematics. These standards include directives for helping students "understand numbers, ways of representing numbers, relationships among numbers, and number systems" as well as "understand meanings of operations and how they relate to one another" and "compute fluently and make reasonable estimates."[42]

Science

National Science Education Standards come from the National Academies of Science and Project 2061 from the American Association for the Advancement of Science. Over the years, these and other organizations have stressed science literacy, hands-on activities for students, and appealing textbooks that promote science literacy. Included in these standards are themes addressing science as inquiry, physical science, life science, earth and space science, science and technology, science and personal perspective, and history of nature and science.[43]

National Social Studies and History

The Standards & Position Statement comes from the National Council for the Social Studies. These standards are based on culture and include a wide variety of areas, including anthropology, geography, history, sociology, civics, economics, and other areas.[44] These themes are based generally on standards prepared by several organizations, including the Center for Civic Education, the Council for Economic Education, the National Geographic Society, and the National Standards for History in Schools.[45]

Physical Education and Health

These standards are produced by the National Association for Sport and Physical Education and reinforce the *National Health Education Standards* (2007) discussed previously. Based on outcomes, the standards identify these important elements: learning skills to perform a variety of physical activities and to be physically fit, encouraging students to engage in physical activities, understanding the benefits of physical activities, and understanding how physical activities make for a healthy lifestyle. Included in the standards are content suggestions for health promotion and disease prevention; health information, products and services; reducing health risks; using communication skills in promoting health; setting goals for good health; and health advocacy.[46]

Technology and Information Literacy Standards (NETS)

These standards are developed by the International Society for Technology in Education (ISTE) and the American Association of School Librarians (AASL). The NETS 2007 standards incorporate skills and concepts relating to basic technology operations and concepts; social, ethical, and human issues; technology productivity tools; technology communication tools, technology research tools, technology problem-solving tools, and decision-making tools.[47] We discussed the closely related AASL's *Standards for the 21st-Century Learner in Action* in Chapter 1.[48]

Business and Commerce

The National Business Education Association issued standards in 1995 that outline major educational objectives for students in business studies. The following selected objectives have been chosen because they seem to influence health-related economics and resources. These particular objectives connect closely with health and globalization issues, which will be discussed more fully in a later chapter. Among others, these objectives include:[49]

- Teamwork, and leadership skills.
- Select and apply the tools of technology as they relate to personal and business decision-making.
- Communicate effectively as writers, listeners, and speakers in social and business settings.
- Use accounting procedures to make decisions about planning, organizing, and allocating resources.
- Apply the principles of law in personal and business settings.
- Develop the ability to participate in business transactions in both the domestic and international arenas.
- Develop the ability to market the assets each individual has, whether he or she is in the labor market or in the consumer goods market.
- Manage data from all the functional areas of business needed to make wise management decisions.
- Utilize analytical tools needed to understand and make reasoned decisions about economic issues, both personal and societal.

A REVIEW OF BASIC INSTRUCTIONAL UNIT DESIGN

Designing instructional units is a well-known process that most school librarians are familiar with. Nevertheless, it is always good to review these tasks in the framework of health information and instruction. Following is a brief review of some important elements advocated by the *National Health Education Standards* for health instructional unit preparation.[50]

- **Time:** Plan time so that a useful and thoughtful unit on health information can be constructed. Time not only means planning but also means time to actually teach the unit and have enough time so content can be learned by students. Commitment to time must be intense and sustainable.
- **Behavior outcomes:** Plan the instructional unit on a clear set of behavioral outcomes.
- **Research-based and theory-driven:** Organize the teaching units based on well-established social, cultural, and cognitive theories. Be aware that new findings in brain research may lead to ways to better plan instructional units.
- **Risk behaviors and attitudes:** Recognize that students need guidance in recognizing risky behaviors and negative health attitudes.
- **Values and norms (peer and family):** Make sure that individual and group values and norms are addressed. Address misconceptions regarding risk behaviors to health and replace them with good health information.

- **Risk perceptions:** Make an effort to strongly consider risk behavior perceptions of students, replacing them with behaviors that will protect against risks.
- **Social pressures and influences:** Plan units that will help students understand how they can effectively deal with peer, family, and other pressures that can interfere with healthy living.
- **Personal competencies:** Health units should also stress building a sense of competency in dealing with health. These include discussions about skills and how skills are learned in a step-by-step fashion; good models of skills; allowing students to practice newly acquired skills; and providing positive feedback and enforcements for newly acquired skills. Allow students ways to connect with good role models and influential persons.
- **Provide useful information and resources:** Information in all units must be current, authoritative, functional, and directed at improving health behaviors and attitudes.
- **Personalize health information:** Design strategies that are student-centered, interactive, and experiential. These will include group discussions, cooperative learning, problem-solving, role-playing, and peer-lead activities.
- **Present age- and developmentally appropriate resources:** Includes information and resources that fit into student's lives. Make sure that all information and materials meet students' needs, interests, and concerns, including social, cultural, and emotional needs.
- **Provide strategies that are culturally inclusive:** Avoid culturally biased materials and teaching methods. Pay attention to gender issues; race, ethnicity, religion, age, physical/mental ability, and appearances. Provide opportunities that recognize diversity as well as multicultural interactions and exchanges. Reinforce positive health ideas and behaviors found in families and communities.
- **Create ways and means of fostering development of faculty and staff:** Create procedures and programs that will encourage teachers to implement health units across the curriculum.

Based on the previous principles, standard procedures for instructional unit development include the following stages, which are self-explanatory:[51]

Stage 1: Pre-Lesson Preparation
1. Goals
2. Content
3. Student entry level

Stage 2: Lesson Planning and Implementation
1. Unit title
2. Instructional goals
3. Objectives
4. Rationale
5. Content
6. Instructional procedures
7. Evaluation procedures
8. Materials

Stage 3: Post-Lesson Activities
1. Lesson evaluation and revision

Avoid rigidity
1. Allow for flexibility.
2. Adapt as needed throughout the unit presentation.

REFLECTIONS

School librarians' involvement in health literacy encompasses a broad range of issues. Teaching and teaching strategies are fundamental, but teaching must be based on knowledge and an understanding of health facts and issues that hinder good health development in youth. These can include local environments, dysfunctional home conditions, peer pressure and attitudes, and the lack of available community resources and information. In addressing some of these problems, this chapter has outlined the importance of assessment and measurement of student learning and provided examples from the field about how these are placed into practice. Later chapters will expand on these processes.

Fortunately, numerous state, provincial, regional, national, international, professional, and for-profit groups offer a multitude of ways to help foster better health for the world's youth. Organizations and agencies play important roles in collectively providing avenues that will help school librarians and teachers become better prepared and more involved in providing good health information and promoting needed and sustainable health literacy instructional programs for youth.

NOTES

1. Welsh, Mary E., and Jennifer A. Murphy. *Children, Health, and Learning: A Guide to the Issues.* Westport, Conn.: Praeger, 2003, pp. 10–22.

2. Miller, John B. *The Holistic Curriculum.* 2nd ed. University of Toronto Press, 2007 (books.google.com/books?id=9wzqAvpb9HEC&dq=holistic+curriculum+definition &source=gbs_navlinks_s). Accessed Dec. 13, 2009.

3. Joint Committee on Health Standards. *National Health Education Standards: Achieving Excellence.* 2nd ed. Atlanta: American Cancer Society, 2007, p. 11.

4. Summerfield, Liane M. "National Standards for School Health Education." ERIC Digest. Available at www.ericdigests.org/1996-2/health.html. Accessed Oct. 28, 2008.

5. Summerfield. "National Standards for School Health Education."

6. Myers-Clark, Susan A., and Suzanne E. Christopher. "Effectiveness of a Health Course at Influencing Preservice Teachers' Attitudes toward Teaching Health." *Journal of School Health*, 71 (Nov. 2001), p. 462.

7. Summerfield, Liane M. "Preparing Classroom Teachers for Delivering Health Instruction." ERIC Digest. ED 460 128. Washington, D.C.: ERIC Clearinghouse on Teaching and Teacher Education, Washington, 2001.

8. Summerfield. *National Standards for School Health Education.*

9. Evans, Carol, and Bethan Evans. "More than Just Worksheets?: A Study of the Confidence of Newly Qualified Teachers of English in Teaching Personal, Social and Health Education in Secondary Schools." *Pastoral Care in Education: An International Journal for Pastoral Care & Personal-Social Education*, 25 (Dec. 2007), pp. 42–50.

10. Myers-Clark, Susan A., and Suzanne E. Christopher. "Effectiveness of a Health Course at Influencing Perservice Teachers' Attitudes toward Teaching Health." *Journal of School Health*, 71 (Nov. 2001), pp. 462–466.

11. Joint Committee on Health Standards. *National Health Education Standards: Achieving Excellence.* 2nd ed. p. 85.

12. Joint Committee on Health Standards. *National Health Education Standards: Achieving Excellence.* 2nd ed. p. 118.

13. Joint Committee on Health Standards. *National Health Education Standards: Achieving Excellence.* 2nd ed. p. 94.

14. "Service-Learning." Available at en.wikipedia.org/wiki/Service_learning. Accessed Dec. 11, 2008.

15. National Youth Leadership Council. Available at www.nylc.org/pages -programs-initiatives-and-Y_RISE_Service_Learning_and_HIV_AIDS_Prevention?oid =3696&null=1229015488393. Accessed Dec. 14, 2008.

16. "The National and Community Service Act of 1990 [as amended through Dec. 17, 1999, P.L. 106–170]. www.csc.ca.gov/aboutus/documents/ncsa1990.pdf. Accessed Dec. 14, 2008.

17. Sakai. Available at sakaiproject.org/product-overview. Accessed Dec. 9, 2009.

18. Joint Committee on Health Standards. *National Health Education Standards: Achieving Excellence.* 2nd ed. p. 120.

19. Learning and Teaching Definitions. Available at admin.exeter.ac.uk/academic/ tls/tqa/Part%203/3Amodapp1.pdf. Accessed Dec. 11, 2008.

20. Teacher Enrichment Initiatives Homepage. Available at teachhealthk-12. uthscsa.edu. Accessed Dec. 15, 2008.

21. "Performance Assessment. Tobacco Free Is the Way to Be." *National Health Education Standards.* 2nd ed. pp. 104–106.

22. California K–12 Book.Org. "Overview of Standards, Curriculum Frameworks, Instructional Materials Adoptions, and Funding," CDE, February 2006. www .californiak12books.org/adoptoverview.php. Accessed March 1, 2009;

23. Mississippi Textbook Catalog. www.schoolbook-ms.com/catalogs/data/MS-Cat4.pdf. Accessed March 3, 2009.

24. Immroth, Barbara and W. Bernard Lukenbill. "Teacher-School Library Media Specialists Collaboration Through Social Marketing Strategies: An Information Behavior Study." *School Library Media Research*, vol. 10 (2007). www.ala.org/ala/mgrps/ divs/aasl/aaslpubsandjournals/slmrb/schoollibrary.cfm. Accessed Nov. 4, 2009.

25. American Association of School Librarians. *Standards for the 21st-Century Learner in Action.* Chicago: American Library Association, 2009, p. 7.

26. American Association of School Librarians. *Standards for the 21st-Century Learner in Action.* p. 63.

27. InspireData, Grades 4–12. "Students and teachers collect data from multiple sources including experiments, library and Internet research, user-created e-Surveys or one of the 100+ subject-specific databases that are part of InspireData. Students' analysis and investigation includes finding the best representation for their data using multiple plot types such as Venn, bar, stack, pie, and axis and time series. InspireData supports STEM initiatives and 21st century skills, and aligns with standards for science, social studies and mathematics." www.inspiration.com/InspireData. Accessed March 2, 2009.

28. Summerfield. *National Standards for School Health Education.*

29. Health Teacher. Available at www.healthteacher.com/about. Accessed Dec. 15, 2008.

30. HECC. Available at www.healthandeducation.org. Accessed Oct. 27, 2008.

31. American Association of School Librarians. *Standards for the 21st-Century Learner*. Chicago: American Library Association, 2008. Available at www.ala.org/ala/mgrps/divs/aasl/aaslproftools/learningstandards/AASL_LearningStandards.pdf. Accessed Oct. 6, 2008.

32. Joint Committee on Health Standards. *National Health Education Standards: Achieving Excellence*. 2nd ed. Atlanta: American Cancer Society, 2007, p. 26.

33. Joint Committee on Health Standards. *National Health Education Standards: Achieving Excellence*. p. 8.

34. Joint Committee on Health Standards. *National Health Education Standards: Achieving Excellence*. pp. 26–27.

35. Joint Committee on Health Standards. *National Health Education Standards: Achieving Excellence*. p. 28.

36. Joint Committee on Health Standards. *National Health Education Standards: Achieving Excellence*. p. 8.

37. Joint Committee on Health Standards. *National Health Education Standards: Achieving Excellence*. pp. 28–29.

38. *The School Music Program: A New Vision: The K–12 National Standards, Pre-K Standards, and What They Mean to Music Educators*. Available at www.menc.org/resources/view/the-school-music-program-a-new-vision. Also at www.education world.com/standards/national/arts/music/5_8.shtml. Accessed Oct. 29, 2008.

39. Education World. Fine Arts—Music. Available at www.educationworld.com/standards/national/arts/index.shtml. Accessed Oct. 29, 2008.

40. Education World. Art. National Standards for Art Education. Available at www.education-world.com/standards/national/arts/index.shtml. Accessed Feb. 7, 2009.

41. Education World. Language Arts. Available at www.educationworld.com/standards/national/lang_arts/index.shtml. Accessed Oct. 29, 2008.

42. Education World. Mathematics. Available at www.educationworld.com/standards/national/math/index.shtml. Accessed Oct 29, 2008.

43. Education World. Science. Available at www.educationworld.com/standards/national/science/index.shtml. Accessed Oct. 28, 2008.

44. Education World www.education-world.com/standards/national/arts/index.shtml. Accessed Feb. 7, 2009. Social Science. Available at www.educationworld.com/standards/national/soc_sci/index.shtml. Accessed Oct. 28, 2008.

45. Center for Civic Education (www.civiced.org/index.php?page=stds); the Council for Economic Education (www.councilforeconed.org); the National Geographic Society (www.nationalgeographic.com/resources/ngo/education/xpeditions/standards/matrix.html); and the National Standards for History in Schools (nchs.ucla.edu/standards). Accessed Oct. 28, 2008.

46. Education World. Physical Education and Health Standards. Available at www.educationworld.com/standards/national/nph/index.shtml. Accessed Oct. 28, 2009.

47. Education World. National Technology Standards. Available at www.educationworld.com/standards/national/technology/index.shtml. Accessed Oct. 28, 2008.

48. American Association of School Librarians. *Standards for the 21st-Century Learner in Action*. Chicago: American Library Association, 2009. Available at www.alastore.ala.org/detail.aspx?ID=2601. Accessed Oct. 28, 2008.

49. "Business Education: An Introduction." ecedweb.unomaha.edu/standards/BusEdStandards.htm. Accessed Sept. 22, 2009. Also see "The National Standards for Business Education." www.nbea.org/curriculum/bes.html. Accessed Sept. 21, 2009.

50. Joint Committee on Health Standards. *National Health Education Standards: Achieving Excellence*. 2nd ed. pp. 13–16.

51. Honolulu College Community College. "Lesson Planning Procedures." honolulu.hawaii.edu/intranet/committees/FacDevCom/guidebk/teachtip/lesspln1.htm. Accessed Nov. 11, 2008.

4

Searching for Health Information and Developing Library Use Skills

BASIC APPROACHES TO SEARCHING

We all know that holistic health information needs are complex and that searching for information can be problematic. For this as well as other reasons, searching for information lies under all the suggested teaching and learning activities we present in this book.

Like all information requirements, holistic health information involves psychological perceptions of self and others. Adding to this complexity is how youth, their families, and institutions that serve them organize socially viable and constructive ways to meet their information needs. Constructive viability includes institutional factors such as the family, schools, and the support mechanisms that school provide. Personal and cultural views that influence information needs and expectations are important, as are elements of life that foster positive decision-making skills in youth. schools, and the support mechanisms that school provide.

Health literacy programs and services in school libraries have benefitted considerably from the works of educators such as Denise Agosto, Sandra Hughes-Hassell, Carol Kuhlthau, and Marcia Bates. In a number of groundbreaking books and papers, Kuhlthau outlines the various processes involved in how youth seek meaning and information. With some minor stylistic rephrasing, we outline her model of the information search process below:[1]

1. **Tasks:** Involves the initiation of selection, exploration of topics, formulation and interaction with collections and resources.
2. **Feelings:** In seeking information, feelings generally begin with uncertainty but can then range from optimism, confusion to satisfaction, or doubt and/or confusion.
3. **Cognitive thoughts:** While involved in the search for information and use of sources and collection, thought patterns can range from vagueness to focused behaviors and increased interests in the search and topic.

4. **Actions:** Involves seeking relevant and pertinent information and the actual exploring and study of the information to documenting what is found.

Marcia Bates used the analogy of picking berries to describe how people generally search for information in online databases. We can also extrapolate this to other types of searching. Her model indicates that the search is not lineal as many models suggest, but it is more naturalistic in that searchers are constantly revising, changing directions, and backtracking as they search for information. This model reflects both the emotional and cognitive levels of searching as indicated by Kuhlthau. Bates states that searchers use the following search strategies in finding information: footnote chasing; citation searching; journal run; area scanning (e.g., browsing); subject searches in bibliographies and abstracting and indexing services; and author searching.[2] Some of these techniques are probably truer for more advanced searchers. Other studies indicate that the more common search approaches are keywords and browsing.[3] This seems especially true of youth when they search.[4]

HEALTH INFORMATION NEEDS

In seeking to add to the research base of the information needs of adolescents, Agosto and Hughes-Hassell surveyed two groups of urban teens in Philadelphia about their information needs. These youth ranged in ages from 14 to 17. One group came from in the Philadelphia Teen Leadership programs of the Free Library of Philadelphia, and the others participated in the after school programs of Boys & Girls Clubs of the city. Of interest to health information is the way these researchers coded the data. Based on their original coding, we have extracted the following health information needs: emotional health; health (e.g., general); physical safety; self-image; sexual safety; and sexual identity.[5] From this coding structure, Agosto and Hughes-Hassell developed a more detailed empirical model.

Although all the aspects of their model are important to adolescent information needs, we have selected the following elements from the empirical model that appear to indicate direct health information needs and relationships:[6]

emotional self familial relationships
emotional safety
reflective self self-image
self-actualization
physical self daily life routine
physical safety
health
sexual self
sexual safety
sexual identity

Taken together, all these studies and models help us teach youth to become more effective searchers and users of health information. But what exactly do youth want to know about health and to whom do they generally turn for this information?

Medical researchers D. M. Ackard and D. Neumark-Sztainer studied adolescents' sources of health care information and beliefs about topics that health care providers should address. This study included a U.S. national sample of 3,575 girls, grades 5 through 12, and 3,153 boys, grades 5 through 12. The study identified subject areas that "are embarrassing for adolescents to discuss with providers." Data indicated that boys and girls used their mothers as the main source for health information. This was especially true of younger adolescents in grades 5 and 6. The health care providers reported that participants were more likely to turn to professionals for health information, including doctors, nurses, and school nurses. But because of the sensitivity of many of the health topics, participants indicted levels of embarrassment in approaching these providers for information. The topics that they most wanted health information included:[7]

- Drugs (65.0%)
- Smoking (58.5%)
- Sexually transmitted diseases (61.4%)
- Alcohol use (56.2%)
- Good eating behaviors (56.8%)

The authors concluded that adolescents do want these topics discussed and that health care providers should not wait for adolescents to broach them but instead to initiate and facilitate these discussions.[8]

Addressing youth, Health Canada (www.hc-sc.gc.ca) list these youth health information needs:

- Alcohol, smoking, and Drugs
- Body image
- Depression
- Diseases
- Family issues
- HIV, AIDS, and STDs
- It's Your Health
- Medication
- Mental health
- Sexuality and relationships
- Sun safety
- Risky behaviors
- Violence and abuse

INFORMATION LITERACY STRATEGIES FOR YOUTH

We know that information technologies (including databases) and the Internet provide a wealth of information on health and other topics. We also know that like all information, we must judge this information must be judged on its merits. Professor Mary Kay Chelton raises some issues about Internet information and information literacy. These statements are based on her overall concerns, with some style and content modifications:[9]

1. How can one teach good information literacy when information systems are so poorly constructed?

2. The use of traditional information resources (e.g., print) has declined in favor of the Internet. Is this good or bad and based on whose viewpoints?

3. The use of the Internet has introduced and/or intensified some social responsibilities that we must address. These include the rise in plagiarism and the massive download of information, such as music.

4. The growth of pornography and illegal content challenges access to useful and legitimate information by youth through filtering and other prohibiting procedures, such as access policies.

5. The responsibilities of caregivers to provide and/or protect youth from Internet information must occur in a legally responsible way.

6. Personal information-seeking introduces new concerns, including responsible social networking and contacts, revealing personal information, and seeking personal psychology needs, such as the need for affection or companions. Other personal needs information that youths must seek out with caution on the Internet includes entertaining, recreation, games, and consumer purchasing. On the surface, these may seem safe, but they can lead to poor choices and bad decisions.

MAJOR SOURCES FOR HEALTH INFORMATION

If we carefully consider the proposition that print sources have declined as sources of information, we may find evidence that puts this into better focus. The Bowker Company projected the publication of 194,353 titles and new editions (excluding nonfiction and juvenile books) in the United States in 2008. In comparison, in 2002, Bowker noted 159,532 titles and new edition (again excluding fiction and juvenile titles).[10] In 2008, that was an increase of only 1.22 percent from 2002. Bowker projected the printing of 10,996 medical books in 2008, compared to 9,495 published in 2002. The represented an increase of 1 percent. Although a great many books are being published, the growth is small.

A 2009 book industry report issued by Bowker showed that women compose the largest group of book buyers. The report also indicated that Generation X (persons born between roughly 1961 and 1981) bought more books online than any other group of purchasers. Twenty-one percent of those surveyed indicated that online advertising and/or notices posted online promoted their awareness of books available for purchase.[11] Do these statistics indicate that traditional sources of print-based information are on the decline? The answer probably lies somewhere in the middle. Print-based information is still important, but electronic resources are popular because they generally offer easier access. Nevertheless, print-based information is often the mainstay of electronic information systems.

A case in point is Gale. This information company describes itself thusly:

Gale, part of Cengage Learning, is a world leader in e-research and educational publishing for libraries, schools and businesses. Best known for its accurate and authoritative reference content as well as its intelligent organization of full-text magazine and newspaper articles, the company creates and maintains more than 600 databases that are published online, in print, as eBooks and in microform.[12]

Databases of special interest to school health instruction and information included in Gale are: *Gale Virtual Reference Library, InfoTrac: Student Edition K–12*; *Global Issues in Context, Gale Virtual Reference Library* (eBooks); *Opposing Viewpoints Resource Center, General Reference Center, Science Resources Center, InfoTrac*; *Student Resource Center* and the Canadian edition; *Health and Wellness Resources Center*; and *Health Solutions*.

One of its resources, *Health Reference Center (Academic)*, offers "60 full-text journals in medicine, nursing, allied and consumer health, full-text reference books, pamphlets, overviews of clinical topics, and indexing and abstracts for over 1500 additional titles covering patient and consumer health information. It is a subset of *Health and Wellness Resource Center*."[13]

EBSCO is also a primary company that offers databases. Its K–12 health-related databases include *Consumer Health Complete* (covering all areas of health); *Health Source: Consumer Education*; *Health Source: Nursing/Academic*; *MedicLatina* (a Spanish language media collection); *Medline, Natural and Alternative Treatments*; and *Science and Technology Collection*.

ACCESSING INFORMATION

The Library Catalog

The library catalog is the heart of the school library media center, and it plays an important role in finding information. With the advent of the online public access catalog (OPACs) in the 1970s, library catalogs offer students quick and easily understood ways to obtain information. Currently, an easier term to use is online catalog. When networked or connected to other libraries' online catalogs, the online public catalog's power becomes further extended.

Students will often need instruction in the worth of using the online catalog and how to use it to their advantage. This is especially true of younger students.

The basic use of the online catalog is to find materials. In 1876, Charles Cutter outlined the major function of the card catalog as being "to help a person find a book when certain factors such as authorship, title, and subject are known; to display what the library holds such as books by authors, subjects, genre of literature; and to help with reader advisement such as finding various editions of a work and to help with literature and subject selection."[14] These principles still hold. Although Cutter restricted his remarks to books, we can now expand them to all kinds of formats.

Records that make up a good online catalog are standardized and meet the rules and principles of existing, recognized standards of cataloging. At the local level, standardized cataloging of records allows for better searching so users can easily find what they need and want. Good records allow for better responses and allow for the retrieval of multiformats. When networking is available, good cataloging allows for effective means of connecting with libraries and school libraries well beyond the local setting.

Through its interface design, the online catalog allows for various ways to access the records contained there. When researching for health information, students need instruction on how to use these interface features:

- Keywords
- Title
- Author
- Subject
- Call number
- ISBN/ISSN numbers
- Phrasing (if available)

Many online catalogs make it easy for students to search by creating bullets with clearly marked search options, such as word or phrase; author; title, subject, series, and periodical title. Online catalogs for students and children will often simplify access to items in their catalog through the use of pictorial icons. For example, health in the SirsDynix systems used by many libraries worldwide offers a series of subject icons to help young users find materials better. For health, the search begins with a general picture of a health care person working and then leads the searcher via pictures through the subject hierarchy to more specific health-related concepts and subjects.

Many online catalogs allow for more precise searching than indicated previously. For example, some interfaces allow for journal title searches, author linked with title, official subject headings included in the controlled vocabulary of the catalog, and retrieval by types of materials (e.g., EBooks, DVDs), by language, by year of publication, and by publisher and/or producer. Beyond that, advanced searches allow for phrase searching, truncation, Boolean searching, proximity searching, and field searching.

The Web Page

A library's Web site also helps extend the influence of the catalog through various links. It offers a means of connecting with health information that is external to the school. A Web site can provide access to existing health information resources throughout the community and links to governmental departments, local service agencies, and those serving larger areas. The careful selection of links to these sources will prove useful to staff, students, faculty, and parents.

Links on the Web site must in accordance with the library's official material selection policy. The selection policy should indicate exactly how the library chooses items are selected for posting on the Web site. The Baltimore County Public Library operates a special section in its catalog that highlights community information that adolescents and their families need and want. The site is called "Connections: Children, Youth & Family Resources," and it presents carefully selected and maintained sites that can meet the needs of youth and their families.[15]

STRUCTURE OF INFORMATION IN DATABASES FOR ONLINE SEARCHES

If you have been teaching access to online databases for some time, the following may seem very repetitious to you. If you need to review how to teach this or have never taught it before, you will find a great deal of help in the next few pages.

Fields and Records

In teaching students how to search for information in databases, a basic knowledge of indexing methods for materials in electronic databases can prove helpful. An extensive introduction is available in Susan Bell's *Librarian's Guide to Online Searching*. A shorter introduction follows.

The primary items in a database record are fields, with each record having a set of fields that holds specific types of information. All individual fields relating to one item (e.g., a periodical article) make a record.

The database includes all the records entered into the particular database. To retrieve the information electronically, important items in each field must be indexed. This means that most words in the title field must be an electronic record and stored in an index. Less important words, such as "a" and "the," are generally placed in a "stop list" and are not indexed for recall. The initial design of the database will include decisions about how and what will be indexed mechanically. For example, certain fields may not be indexed. Decisions about how certain grammatical constructs, such as contractions and possessives, are indexed must be decided. Decisions should be made as to how phrasing. The careful design and indexing of the database will allow for rapid searching of vast amounts of information.[16]

Boolean Logic and Operations

Boolean logic is a mathematical model that illustrates both the interconnection of concepts and the exclusion of relationships and allows for the combining of terms in an electronic database. The Boolean operatives are AND, OR, and NOT. For example, a search for information on types of healthy foods often mentioned in health such as diet management, includes apples and oranges. Using Boolean operatives, you can write this search can be stated as: apples AND oranges. This will narrow the search down to only those records that have those words in common. But pineapples is also a healthy fruit, but we do not want that to turn up in our search, so we can add NOT to our search to reject all records that have pineapples in them: apples AND oranges NOT pineapples (Figure 4.1).

Venn Diagrams

Venn diagrams are used with Boolean operations to illustrate concept relationships. These relationships can be sets, groups, or objects that share commonality or unwanted concepts. Venn diagrams are used to illustrate relationships and intersections between and among groups of objects that share something in common.[17]

Truncations and Wildcards

Truncation means to cut something short. Truncation in online searching uses symbols to shorten a word and allows variations of the word. For example, "child*" will retrieve childhood, and children.

Using wildcards means to put a symbol to replace a letter within the word. Wom?n will retrieve women and woman.[18]

Phrase and Proximity Searching

Phrase-searching brings together items that are better connected by word phrases. For example, most online catalogs use enclosed quotation marks around the desired phrase. For example, "child care" and "Centers for Disease Control" will help eliminate a vast amount of items relating to child and/or children and will retrieve only those child care items that relate to the Centers for Disease Control.[19] Online catalogs also allow for the identification of works in proximity to each other. For students that are interested in this technique refer them to Patrologia Latina Database "Proximity Search (Near, Followed by, Exact)" at pld-old.chadwyck.com/help/hlp_prox.htm.

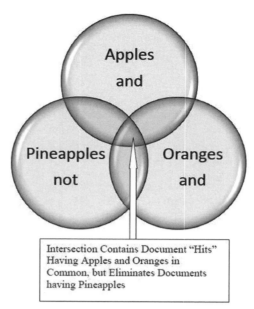

Figure 4.1.
Venn diagram: Searching for apples AND oranges, but NOT pineapples.

Controlled and Natural Language

Many databases are organized based on a controlled vocabulary. That is, all subjects or descriptor terms that attached to records by a vender (or cataloger or subject specialists) are selected from a list of official terms designated especially to be used in that database. A controlled vocabulary provides for consistency in connecting similar records, providing the user with direct access to the records in the database. It frees the user from having to keyword-search all variations of how the subject might be expressed.[20]

Natural language searching uses words or keywords that are naturally found in the record and which are based on a language. Natural language statements are words that are embedded in the document's narration. Natural language words are found throughout the document, including title words as well as words found in the narrative text. In using natural language searching, the researcher in a search simply enters a word or words from a spoken language and the computer will then search for the occurrence of that word(s) throughout the database. Most databases accommodate natural language searching. Many commercial databases accommodate both natural language and controlled vocabulary searching.[21]

Subject Heading Lists and Thesauruses

Students and teachers researching terms in a health vocabulary can use an official, established list of authoritative subject headings or descriptors with database searches. These can be subject headings that require a controlled vocabulary (terms selected as official descriptors) or a thesaurus. Some of the better known controlled vocabularies include the *Library of Congress List of Subject Headings*, *Medical Subject Headings*, and the *Sears List of Subject Headings* (Figure 4.2).

Figure 4.2.
Library of Congress List of Subject Headings. Courtesy of the Library of Congress.

In introducing health terms, a thesaurus can be useful. A thesaurus is "A book list of words in groups of synonyms and related concepts."[22] *Roget's Thesaurus* is one of the better-known general thesauruses. Thesauruses take on a more specialized meaning when applied to databases. When developed for the indexing of records in a particular database, it is a controlled vocabulary or "a structured list of approved subject headings (preferred terms) showing the relationships between them. The relationships include broader (parent) terms, narrower (child) terms, and related terms."[23] A free online medical thesaurus, *The Missouri Medical Informatics Thesaurus* by N. J. Ogg, M. E. Sievert, Z. R. Li, and J. A. Mitchell, is available at https://www.researchgate.net/publication/14609693_The_Missouri_Medical_Informatics_Thesaurus.

Field Searching

Field searching can be effective in searching, as it allows us to narrow the amount of data that the computer must process. For example, field searching allows us to search author fields, title fields, and subject fields. A search is more efficient when field searching is used in combination with keywords or a controlled list of subject descriptors.[24] WorldCat's advanced search offers some examples of field searching. For example, if we want a book on blindness and Helen Keller but we do not know any titles, according to the instructions from WorldCat (http://www.worldcat.org/advancedsearch), we would type these entries into appropriate fields.
WorldCat Instructions:

Enter search terms in at least one of the fields below

Keyword: Blindness

Title: _____

Author: Keller

Because we did not know the exact title, we would leave the title field blank. This should be enough information to retrieve *The Story of My Life* by Helen Keller.

THE PROCESS OF SEARCHING

The terms and concepts discussed previously are important for students to understand as they seek heath information. Also important is understanding the stages and processes involved in a complete or holistic search. This process has been described in many ways, but they all have similarities. For librarians, these elements reflect the strategies that are customarily used to answer simple as well as complex reference question.[25] Figure 4.3 illustrates both a simple question or topic search and an advanced research approach.

---

1. Basic Search Approach:

Question: What is the name of the virus that causes chicken pox?
- What is the question or topic?
- What tasks are involved in understanding the question?
- What are the most likely sources to answer the question or topic? How can they be identified and judged?
- Where are they located? How can they be reached in a timely manner?
- What is the best way to use them? Do they require special knowledge?
- How can the information be retrieved and then recorded and stored?
- How should the information be interrelated, analyzed, evaluated, and synthesized?
- Once the answer is found or the topic well-searched, how should it be presented?
- How can the search tasks be assessed in terms of overall learning?
    - *Source:* Thomas, Nancy Pickering. *Information Literacy and Information Skills Instruction: Applying Research to Practice in the School Library Media Center.* 2nd ed. Westport, Conn.: Libraries Unlimited, 2004, p. 46.

2. Research Approach:

Question: What public health programs are in place in the United States to protect children against chicken pox?
- Define and narrow the topic to be researched. (Specify exactly terms that are appropriate to the research topic.)
- Prepare for the search.
    - Identify the parts and subparts of the topic.
    - What subjects or keywords are generally associated with the topic? Develop a list of likely search terms.
- Be sure to consult subject heading lists and appropriate thesauruses for terms during and before the search.
- Conduct the search.
    - Determine the relevant sources of information associated with the research topic (books, journals). Along with books, identify the most appropriate online databases. When possible, use the online catalog for identifying books, journals, and databases.
    - In searching, focus on finding only the most relevant sources. Be prepared to discard citations as you refine your search.

 – Use Boolean search logic to help locate information.
 – Develop a means of taking notes, duplicating, and recording your findings.
• Prepare the research product.
 – Read and evaluate the information.
 – Select, interpret, and synthesize the information.
 – Make sure that this analysis meets the needs required by the research topic.
 – Write a paper or present your findings in an appropriate information package or product.
• Evaluate the process and assess what was learned about the topic as well as the search process.
 – *Source:* Elizabeth Schneider and Russell K. Schutt. "Finding Information." In Daniel F. Chambliss and Russell K. Schutt. *Making Sense of the Social World. Methods of Investigation.* 2nd ed. Pine Forge Press, 2006, pp. 283–293.

Figure 4.3.
Elements in basic and advanced research approaches.

COLLECTION DEVELOPMENT CONSIDERATIONS FOR HEALTH DATABASES

Databases acquired for schools must have clear collection development guidelines. The Collection Development Policy for the Texas K–12 TexShare Database Program for Texas schools provides these useful suggestions for general database selection.[26] Most, if not all, of these guiding principles apply directly to health materials.

TEXSHARE GUIDELINES AND PRINCIPLES FOR ACCESS AND REVIEW

These guidelines recognize that local school districts' policies and procedures prevail associated with limited access of students to some of the materials in these databases, but the guidelines also recognize the need to protect the rights of students to have access to materials that might be challenged. Unfortunately, some topics in health are considered by some parents and other members of the surrounding community as unfit for school libraries. This can apply to databases.

Rationale for Selection of Materials

• Are for both curriculum and enrichment beyond the curriculum and are to include interests, abilities, learning styles, and maturity levels.
• Are to encourage "factual knowledge, enjoyment, literacy appreciation, aesthetic values, and societal standards and that promote lifelong learning and reading habits."
• Include "both side of controversial issues" that will promote critical thinking and analysis in students, leading to informed decision-making.
• Represent ethnic, religious, and cultural groups and highlight their contributions "to the national heritage and world community."
• Present "a wide range of background information that enables students to make intelligent choices in their daily lives."

Rationale for Challenged Materials

The state-supported databases for Texas public and private schools offer these guidelines and principles to ensure access to databases and to offer means to challenged materials.[27]

- Any resident or employee in the school district may challenge access to database materials.
- Challenged materials are subjected to reconsideration process.
- A parent's right to object to reading and reviewing of database materials is limited to only his or her child or children.
- With all challenges, the right of access to material, such as reading, listening, and viewing, should be considered.
- The school district has the authority to limit or not limit access to materials during the reconsideration process.
- The major criteria for determining the appropriateness of the materials are based on their educational use and not the "ideas expressed therein."
- The decision to remove challenged materials "should not necessarily be interpreted as judgment irresponsibility" on the part of professionals who made the decision to acquire the database.

As with all information in the school library media center, the rights of access must be protected from unreasonable and unjustified challenges.

HEALTH DATABASES

Selected Free Access Databases Available on the Internet

The Internet offers numerous free and easily accessible health-related databases. These include many that have been created by various government agencies. Listed below are some of the major databases created by the U.S. federal government.

MedlinePlus

MedlinePlus is a site that is free on the Internet. Begun in 1998, it is an important medical database developed by the U.S. National Library of Medicine. It is designed to be especially helpful in providing the lay public with accessible and accurate health information. All materials listed are based on evaluation guidelines and are selected by health sciences librarians. The site is free of advertisement and has no link to commercial interests. Along with citations to available information, MedlinePlus offers full texts of articles appearing in important references sources, including medical dictionaries, newspapers, and pharmaceutical sources. Medical terminology and search terms are constructed to be understandable by the consumer. For example, "breast cancer" is the preferred term, not "breast neoplasms" Special sections are designed to be used by children and teenagers. The site is also available in Spanish.[28]

MedlinePlus not only provides accurate information, but it offers a wealth of information not easily found elsewhere, such as:[29]

- Correction pronunciation of medical terms
- Locations of local doctors, hospitals, and medical libraries
- Recent health news (within the past 30 days)
- Information, including illustrations from health encyclopedias

- Information about prescribed and over-the-counter drugs
- Evidence-based information on alternative medicines
- Links to other health-related resources
- Self-administered health quizzes, calculators, and assessment guides
- Information for special needs groups, such as easy-to-read pages in both English and Spanish, and resources for low visual users

Many of these topics lend themselves to instruction in many areas of the curriculum. The National Library of Medicine also provides Medline and PubMed. These are more technical and are directed at the medical professional. MedlinePlus will often direct its users to these when appropriate.

Medline

This is an advanced database that is useful in advanced secondary programs offering a dedicated medical curriculum. It "provides authoritative medical information on medicine, nursing, dentistry, veterinary medicine, the health care system, pre-clinical sciences, and much more. Created by the National Library of Medicine, Medline uses MeSH (Medical Subject Headings) indexing with tree hierarchy, subheadings and explosion capabilities to search citations from over 4,800 current biomedical journals" (pioneer.utah.gov/research/health.html). Included are citations from Index Medicus, the International Nursing Index, and the Index to Dental Literature, Premedline, Aidsline, Bioethicsline, and HealthSTAR. It offers free access through the NLM gateway at gateway.nlm.nih.gov/gw/Cmd.

Federal Drug Administration (FDA)

The FDA maintains an online database for children and adolescents (Kids & Teens) that provides health information along with instructional approaches to leaning about health. These include songs, quizzes, interactive games, and crossword puzzles. The site is divided into two sections: one for children and the other for adolescents. For example, in the Kids section, Food Safety & Nutrition is presented with subdivisions (links) that lead to more specific information about the topic, such as hand washing. The Students & Teachers section provides links to several information resources, including a food science curriculum or and high school students.

U.S. Department of Health and Human Resources (HHS)

HHS is the U.S. government's "principal agency for protecting the health of all Americans and providing essential human services, especially for those who are least able to help themselves." Included in its activities are conducting research, protecting and promoting public health, food and drug safety, and other activities. Its Web site includes HHS for Kids, which is an extensive listing of its various services and instructional units produced by various departments within HHS, such as the CDC and FDA. For example, "The ABCs of Bullying: Addressing, Blocking, and Curbing School Aggression" is an online course for educators addressing the causes of bullying and some strategies to cope with it. "Powerful Bones, Powerful Girls" is a colorful guide for girls on how to eat right and exercise to maintain good bones.

U.S. Department of Agriculture (USDA)

The National Library of Agriculture, an agency of the USDA, provides a Web site that addresses many health-related issues, including food and nutrition, dietary needs, food safety, food inspection, and physical activity and nutrition. The site also offers a link to the Children's Nutrition Research Center, operated by the Baylor College of Medicine.

Selected Commercial Consumer Health Information

Commercial databases are widely available, and they are expensive. Many school library media centers have access to these at a reduced price through cooperative arrangements. For example, in Texas, selected commercial databases are supported by funding from the Texas Legislature. The operation arm of the services is administered through Education Service Center 20, which is located in San Antonio. In bringing these databases to schools around Texas, the center cooperates with the Texas Education Agency and the Texas State Library and Archives Commission.[30] The following discussions include descriptions of commercial health databases that are widely available to schools, public libraries, and higher education institutions.

Consumer Health Complete (CHC)

CHC is a product of EBSCO Publishing. The publisher claims it is "the single most comprehensive resource for consumer-oriented health content." The content covers all areas of health and wellness and offers full-text access to articles, reference books, and encyclopedias. Its information content is extensive, covering both mainstream medicine as well as complementary and holistic approaches to health. It has specific coverage on "aging, cancer, diabetes, drugs & alcohol, fitness, nutrition dietetics, children's health" and also highlights the particular health issues of men and women. Some of the specific references materials included are *Columbia University Children's Medical Guide*, *American Medical Association Complete Medical Encyclopedia*, *Mayo Clinic Family Health Book*, and the *Royal Society for Medical Health Encyclopedia*.[31]

Library Accessible Databases

Often, very useful commercial databanks are available to cardholders through public and university libraries. For example, the Austin Public Library provides these:[32]

Health and Medicine Resource Center
Includes information from the *Gale Encyclopedia of Medicine*, *Mosby's Medical, Nursing and Allied Health Dictionary*, and the *Medical and Health Information Directory*. Also find information about drugs, the latest health news, and health assessment tools.

Health Resources: Consumer Edition
Offers authoritative health-related information, including the full text of nearly 300 consumer health magazines. Also included are more than 4,500 *Clinical Reference Systems* reports (in English and Spanish); *Clinical Pharmacology*, which provides access to 1,100 drug monograph entries and 2,700 patient education fact sheets; and *Merriam-Webster's Medical Desk Dictionary*.

Alt HealthWatch

Focuses on the many perspectives of complementary, holistic, and integrated approaches to health care and wellness, and it provides full-text articles from more than 180 international and often peer-reviewed journals, reports, proceedings, and association and consumer newsletters. In addition, there are hundreds of pamphlets, booklets, special reports, original research, and book excerpts.

Natural & Alternative Treatments

This is a complementary and alternative medicine database designed for the consumer-health researcher.

Health Reference—Academic

A one-stop, full-service resource for health-related research, it provides an integrated collection of general interest health and fitness magazines, medical and Professional periodicals, reference books, and pamphlets.

Health Source: Nursing/Academic

This is similar in content to Health Reference—Academic.

Magill's Medical Guide

This covers diseases, disorders, treatments, procedures, specialties, anatomy, biology, and issues in an A–Z format, with sidebars addressing recent developments in medicine and concise information boxes for all diseases and disorders.

Health Organization Directory

This directory provides access to Gale's *Health Organization Directory* for organizations, agencies and institutions, publications and other information resources, and health.

HEALTH LITERACY: CHALLENGES TO HOLISTIC HEALTH INFORMATION

Health literacy goes well beyond searching health-related databases. It involves the health care system that youth have to negotiate, their culture and society, and their education system. Underlying all of this is the ability to think critically and to solve problems, to be responsible, productive, and self-directed, and to communicate effectively. Although these ideas are reflected in standards such as the *National Educational Standards* that are widely used to construct health curricula, research indicates that the *Standards'* effects are uneven among schools in terms of content, consistency of delivery, and time spent on health instruction.[33]

Researchers Brown, Teufel, and Birch found in a survey of 7 states that youth ages 9 to 13 had difficulty understanding health information and felt that "kids" can do little to affect their health futures. Unfortunately, those surveyed had little interest in health as taught in school. These researchers suggested that more attention should be given to teaching students how to use more unconventional sources of health information, such as parents, medical personnel, and the Internet.[34]

No matter where students turn to for health information, health literacy deserves extensive consideration. Research shows that a number of factors influence health literacy. These include:

- Ability to read and write (literacy) and the ability of their parents to read and write
- Evaluate the credibility of health information
- Think critically about health and health information

- Access and evaluate health information from the mass media (e.g., medial dramas)
- Acquire and place health information within their daily activities and social life[35]

We do know from research that adolescents search for health information on the Internet.[36] Overall health literacy is important here. Students have a number of problems with understanding that all medical information found on the Internet is not accurate and free of commercial and personal biases and should not always be used to make health decisions.[37] Beyond that, students face a number of problems when they search online, whether it is the Internet or databases. These include:

- Spelling medical terms correctly
- Ability to construct a search process
- Describing disease symptoms and medical situations
- Ability to determine appropriate information retrieved from search engines
- Ability to place health information into personal and local situations
- Ability to identify reliable and trusted sources[38]

Recommendations based on these and other problems suggest that students' uses of online health information must be carefully directed. This includes offering correct instruction on how to identify information that is incorrect or capable of being misunderstood. Teaching students to construct a reliable search strategy is a continuing issue. Filtering is clearly associated with health information and literacy in that needed information is simply not accessible at times when it is most needed.[39]

HOLISTIC HEALTH INFORMATION INSTRUCTIONAL PLAN

Providing students with health information skills is important no matter where they search for information. As electronic resources are one of the major preferred sources, it is imperative that we provide students with solid instruction on how not only to access information but to also evaluate it. Suggested learning outcomes and instructional activities to meet these goals are presented in the following discussion.

Learning Outcomes

Students will:

- Define terms used in searching for information online.
    Online catalog
    Online databases
    Search vocabulary
    Subject headings
    Descriptors
    Keywords
    Search fields
    Venn diagram
    Search logic (Boolean logic)
- Demonstrate how to find information on health topics by:
    Developing a logical search strategy

Explaining how to select appropriate health topics as well as, keywords and subject, terms for their topics

- Demonstrate how to select online databases, including the online catalog that meets the logic of their search strategy.
- Activate and explain the basic operations of databases and/or online catalogs.
- Explain the uses of a menu bar, a toolbar, and a scrollbar in online searching.
- Execute appropriate note-taking and documentation of their findings as they search.
- Development standards for what they need and evaluate information they retrieve, eliminating information that does not meet their search strategy and standards.
- Explain their search strategies and findings upon request.
- Produce an appropriate product based on their search.
- Demonstrate the historical development of electronic information transfer (based on abilities and age).

Questions and/or Activities (Adjust According to Age and Abilities)

For Older Students

Begin with a review:

1. Review with students how to use the online catalog, paying attention to the use of the catalog's interface to locate materials by keywords, title, author, subjects, and, if available, phrases.
2. Introduce students to criteria for evaluating Web sites for use. Consider these points:
   - **Authority:** Who developed the Web site or database? Have students brainstorm ideas about how to judge authority?
   - **Audience:** For whom was it developed?
   - **Scholarship:** What determines scholarship and its audience (academic, professional audiences)? How does popular health material differ from scholarly health materials? What are the characteristics of a "popular audience"?
   - **Bias:** Is there a biased or direct commercial viewpoint advanced by the author or commercial companies?
   - **Currency:** Is the database or Web site up to date? How can you determine this?
   - **Links:** Are links to other sources provided? Do they take you to appropriate sites? Are they working?
   - Is the Web site or database easy to search? Is the search interface transparent or readily understood?
   - Is the Web site artistically pleasing? Are colors, arrangements, and fonts appropriately used and appealing? Have students brainstorm ideas about what makes Web site visually appealing and useful.
3. Introduce the concept of "appropriate use":
   - Is use of the Web site restricted by copyright? Explain to students the basic elements of current copyright, including fair use rights (library.albany.edu/usered/webeval/we4.html).
   - Explain how to cite materials from Web site and databases. Use examples from standard style manuals, such as the *APA Manual of Style*, the *Chicago Manual of Style, Turabian*, and the *MLA Style Manual* (en.wikipedia.org/wiki/Style_guide).
4. Introduce and/or reinforce the evaluation of Internet information.
   - Ask students to identify a Web site that does not appeal to them and one that they like and then ask have them compare the two in terms of evaluation criteria and personal use and needs.

5. Introduce the concept and history of electronic information transmission. Explain that the Internet was not the first device to use electronic transmissions as a way of carrying information. For example, give students some background information involving the telephone and cable transmissions. Do this by selectively sharing items from the following chronology. Help students see the relationship between the early development of electronic communications and modern-day computer technology. [Note: This chronology is based on "History of the Internet" (dave@cs.cf.ac.uk. All quoted materials are from "History of the Internet" or as otherwise cited]).

   1836. Telegraph. Cooke and Wheatstone patented the telegraph. This was the beginning of electronic communications.

   1844. Morse Code. Developed as a means of communication. This used a binary system of on/off singles (0/1). Binary is the way that computers transmit information today.

   1858–1868. Transatlantic cable. The successful laying of the cable permitted instantaneous communication across the Atlantic.

   1868. First commercially successful transatlantic telegraph cable completed between the UK and Canada, with land extension to the United States. Today, cable connects all continents and is still an important means of communication.

   1876. Bell invents and patents the telephone. Telephone linkage "provides the backbone of Internet connections today and modems provide Digital to Audio conversions to allow computers to connect over the telephone network."

   1937. United States connections. Connected to 68 countries via HF (high frequency radio), with 93 percent of the world's telephones now interconnected by wires and radio transmissions.

6. Introduce and/or review of search techniques.
   * Introduce or review these concepts with students. If needed, use the explanations of the concepts as discussed previously: fields and records, Boolean logic and operations, and Venn diagrams.

7. Searching for biographical information (see Chapter 6).
   * Have students conduct online searches for personalities: Lucinda Williams, Julie Andrews, Robert Plant, Bonnie Tyler, Amanda Parker, Davey Havok, Freddie Mercury, Whitney Houston, Belle Midler, Lee Ryan, Elton John, Madonna, Joni Mitchell, Charles Drew, Walter Reed, and Clara Barton.

8. Searching for health conditions: sports, dance, and music (see Chapter 6).
   * Ask students to search for these common health conditions: bursitis, carpal tunnel syndrome, hearing loss in musicians, performance stress in music, dance and sports, tendinitis, tenosynovitis, sprains and strains, knee injuries, swollen muscles, Achilles' tendon injuries, pain along the shin bone, fractures, and dislocation (www.nlm.nih.gov/medlineplus/sportsinjuries.html).

9. Searching for health Issues and globalization (see Chapters 7 and 9 for other health issues).
   * Ask students to search for information concerning food and food culture; child growth and development; community health and hygiene; and infection prevention; prevention and control of epidemics; and importance of immunization. Research this question: "how globalization is promoting both the rapid spread and the effective treatment of highly contagious diseases [and] the growing debate over the use and future of genetically modified organisms (GMOs)" (www.globalization101.org/issue_main/health).

10. Searching for health themes in literature and the arts (see Chapter 6).
    * Ask your students to research ways that illnesses are used in fiction, drama, and music, such as opera, to develop a theme (e.g., personality of the main characters, psychological and sociological environments of the main characters, family circumstances). Research ways that health themes have been used in the visual arts, such as in paintings. Research medical art as well as art used to promote healing.

For Younger Students

Provide a basic overview of the online catalog with exercises:

- Demonstrate to students how to use the online catalog. Show them how to manage the online catalog by using its interface features.
- Explain to students how to find books in the library that are listed in the online catalog.
- Show students how to search for subjects, names of authors, and keywords or phrases in the online catalog. Provide examples, such as favorite authors, subjects, titles, and keywords.
- Type in a word that is misspelled to illustrate how the catalog will ask for the correct spelling.
- When students are familiar with the online catalog interface, have them keep a simple "health journal." Explain that it is necessary when finding information to keep a careful record of what you find as you search and that they should carefully consider what to write in their journal about what they find. If needed, provide sheets for the journal that offer guides as to what to include in the journal. Talk with students and have them help you create a list of health-related words, such as "medicine," "illness," "disease," "nurses," and "doctors." With an over-head projector, enter their selected words in the online catalog.
- Make sure that students understand the different difference between the local online catalog and a database. To explain this, have students select the name of an important person or an organization that has made a significant medical discovery or contribution to health care. Instead of the online catalog, select appropriate databases for students to use in their searches. Make sure that they understand the basic operations of the database they select for their search. Have them also search for their selected name in the local online catalog. After the searches, have students compare what they found in the two sources. Some suggested names:
  - Jonas Salk (polio vaccine)
  - Pasteur Institute (famous research institute)
  - Charles Drew (perfected blood plasma technology)
  - Tgnoz Semmelweis (discovered the cause of childbirth fever)
  - Joseph Lister (antisepsis and modern surgery)
  - Louis Pasteur (linked microorganisms to disease)
  - Gregor Mendel (genetics in plants)
  - James Lind (discovered the cause of scurvy)
  - International Red Cross and Red Crescent
  - March of Dimes campaigns
  - Madam Currie (radiation)
  - Clara Barton
  - Florence Nightingale
- Explain to students the meaning of keywords and how the online computer allows for searching by keywords. Explain that this is a useful approach when you do not know the exact subject, author, or title. Have students list some keywords relating to health and then have then search for at least two of these words in the online catalog. Before the search, check to make sure the words are spelled correctly.
- If the online catalog has a visual approach, explain to students that the online catalog's "visual" approach is helpful in finding subjects and topics. Demonstrate how to do a visual search by linking to the health icon and its subdivisions. Have students practice by using a visual approach. Have students write down two items on health that they found by visual searching. Ask students to make comparisons between their keyword searching and their visual search. Ask if they found the same items or different items.

If the library has little in the way of health materials, include a very broad definition of health, including first aid, nutrition, exercise, hospitals, ambulances, rescue, emergency, and various illnesses, such as smallpox.

REFERENCE MATERIALS FOR HEALTH INFORMATION

A number of reference books are available online. We have discussed some of these already. Some of these are easy to understand and use, while others present challenges to inexperienced users; therefore, it is always necessary to give some guidance to all ages and abilities in how to use both the online and the print-based reference materials. Select these terms and concepts based on the maturity and abilities of students in their individual classes.

- Explain that reference information that you find online and in print have basic characteristics. Introduce the index and explain how to use an index in a print-based reference book, such as an encyclopedia. Explain to students that information in a print-based reference book can be arranged in several ways, including in alphabetic order and by categories (large subject areas). Introduce the concept of the table of contents and explain that if you want to find materials that are contained in large subject areas, you need to use both the table of contents and the index. Have students brainstorm some health topics and then have them search for information related to their terms by searching in the library's print encyclopedias. To start, use some of the keywords listed previously.
- Introduce students to an online reference, such as *Britannica Online School Edition, PreK–12*. Explain that finding information in *Britannica* and other online databases is similar to finding items in the online catalog. Explain that the search requires a keyword or keywords and the advance search allows for additional search terms, such as author, title, subject, and a combination of keyword concepts. Demonstrate this by using the keyword search and the advance search interfaces. When students understand these concepts, help them create a list of general health terms and then have them practice searching the *Britannica Online School Edition* or other appropriate online reference.
- Have them note-take and record in their online journal what they find in their "Online Journal." Some search terms include "allergies," "bacteria," boils," "diabetes," "depression," "ear infection," "high blood pressure," "headaches," "sinuses," "smoking," "spider bites," "sun and skin damage," and "tattoos." A convenient source for common medical terms is MedicineNet.com. Have your teachers introduce this by asking students to find medical and health terms on which they would like to find information.

RESOURCES

Support resources for both librarians and teachers are important for these technical aspects of searching. Selected resources that support instruction in searching for information are found in Appendix A.

REFLECTIONS

This is an age in which most students are exposed to computers and the Internet, but that does not mean that they are expert users of those resources. Some may be skilled at the use of the technology but have little awareness of how to critically evaluate what they find through electronic means. Students need help and instruction in what to use and think about the Internet in context of what they are learning and need to learn. The school librarian needs not only to involve students, but they need to collaborate extensively with classroom teachers, subject specialists, and school staffs to fully bring the power of electronic information to students.[40] Collaboration and networking with parents and health providers is especially important as we face new challenges to health and wellness.

NOTES

1. Kuhlthau, Carol. "Information Search Process." www.cite.hku.hk/events/doc/2005/CITE-7July2005.pdf. Accessed Sept. 28, 2009.

2. Bates, M. J. "The Design of Browsing and Berrypicking Techniques for the Online Search Interface." 1989. www.gseis.ucla.edu/faculty/bates/berrypicking.html. Accessed Sept. 28, 2009.

3. Wang, Ben. "Efficient Indexing Structures for Similarity Search in Content-Based Information Retrieval." Ph.D. dissertation, University of Essex (United Kingdom), 2007. Abstract in *Dissertation Abstract International*, C, 68/04, p. 1053, Winter 2007.

4. Hirsh, Sandra Goldstein. "The Effect of Domain Knowledge on Elementary School Children's Information Retrieval Behavior on an Automated Library Catalog." Ph.D. dissertation, University of California, Los Angeles, 1996. Abstract in *Dissertation Abstraction International*, A, 57/11, p. 4580, May 1997.

5. Agosto, Denise E. and Sandra Hughes-Hassell. "Toward a Model of the Everyday Life Information Needs of Urban Teenagers, Part 2: Empirical Model." *Journal of the American Society for Information Science and Technology* 57, 11 (published online June 2006): 1418–1426.

6. Hughes-Hassell, Sandra and Denise E. Agosto. "Planning Library Services for Inner-City Teens: Implications from Research Sources. *Public Libraries* 45 (Nov./Dec. 2006): 57–63.

7. Ackard, D. M. and D. Neumark-Sztainer. "Health Care Information Sources for Adolescents: Age and Gender Differences on Use, Concerns, and Needs." *The Journal of Adolescent Health: Official Publication of the Society for Adolescent Medicine* 29 (Sept. 2001): 170–176.

8. Ackard and Neumark-Sztainer.

9. Chelton, M. K. "Future Direction and Bibliography." In *Youth Information-Seeking Behavior Theories, Models, and Issues*. Mary K. Chelton and Colleen Cool, eds. Scarecrow Press, 2004, pp. 387–397.

10. New Book Titles and Editions, 2002–2008. www.bowker.com/bookwire/IndustryStats2009.pdf. Accessed Sept. 30, 2009.

11. "Bowker Publishers First Consumer-Focused Research Report for Book Industry." www.bowker.com/index.php/press-releases/567-bowker-publishes-first-consumer-focused-research-report-for-book-industry. Accessed Sept. 30, 2009.

12. Gale. www.gale.cengage.com/about. Accessed Oct. 2, 2009.

13. "Health Reference Center (Academic)." www.lib.utexas.edu/indexes/titles.php?id=174. Accessed Oct. 2, 2009.

14. Intner, Sheila S. and Jean Weihs. *Standard Cataloging for School and Public Libraries*. 4th ed. Westport, Conn.: Libraries Unlimited, 2007, p. 2, quoting Charles A.

Cutter. *Rules for a Dictionary Catalog.*, 4th ed. Washington, D.C.: Government Printing Office, 1904, p. 12.

15. Baltimore County Public Library. "Connections: Children, Youth, & Family Resources." www.bcpl.info/commpg/connections/connections.html#What%20Is%20the%20Connections. Accessed Oct. 4, 2009.

16. Bell, Suzanne S. *Librarian's Guide to Online Searching.* 2nd ed. Westport, Conn.: Libraries Unlimited, 2009, pp. 4–11.

17. Venn diagram. wordnetweb.princeton.edu/perl/webwn?s=venn%20diagram. Accessed March 20, 2010.

18. University of Texas at Austin. Library Catalog. "Advance Keyword Search." catalog.lib.utexas.edu/search/X. Accessed Oct. 4, 2009.

19. University of Texas at Austin. Library Catalog. "Advance Keyword Search."

20. Bell, pp. 24–26.

21. Natural language query. encyclopedia2.thefreedictionary.com/natural+language+query. Accessed Oct. 2, 2009.

22. InfoSkills Glossary. www.newcastle.edu.au/service/library/tutorials/infoskills/glossary.html. Accessed Oct. 4, 2009.

23. Google Dictionary. www.google.com/dictionary?hl=hu&sl=en&tl=en&q=thesaurus. Accessed March 9, 2010.

24. Bell, p. 26.

25. Cassell, Kay Ann and Uma Hiremath. *Reference and Information Services in the 21st Century: An Introduction.* Neal-Schuman, 2006, pp. 31–50.

26. "K–12 TexShare Database Program. Collection Development Policy, Approved by TexShare Advisory Board, January 26, 2007." esc20.net/k12databases/pdf/K12CDPOLICY_APPROVED.2007-01-26.pdf. Accessed Oct. 7, 2009.

27. "K–12 TexShare Database Program. Collection Development Policy, Approved by TexShare Advisory Board, January 26, 2007."

28. Schloman, Barbara F. "Information Resources: MedlinePlus: Key Resource for Both Health Consumers and Health Professionals. *OJIN: The Online Journal of Issues in Nursing.* March 7, 2006. www.nursingworld.org/MainMenuCategories/ANAMarketplace/ANAPeriodicals/OJIN/Columns/InformationResources/MedlinePlus_1.aspx. Accessed Oct. 5, 2009.

29. Schloman.

30. "K–12 Databases Program." esc20.net/k12databases/default.htm. Accessed Oct. 7, 2009.

31. Consumer Health Complete™. www.ebscohost.com/thisTopic.php?marketID=1&topicID=541. Accessed Oct. 7, 2009.

32. Austin Public Library Online Databases. Descriptions provided by the Austin Public Library. www.austinlibrary.com/databases/index.cfm?action=subject&id=013. Accessed Oct 7, 2009.

33. Brown, Steven L., James A. Teutel, and David A. Birch. "Early Adolescents Perceptions of Health and Health Literacy." *Journal of School Health* 77 (Jan. 2007): 7–15.

34. Brown, Teutel, and Birch.

35. Manganello, Jennifer A. "Health Literacy and Adolescents: A Framework and Agenda for Future Research." *Health Education Research* 23 (no. 5): 940–947. www.unitedhealthfoundation.org/download/Manganello.pdf. Accessed Oct. 7, 2007.

36. Gray, Nicola J. and Jonathan D. Klein. "Adolescents and the Internet: Health and Sexuality Information." Abstracted in *Find-Health-Articles.Com*. Sept. 20, 2006. www.find-health-articles.com/rec_pub_16932046-adolescents-internet-health-sexuality-information.htm. Accessed Oct. 5, 2009.

37. Kortum, Philip, Christine Edwards, and Rebecca Richard-Kortun. "The Impact of Inaccurate Internet Health Information in a Secondary School Learning Environment." Abstracted at Find-Health-Articles.com. www.find-health-articles.com/rec_pub_18653441-the-impact-inaccurate-internet-health-information-secondary-school.htm. Accessed Oct. 5, 2009.

38. Gray, Nicola J. and others. "The Internet: A Window on Adolescent Health Literacy." *Journal of Adolescent Health* 37 (Sept. 2005): 243. Abstracted from Medline.

39. Gray, Nicola J. "Health Information on the Internet—A Double-Edged Sword?" *Journal of Adolescent Health* 42 (May 2008): 432.

40. Thomas, Nancy Pickering. *Information Literacy and Information Skills Instruction: Applying Research to Practice in the School Library Media Center*. Libraries Unlimited, 2004, pp.132–157.

5

Materials for Health Instruction and Information

MAKING GOOD SELECTIONS

Selecting resources for a holistic health curriculum is crucial. School librarians—together with teachers and based on official materials selection policies—make decisions about how to acquire materials that will best meet instructional and informational needs of students. The instructional suggestions that follow in subsequent chapters involve teaching that relies on well-selected and effective materials.

Materials for health instruction and information are widely available. These include books for personal information, classroom instruction, references books, periodicals, electronic materials, pamphlets and brochures, and posters (Figure 5.1). This abundance makes selecting the appropriate materials difficult based on specific needs and specific audiences. This is coupled with the fact that health information is complex and diversified and requires health information skills to select what is appropriate. Fortunately, in her book *Understanding Healthcare Information*, Lyn Robinson offers us help in making sense out of this vast sea of information through her knowledge and reporting on reputable health information providers.[1]

Sources of materials include commercial publishers that offer publications and databanks; nonprofit and health advocacy groups that provide listings and other types of information packages; public and other types of libraries and informant centers that highlight sources for information; and government documents of all types that are published to meet their mandates.

Based on an informal survey by Lea K. Starr, Canadian librarians who deal with health issues recommend the following publishers as dependable and reputable.[2]

American Medical Association (www.ama-assn.org)
> The bookstore of the AMA provides a vast array of materials suitable for medical professionals as well as laypeople.

Figure 5.1.
Attractive and useable collections of health information are necessary for good health.
Courtesy of the University of Texas (at Austin) Libraries.

Canadian Medical Association (www.cma.ca)
Excellent resources of information about health issues in Canada
Facts on File (factsonfile.infobasepublishing.com/newsservices.asp)
Provides reference and instructional health materials for a wide variety of needs
Gale (www.gale.cengage.com)
Offers a variety of health information resources, both in print and online
Guilford (www.guilford.com)
Guilford's list of publications includes useful resources for teachers in addressing the broad needs of health care. The line of geographical and social science materials address some issues encountered with globalization.
Hazelden (www.hazelden.org/web/public/publishing.page)
Hazelden Publishing and Educational Services specializes in trade books that address issues relevant to alcoholism, drug addiction, and closely related psychology issues.
Jossey-Bass (www.josseybass.com/WileyCDA)
The inclusive listing of materials from Jossey-Bass provides information for professional educators who teach and/or are interested in health and other subject in the K–12 curriculum.
O'Reilly (oreilly.com/about)
Well-known California firm that offers a variety of sophisticated health care resources
Springhouse (www.lww.com/springhouse-publisher)
Offers a line of professional materials for nursing, including some reference titles that will be useful for teachers of health in secondary health education classes

As mentioned, various governments offer a variety of information resources. In the United States, www.health.gov is a portal to the Web sites of a number of multi-agency health initiatives and activities of the U.S. Department of Health and Human Services (HHS) and other federal departments and agencies.

Many if not all states in the United States as well as provinces and other governmental regions in other countries have health departments that provide information in various formats. For example, the North Dakota Health Department's Education

Technology Division offers distance-learning programs and other resources on topics such as emergency, public health, and medical services. Among others, it offers production services, satellite transmitted programs, Web casting, and interactive video conference programs. A more complete description of its offerings is available at www.ndhealth.gov/ET/Instructions.htm.

In Canada, Health Infoway provides similar services. It is

[An] independent, not-for-profit organization funded by the Federal government. Infoway jointly invests with every province and territory to accelerate the development and adoption of electronic health record projects in Canada. Fully respecting patient confidentiality, these secure systems will provide clinicians and patients with the information they need to better support safe care decisions and manage their own health. Accessing this vital information quickly will help foster a more modern and sustainable health care system for all Canadians. (www.sources.com/listings/Subscribers/L3441.htm)

The Department of Health (DH) in the United Kingdom offers information about government policies and up-to-date news on health issues. The department also maintains a publication program. Its Web site is at www.dh.gov.uk/en/index.htm. Australia's government health information portal is maintained by the Department of Health and Aging. Among its various information resources are publications that are of use in instructional programs. Its Web site is at www.health.gov.au.

CRITERIA FOR GOOD SELECTION

One of the hallmarks of health information literacy is to help students understand health information and to make positive decisions about their own health as well as practice good health behaviors. Having access to reliable health information is an important beginning in this process. Teachers, school librarians, and other health care providers have an abundance of selection aids and resources to help them in the important process of selection materials. Primary among selection criteria are:

- Accuracy
- Authority
- Currency
- Usability within its format and intended audience
- Available when ordered
- Easy to acquire within the usual acquisition procedures including
- Interlibrary loan access

Going beyond these elementary concepts, comprehensive health information literacy requires students to apply health information in complex, accurate, and comprehensive ways. This complexity requires students to understand the breadth and depth of accurate health information and how to draw conclusions from this information.[3] Health information literacy taught through a holistic curriculum can help students avoid misunderstanding or disregarding the relationship of health information to personal health situations.[4]

ENSURING INFORMATION QUALITY

MedlinePlus outlines the following points that will help ensure good quality health information. These criteria concerns online resources, but one can apply them to almost any health information product. These include:

- Use recognized authorities (editorial boards, credentials, posted selection guidelines and policies, author identifications, author credentials, contact information).
- Look for unreasonable health claims not based on established science.
- Avoid resources that use obscure language and offer reading difficulty to the average user of the resource.
- Look for well-constructed design features, such as color, fonts, layouts, and spacing of information.
- Check for accuracy of information (dates of documents posted on sites, information citations, information resources).
- For Web sites, consider currency of links, how items are updated, and how protection of privacy is provided.
- Beware of biases that might include publishers, site sponsorships, and misapplications of information in support of a viewpoint.

Understanding social and cultural aspects of information needs and how information products are designed are necessary. Instructional designs and instructional needs are likewise paramount to making good selection decisions. Social and cultural considerations include:[5]

- Peer pressure and acceptance of information and its formats
- Community and family influences on how to accept health information
- Commercial advertising and promotion of health items and information
- Preferred information-seeking behaviors
- Lifestyles and awareness of health information needs.

As stated, these criteria can be applied to a wide variety of health information products and reinforced with an understanding of what is generally considered appropriate for age and grade levels, instructional needs, and cognitive and learning skills.

E-HEALTH: ELECTRONIC HEALTH INFORMATION FOR YOUTH AND THEIR CAREGIVERS

The Internet offers an abundance of health information appropriate for students and their caregivers. The following list is by no means exhaustive, but it does show the great variety of sites that offer health information.[6,7] For the most part, these are not-for-profit sites, but those that have a commercial aspects are so marked.

Above the Influence. An attractive site offering straight talk about drug use and abuse. In addition to useful information, it provides games and personal stories. Available at www.above theinfluence.com.

AdiosBarbie.com. This site provides guidance on how to be realistic about body types. It is aimed at helping people feel comfortable with their bodies and not to evaluate themselves based on impossible standards of looks. It offers interactive videos, games, helpful information about diets, and other resources. Available at www.adiosbarbie.com.

Advocates for Youth. A site supporting policies and programs focused on assisting teens and young people form and practice responsible decisions about reproductive and sexual health. Provides advocacy and program information, news, publications, lesson plans, and useful facts. Available at www.advocatesforyouth.org.

Adolescence Directory Online. Adolescence Directory Online supports educators, counselors, parents, researchers, and teens by offering links and other forms of information on issues of interest to youth and their caregivers. Available at site.educ.indiana.edu.

Alternative Medicine. "[A] jumpstation for sources of information on unconventional, unorthodox, unproven, or alternative, complementary, innovative, [and] integrative therapies." Available at www.pitt.edu/~cbw/altm.html.

Alt HealthWatch. "[I]ndexes over 140 full-text journals concerning complementary, holistic or alternative health care and wellness. Twenty-eight of these journals are peer reviewed. . . . In addition, the database includes full-text pamphlets and reports." Available at www.ebscohost.com/thisTopic.php?topicID=25&marketID=1.

American Medical Association. Provides information on American medicine and concerns for medical care; includes list of the AMA's publications, most of which are technical in character. Available at www.ama-assn.org.

Band-Aides and Blackboards. This colorful and user-friendly Web site provides information and resources on problems and issues concerning "children with chronic illness and special health care needs in school." Separate sections of the site support the needs of children, teens, and adults, including parents, health professionals, and educators. Available at www.lehman.cuny.edu/faculty/jfleitas/bandaides.

BBC. The BBC has a number of useful Web sites dealing with health. Its "BBC Schools: Learning Resources for Home and School," along with other topics, provides useful health and socially related information associated with the British national curriculum (www.bbc.co.uk/schools). An abundance of heath information is found throughout its postings, including "BBC Health." Available at www.bbc.co.uk/health.

Center for Mental Health Services Knowledge Exchange Network. The KEN Center is a Web site produced by the Center for Mental Health Services, a federal government agency. It provides access and information involving programs, services, consumer mental health information, publications, and useful resources for professionals. It offers a special children's section. Available in part at mentalhealth.about.com/library/2010/inf/blrc12.htm.

Center for Substance Abuse Prevention. CSAP, a division of the U.S. Substance Abuse and Mental Health Services Administration (SAMSHA), presents information about alcohol and drugs as well as effective prevention programs. This is useful source for professionals, families, and teens. Available at prevention.samhsa.gov.

Center for Young Women's Health. This colorful site provides an abundance of health publications written for teens concerning such topics as growth and development, reproductive and sexual health, nutrition, and eating disorders. Information is also offered for parents and health professionals. Available at www.youngwomenshealth.org.

Child Advocate. "ChildAdvocate.net serves the needs of children, families and professionals while addressing mental health, medical, educational, legal and legislative issues." Provides references to health sources. Available at www.childadvocate.net.

Children's Page. Available through MedlinePlus. The site says: "Kids, this page is for you. Learn about everything from how the body works to what happens when you go to the hospital. There are quizzes, games and lots of cool web sites for you to explore. Have fun!"

Available in Spanish. See Teen's Page. Available at www.nlm.nih.gov/medlineplus/childrenspage.html.

Child Welfare Information Gateway Adoption Information Clearinghouse. A service of the Children's Bureau, Administration for Children and Families, U.S. Department of Health and Human Services, that "provides access to print and electronic publications, websites, and online databases covering a wide range of topics from prevention to permanency, including child welfare, child abuse and neglect, adoption, and search and reunion." Available at www.childwelfare.gov.

Consumer Health Complete. "[T]he single most comprehensive resource for consumer-oriented health content. CHC provides content covering all areas of health and wellness from mainstream medicine to the many perspectives of complementary, holistic, and integrated medicine. This full-text database covers topics such as aging, cancer, diabetes, drugs & alcohol, fitness, nutrition & dietetics, men's & women's health, and children's health." Available at www.ebscohost.com/thisTopic.php?marketID=1&topicID=541.

Cool Nurse. More topics are covered here than at many other Web sites. Information includes prescription drug abuse, a condom tutorial, depression, diets, tattoos and body art, and anorexia and bulimia. It presents the tough topics on the homepage, right up front, and addresses them head-on. This has a section for women and men as well as quizzes, a place to ask questions, and hotline numbers. Some of the content is advanced, especially that dealing with sex. This is a commercial site with advertisements, published by Hillclimb Media Seattle. Available at www.coolnurse.com.

eLibrary Curriculum Edition. A curriculum and reference resource for grades K–12, containing reference materials, periodicals, and digital items. Includes health and medical information as well as a knowledge base of educational standards. Available at www.proquestk12.com/productinfo/elibrary_ce.shtml.

Facts On File's Health Reference Center. "[A] comprehensive encyclopedic database containing thousands of hyperlinked entries organized into four major categories: conditions and diseases, mental health, health and wellness, and body systems. It provides clear information on the causes, cures, key research, medical terms, symptoms, treatments and trends, and organizations in each field of study. Each content area is searchable by keyword and [an index]." A list of links also allows users to easily find more focused topics within subject areas. Available at www.fofweb.com/SellSheets/046964.pdf.

Family Village. The Village helps families with children who have special needs. The site presents a variety of Internet links as well as Web-based information and resources on "specific diagnoses, communication connections, adaptive products and technology, adaptive recreational activities, education, worship, health issues, and disability. Available at www.halfthesky.org/work/familyvillage.php.

For Kids. Especially designed for children and teens, the site offers information on a variety of issues of importance and interest to teens and younger children. Provides links to a variety of colorful and interest sites. Available at www.fda.gov/ForConsumers/ByAudience/ForKids/default.htm. http://www.freevibe.com.

GirlsAllowed! An interactive site sponsored by Corporate Alliance to End Partner Violence. The site offers girls information and tools supporting the "development and maintaining healthy relationships with friends, partners, and others." It offers activities for girls, parents, educators, and group leaders designed to promote discussions between parents and adults and girls. The site requires Macromedia Flash Player for operation. Available at www.girlsallowed.org/index_yes.html.

Girls Health.gov. Sponsored by the Office on Women's Health of the U.S. Department of Health and Human Services. The site presents a wealth of health-related information for girls 12–16 as well as information for parents and caregivers and girls with disabilities and/or chronic illness. Available at www.girlshealth.gov.

Girls Incorporated. A national, not-for-profit organization that provides educational programs based on research for high-risks American girls. The site provides links, resources, fact sheets, and publications. The site also offers a section for adults. Available at www.girlsinc.org/girls -inc.html.

Girlpower. Sponsored by the U.S Department of Health and Human Services. As a public education campaign, this site—available within the department's Web site—helps brings research and news helpful to girls and their emotional development. Available through mentalhealth .samhsa.gov/publications/allpubs/ca-0038/default.asp.

Go Ask Alice. Provides a large amount of information for teens, including sexuality issues. Sponsored by Columbia University. Available at www.goaskalice.columbia.edu.

Grolier Online. An online subscription system constructed around the company's existing seven encyclopedia databases, containing age-appropriate information and resources, including health information. General description available at go.grolier.com/faq.php.

Health & Wellness Resource Center. A subscription-based resource that "provides reference material as well as full text periodicals and pamphlets from a wide variety of authoritative medical sources" General description available at www.gale.cengage.com/Health/HealthRC/ about.htm.

Health Information for Teen/Health Information for Kids. This service of the U.S. Food and Drug Administration provides factsheets on special issues of concern to teens and children and offers a serious approach to health issues of special interests to adolescents. Information provided includes drug and alcohol use and abuse, birth control methods, and information on diseases that often affect teens, such as mononucleosis. Available at www.fda.gov/ForConsumers/ ByAudience/ForKids/default.htm.

Health Source: Consumer Edition. This commercial source is a rich collection of consumer health information providing access to nearly 80 full-text, consumer health magazines, including *American Fitness, Better Nutrition, Fit Pregnancy, Harvard Health Letter, HealthFacts, Men's Health, Muscle & Fitness, Prevention, Vegetarian Times,* and many others. This database also includes searchable full text for current, health-related pamphlets and more than 130 health reference books. General description available at www.ebscohost.com/ thisTopic.php?marketID=1&topicID=82.

Himmelfarb Health Science Library: Internet Resources. This site provides an extensive list of links to health related Web sites. Some sites are technical, while others are consumer- and student-orientated. Available at www.gwumc.edu/library/eresources/inetres.cfm/subject/ Environmental-Occupational-Health.

IWannaKnow.org. A colorful site that offers sexual and STD information for teens. Information provided by the American Social Health Association. The information is available for teachers, parents, and other caregivers. Spanish-language access is also provided. Available at www.iwannaknow.org.

KidsHealth. Provides information for both teens and younger children as well as parents. The site is divided into categories addressing various audiences. Sponsored by the Nemours Foundation. See TeensHealth. Available at kidshealth.org.

KidSpace. A service of the Internet Public Library, this site offers numerous links to health and safety site for children. See TeenSpace. Available at www.ipl.org/div/kidspace.

The Lancet. Although primarily intended for physicians and other medical personnel, *The Lancet,* by most accounts, is one of the oldest peer-reviewed and important international medical journals. It is important to consumers of health care information because of its international coverage of medical events and situations and its editorial approaches to important medical issues affecting society. Available at www.thelancet.com.

LD Online. Presents information, including multimedia, on learning disabilities for children, parents, educators, and professionals in a variety of fields. Available at www.ldonline .org.

Let's Face It. The Dentistry Library at the University of Michigan School of Dentistry, through this attractive and user-friendly site, provides information and resources especially useful for dental and teeth care. Updated frequently. Available at desica.dent.umich.edu/faceit/.

Medical Library Association. For over 100 years, this association has been primarily concerned with making health care information accessible to medical professionals as well as to the general public. Its publication programs include a variety of pamphlet materials aimed at the health information consumer. CAPHIS is the Consumer and Patient Health Information Section of the Medical Library Association. Available at www.mlanet.org.

National Eating Disorders Association. This site offers information on eating disorders and their prevention. It offers treatment referrals, advocacy information, links to resources, and success stories in overcoming various disorders. Available at www.nationaleating disorders.org.

National Center for Learning Disabilities. This organization "strives to increase opportunities for all individuals with learning disabilities to achieve their potential." The site provides information for people with learning disabilities, professionals serving them, news reports, important research, and advocacy information. Available at www.ncld.org.

National Dissemination Center for Children with Disabilities. Provides "comprehensive information on the entire spectrum of issues involved in living with, caring for, and educating a child or youth with disabilities." The site includes information on educational issues for youth ranging in age to 22. Coverage includes laws, news, research, and factsheets on specific types of disabilities. Available at www.nichcy.org/Pages/Home.aspx.

National Institute for Mental Health. NIMH's Web site provides education materials about mental health for concerns both consumers and practitioners. Available at www.nimh .nih.gov/index.shtml.

National Library of Medicine Databases. Provides useful electronic databases offering extensive and freely accessible medical information throughout the world. The services include Medline, MedlinePlus and PedMed. MedlinePlus is designed to be of use to the general public, and it has features that are user-friendly and that have subject approaches that have been preformulated with MEDLINEMedline. All these databases as well as a host of other health information are described by NLM on its site at www.nlm.nih.gov.

Native Health Databases. Contains bibliographic information and abstracts of health-related articles, reports, surveys, and other resource documents pertaining to the health and health care of American Indians, Alaska Natives, and Canadian First Nations. The site offers search options for finding detailed information. Available at https://hscssl.unm.edu/nhd.

Natural & Alternative Treatments. Offers a complementary and alternative medicine database designed specifically for the consumer health researcher. Updated frequently. Available at www.ebscohost.com/thisTopic.php?marketID=6&topicID=114.

Nature. This is one of the premier scientific journals in the world. It is available both in print and electronic form, and it is archived back to 1869. Available at www.nature.com/nature/ index.html.

Oasis Magazine. Sponsored by the National Coalition for Gay, Lesbian, Bisexual & Transgender Youth, this site provides useful information for educators, including a searchable database, a chat forum, and school and library resources. Available at www.oasisjournals.com/resources.

Parents, Families and Friends of Lesbians and Gays. Known as PFLAG, this organization through its Web site emphasizes the health and social issues of GLB youth and their families and friends. Its programs include support, education and training, advocacy, publications, and development of local chapters. Available at community.pflag.org.

Positive.org. Sponsored by the Coalition for Positive Sexuality (CPS), this nonprofit organization offers appealing, straightforward, and positive sex education materials for teens. Available at www.positive.org.

Sex, Etc. A service of the Network for Family Life Education. The site is created by teens for teens. In addition to sexual information, it offers information on emotional health, abuse, body image, alcohol, and drugs. Available at www.sexetc.org.

Something Fishy. A site concerned with eating disorders, such as anorexia, bulimia, and excessive overeating. The site provides a wide array of information and support resources. Available at www.something-fishy.org.

Suicide Awareness Voices of Education. SAVE is a source for educational materials about suicide. It provides information directed at teens. Available at www.save.org.

TeenGrowth. A commercial site that provides real-world answers and options about birth control, pregnancy, and personal hygiene. It includes fun trivia and quizzes where teens can test their knowledge of pregnancy and sex. Q&A information is provided by board-certified physicians. Available at www.teengrowth.com.

Teen Health. Information here is provided by the Cincinnati Children's Hospital and Medical Center, with emphasis on health conditions, treatments, wellness, and physical and emotional development. Available at www.cincinnatichildrens.org.

Teen Health & Wellness: Real Life, Real Answers. This is a subscription-based resource from the extensive line of health books for teens in the publisher's Coping series. This interactive database "provides students with comprehensive curricular support and self-help tools on topics including diseases, drugs, alcohol, nutrition, fitness, mental health, diversity, family life, and more." *Library Journal* said this about the resource: "A one-stop self-help resource and fully interactive online community center for teen health and wellness . . . authoritative." The site offers an interactive hotline service. Available at www.teenhealthandwellness.com/static/publicabout.

Teen Health and the Media. A service of the University of Washington created to help teens understand the role of media on health issues, attitudes, and behaviors. Discusses how media influences attitudes about sexuality, body image, nutrition, drugs and alcohol, and violence. Available at depts.washington.edu/thmedia.

Teenage Health Freak. Written in diary and cartoon form, this is a visually interesting approach to health information of interest to teens. Information is often given in conservational forms and includes information on sexually transmitted infections, smoking, weight and body images, moods, and cold sores. Available at www.teenagehealthfreak.org/homepage/index.asp.

Teen Health. This Canadian site provides a wide variety of health information topics, including sex and relationships, smoking, and mental health. It provides links to other Canadian health information sites. Available at www.chebucto.ns.ca/Health/TeenHealth. If unavailable contact publichealthservices(at)cdha.nshealth.ca

TeenHealthFX. Provided by Atlantic Health Systems, this site provides medical information largely in a question-answer format. Questions are answered by a wide variety of medical professionals. Available at www.teenhealthfx.com.

TeensHealth. Provides access by subject categories to such topic as body, sexual health, drugs, and alcohol. Offers links to featured articles, hot topics, expert answers, journals, etc. Delivers clear and concise answers to health-related topics in a language that teens can understand. The Web site is also accessible in Spanish. Available at www.kidshealth.org/teen.

Teens' Page. The site states that it just for teens and not their parents. It is "about health and safety for teens. There are quizzes, games and lots of cool web sites for you to explore. Have fun!" A companion Spanish site is also provided. Available at www.nlm.nih.gov/medlineplus/teenspage.html.

TeenSpace. Operated by the Internet Public Library, this site provides an abundance of links to sites dealing with teen health and sexual issues. Available at www.ipl.org/div/teen.

Teenwire. This is a service offered by Planned Parenthood. The site provides an abundance of information and news about teen sexuality, sexual health, and relationships. Available at www.plannedparenthood.org/teen-talk.

Testicular Cancer Resource Center. A not-for-profit resource center that offers information on the diagnosis and treatment of testicular cancer as well as the testicular self-exam (TSE). Testicular cancer is the most common cancer for young men between the ages and 15 and 35. The site addresses the information needs of caregivers, patients, family, friends, and physicians. Available at tcrc.acor.org/about_us_main.html.

U.S. Food and Drug Administration. This is the central homepage for the FDA. It offers links to an abundance of information concerned with its governmental missions and mandates. Included here are a wide variety of health information, such as food safety and regulations, drugs, medical devices, biologics, cosmetics, and radiation safety and issues. Available at www.fda.gov.

Working Safely: Advice for Kids. Sponsored by FamilyDoctor.org, this commercial site gives youth information about work and how to stay safe at work and recreation. It suggests links to other work-related sites. Available at http://familydoctor.org.

Young Men's Health. Through health information sheets prepared for young men, this attractive site operated by Children's Hospital Boston offers information on nutrition, acne, athlete's foot, sexual health, stress, and depression. Available at www.youngmenshealth site.org.

Young Women's Health. This site is operated by the Oregon Health and Science University. The site includes book reviews of interest to young women and information about research in women's health as well as crisis and emergency links. Available at www.ohsu.edu/xd/health/services/women/index.cfm.

Youth Guardian Services. This is an attractive youth-managed and operated not-for-profit site that offers support and services through the Internet for gay, lesbian, bisexual, transgendered, questioning, and straight youth. E-mail addresses of resource sites arranged by age and interests topics are available at www.youth-guard.org.

YouthResource. A Web site that is constructed and maintained for and by gay, lesbian, bisexual, transgender, and questioning (GLBTQ) young people ages 13–24. It provides support, education, and information about issues concerning GLBTQ youth. Available at www.amplifyyourvoice.org/youthresource.

SELECTION AIDS AND SOURCES: OFFERING ACCESS TO HEALTH INFORMATION

The following list of health selection aids is an update of a list appearing in *Health Information for Youth: The Public Library and School Library Media Center Role* (Libraries Unlimited, 2007) by the authors.

A to Zoo: Subject Access to Children's Picture Books. **By Carolyn W. Lima and John A. Lima.** 7th ed. Westport, Conn.: Libraries Unlimited, 2006. This has become a standard reference resource for collection development and reader's advisement that includes over 4,000 titles published since 2001. It includes information on fiction and nonfiction picture books for children. Subject and bibliographic guides are provided, along with title and illustrator indexes.

Adventuring with Books: A Booklist for Pre-K–Grade 6. **By Amy A. McClure and Janice V. Kristo.** 13th ed. Urbana, Ill.: National Council of Teachers of English, 2002. A longtime favorite, it lists more than 850 books published between 1999 and 2001 suitable for children for research, learning, and pleasure reading

ALA's Guide to Best Reading. Chicago: American Library Association. This is an ongoing series that list and annotates books that are considered "best" for the given year under review. Includes books listed in *Notable Children's Books, Notable Books, Editor's Choice*, and *Best Books for Young Adults*. Includes the best in fiction, nonfiction, and poetry for all ages.

ARBA In-Depth: Health and Medicine. **By Martin Dillon and Shannon Graff.** Libraries Unlimited. 2004. "Provides focused help for . . . health and medicine collection development needs. Critical reviews of quality reference titles by subject-experts cover general and specialized titles in the areas of: Medicine, Nursing, Pharmaceutical Sciences, and Nutrition."

Best Books for Children: Preschool through Grade 6. **By Catherine Barr and John T. Gillespie.** 8th ed. *Children's and Young Adult Literature Reference* series. Westport, Conn.: Libraries Unlimited, 2005. Includes more than 25,000 in-print titles for children in grades K–6. Arranged by themes, with concise annotations.

Best Books for High School Readers: Grades 9–12. **By Catherine Barr and John T. Gillespie.** 2nd ed. *Children's and Young Adult Literature Reference* series. Westport, Conn.: Libraries Unlimited, 2009. This second edition includes 1,500 titles published from 2004 through 2008. Provides bibliographic information as well as review sources.

Best Books for High School Readers: Grades 9–12. Supplement to the First Edition. **By John T. Gillespie and Barr, Catherine, eds.** Westport, Conn.: Libraries Unlimited, 2006. Includes over 2,600 highly recommended titles published from June 2004 to June 2006. Arranged thematically, this resource provides, in the words of the publisher, "state-of-the-art reading guide and selection tool for teen reading material, both fiction and nonfiction."

Booklist. Presents reviews of recommended books, nonprint items, and computer programs for use in school library media centers and public libraries. Essays and reviews cover special topics, such as easy-to-read and foreign language materials. Through its Booklist Publications imprint, it issues bibliographies, lists, and special monographs designed to help in the selection of materials (www.ala.org/booklist).

Books for You: An Annotated Booklist for Senior High. **By Kylene and Teri Lesesne.** 14th ed. Urbana, Ill.: National Council Teachers of English, 2001. Presented here is a thematic listing of more than 1,000 books for high school students. Arranged by themes, readers (teachers, librarians, students, and parents) are encouraged to explore many areas. Award-winning books are highlighted in an appendix.

The Book Report. See *Library Media Collection*.

Book Review Digest. First published by the H. W. Wilson Company in 1905, it is designed to provide bibliographic citations and digests of reviews of books as they appear in the professional and literary press. Includes children and young adult reviews along with bibliographic and acquisition information. Its electronic format is *Book Review Digest Plus*, with links to reviews it cites (www.hwwilson.com/databases/brdig.htm).

Books in Print. First published by the R. R. Bowker Company in 1948. *Subject Guide to Children's Books in Print* followed in 1970. These sources were not originally considered selection aids but more as acquisition aids, providing school library media center specialists and public youth librarians with convenient access to information on the availability of books within the book trade market. In recent years, *Books in Print* has become more useful as a selection aid through its publishing of abstracts of reviews of selected items. Its electronic version *Book in Print Plus* has expanded this to include reviews of children and young adults books as well as special services, such as award books and guides to materials according to grade, reading, and special interests needs (www.bowker.com).

Bulletin for the Center for Children's Books. Offers reviews of children's books and books for adolescents. Reviews are brief, but rating scales offer recommendation suggestions as well as suggested audience and uses (e.g., R for recommended; NC for those not recommended; SPC indicates that subject matter or treatment will tend to limit the book to specialized collections). Reading levels for each book are also provided (bccb.lis.illinois.edu).

Consumer Health Information Source Book. **By Alan Rees, ed.** 7th ed. Westport, Conn.: Greenwood Press, 2003. An impressive guide to popular print and electronic health information for general consumers. Includes newsletters, pamphlet titles, health information clearinghouses, toll-free hotlines, health-related resources and referral organizations, online services and CD-ROM products, selected Web sites, and a listing of supportive professional medical textbooks and monographs.

Drug Information: A Guide to Current Resources. **By Bonnie Snow.** 3rd ed., New York: Neal-Schuman, 2008. "More than a bibliography, this readable guide brings together the best resources plus practical advice on everything from expert search techniques to core collections for libraries."

The Horn Book Guide to Children's and Young Adult Books. Attempts to list and comment on all children's and young adult books published in the United States. Although comments are brief, the guide provides a rating scale indicating the quality of the book and includes a guide to genre and subject areas. See http://www.hbook.com/guide.

The Horn Book Magazine: About Books for Children and Young Adults. A fine literary review and discussion journal devoted to promoting reading and culture through the reviews and critical analysis of books for children and young adults. Various sections or departments include reviews of newly published books, recommended paperbacks, new editions and reissues, and science books. Special columns are devoted to discussing young adult books, re-reviewing older books, and reviewing Canadian books. It also publishes *The Horn Book Guide*, which is a rather complete listing with annotations and brief reviews of children's and young adult books published in the United States (www.hbook.com).

Introduction to Reference Sources in the Health Sciences. **By Jo Anne Boorkman, Jeffrey T. Huber, and Jean Blackwell.** 5th ed. New York: Neal-Schuman, 2008. Includes descriptions and advice on important health information sources, including electronic resources.

Kirkus Reviews. Kirkus offers long and detailed reviews of fiction and nonfiction books for adults, adolescents, and children. Reviews are intended for booksellers and librarians and appear before the books are published, allowing librarians and bookstores to stock in anticipation of demand. The children's section, which must be subscribed to apart from the basic subscription, offers special lists, such as holiday books. Both formats are available only by subscription. See www.kirkusreviews.com.

Kliatt Young Adult Paperback Book Guide. Publishes reviews of paperback books, young adult hardcover fiction, audiobooks, and educational software appropriate for young adults in classrooms and libraries. Reviews include most fields of interest: fiction, literature and language arts, biography and personal narratives, education and guidance, social studies, history and geography, sciences, the arts, and recreation (Kliatt Young Adult Paperback Book Guide, 33 Bay State Road, Wellesley, MA 02481; 781-237-7577).

Library Media Collection. According to the publisher "[b]lending the best of its predecessors *The Book Report, Library Talk* and *Technology Connection, LMC* delivers proven, real-world practical information, professional development, and educator-developed book and technology reviews seven times each school year" (www.linworth.com/lmc).

The New Walford, Volume 1: Science, Technology, and Medicine. **By Ray Lester, ed.** New York: Neal-Schuman, 2005. "This comprehensive guide classifies over twenty types of print and electronic reference resources—General Introductions; Dictionaries, Thesauri, and Classifications; Associations and Societies; Libraries, Archives, and Museums; Digital data, image, and text collections; directories and encyclopedias . . . provides thorough coverage of over 150 subject areas with the guidance of over a dozen subject specialist" (publisher).

Notable Books for Children. Chicago: Association for Library Service to Children. Annual. An annual list of books considered to be the best published during the preceding year by a committee of professionals. Listing includes fiction and nonfiction. The association also annually publishes its Notable Films and Videos for Children. Often, its listings include items related to health and society. See also Young Adult Library Services Association in this list.

Parents Choice Foundation. An online source for reviews and discussions intended for parents and educators, including librarians. It provides written reviews in all areas of children's media, including books, television, home video, recordings, toys, music, recordings, and computer software (www.parents-choice.org).

Publishers Weekly: The Book Industry Journal. A trade journal that offers broad coverage of events in the book trade, including children's and young adult publishing. Reviews are offered for books just released by various publishers (www.publishersweekly.com).

School Library Journal. Serves children and young adult public librarians and school librarians as a dependable review source. It contains review sections on computer software, audiovisual media, and fiction and nonfiction books. Reviews are written by professionals knowledgeable about the needs of youth and their education (www.schoollibraryjournal.com).

Science Books and Films. Published by the American Association for the Advancement of Science in six print issues per year. It reviews print, film, and software materials in all areas of the sciences for all ages. Reviews are directed at all types of librarians and educators. *Science Books and Films Online* is its companion that is included in a subscription to *SB&F* (www.sbfonline.com/Pages/welcomesplash.aspx).

Sexuality Information and Education Council of the United States (SIECUS). *Guidelines for Comprehensive Sexuality Education.* 3rd ed. New York: The Council, 2004. Outlines the council's approach to sexual health. A complete copy is available at www.siecus.org/_data/global/images/guidelines.pdf.

Teacher Librarian: The Journal for School Library Professionals. An independent school library journal that addresses the needs of professionals who work with children and young adults. In addition to reviews of books and nonprint media, it features articles on current issues and trends. Reviews cover children and young adult books, new nonfiction, best sellers, video materials, computer software, and Internet resources. It also profiles authors and illustrators. *Teacher Librarian* is a continuation of *Emergency Librarian*, published from 1973 to 1998 (www.teacherlibrarian.com).

Voice of Youth Advocates (VOYA). A hard-hitting review (sometimes opinionated) and discussion journal intended to help librarians who work with adolescents. It reviews films, video games, and fiction of all kinds. It also provides good coverage of nonfiction items, including health related issues (www.voya.com/whatsinvoya).

Wilson Co. (H. G.). *The Wilson Core Collections* **(formerly** *The Wilson Standard Catalogs***).** The Core Collections series offers several basic guides to collection development. Guides in this series present core collections of titles based on expert recommendations for elementary, middle, junior high, and senior high school library media centers. In addition, the Core Collections series includes guides to fiction, graphic novels, and nonfiction for public libraries and nonprint materials. In keeping with the company's philosophy of service, all recommendations made by this series are based on professional, expert opinions. All titles in the Core Collections series are available in print and electronic formats (www.hwwilson.com/Databases/stcatelect.htm).

Young Adult Library Services Association. The association maintains impressive, highly selected lists of books and nonprint materials for young adults. Many of these address health issues. For a complete catalog of these lists, consult the association's Web site at www.ala.org/ala/mgrps/divs/yalsa/booklistsawards/booklistsbook.cfm.

Your Reading: An Annotated Booklist for Middle School and Junior High. **By Jean E. Brown and Elaine C. Stephens.** 11th ed. Urban, Ill.: National Council of Teachers of English, 2003. Intended to be used by teachers, students, and parents in selecting good and interesting books to read, this source offers a variety of books, fiction and nonfiction, for the middle and junior high child.

Other important and useful guides include the National Science Teachers annual list of outstanding trade books in science and the National Council of Social Studies annual list of outstanding trade books in the social sciences.

HEALTH BOOKS IN SERIES AND FILMS

Various publishers publish a great many books on health in series. A direct approach to finding such series is through any of the book acquisition services. For example, using the keywords "health series" in the *Books in Print* electronic database within its Children's Room section and limiting the search by the various options will most likely produce a number of hits, with many of these including reviews as well as annotations. Publishers indexed here include Franklin Watts's *Human Health and Disease* series published by Scholastic Library Publishing; Curriculum Concepts (New Zealand); Image Paths Inc.; Heinemann Library; Scholastic Library Publishing; Marshall Cavendish Corp.; and Kids For Health, Inc. Kids for Health also has a series of health-related videos.

Rosen Publishing Group's *Coping* series is a series of well-reviewed books intended for adolescents and addressing some of their major concerns. The publisher states: "This informative, up-to-date series can provide the information many teens need to help them make informed choices." Some examples include: *Coping When a Parent Has AIDS* by Barbara Hermie Draimin; *Coping with the Death of a Brother or Sister* by Ruth Ann Ruiz; *Coping with a Drug Abusing Parent* by Lawrence Clayton; *Coping with Cross-Cultural and Interracial Relationships* by Sandra Lee Smith; *Coping with Special Needs Classmates* by Sherri McCarthy-Tucker; *Coping with School Age Fatherhood* by Michael Pennetti; *Coping with a Physically Challenged Brother or Sister* by Linda Lee Ratto; *Coping with Mental Illness* by Barbara Moe; and *Coping with Being Physically Challenged* by Linda Lee Ratto (www.rosenpublishing.com).

Omnigraphics' trade list includes these timely titles in its *Teen Health* series: *Abuse and Violence Information for Teens; Accident and Safety Information for Teens; Alcohol Information for Teens*, 2nd ed.; *Allergy Information for Teens; Asthma Information for Teens*, 2nd ed.; *Cancer Information for Teens*, 2nd ed.; *Complementary and Alternative Medicine Information for Teens*; *Diabetes Information for Teens*; *Diet Information for Teens*, 2nd ed.; *Drug Information for Teens*, 2nd ed.; *Eating Disorders Information for Teens*, 2nd ed.; *Fitness Information for Teens*, 2nd ed; *Learning Disabilities Information for Teens*; *Mental Health Information for Teens*, 3rd ed.; *Mental Health Information For Teens*, 2nd ed.; *Pregnancy Information For Teens*; *Sexual Health Information for Teens*, 2nd ed.; *Skin Health Information for Teens*, 2nd ed.; *Sleep Information for Teens*; *Sports Injuries Information for Teens*, 2nd ed.; *Stress Information for Teens*; *Suicide Information for* Teens; and *Tobacco Information for Teens* (http://www .omnigraphics.com/category_view.php?ID=46).

Health libraries are excellent sources for films and visuals. Film libraries are often maintained by government agencies, ranging from national to state, provincial, and local providers. Of interest to teachers is the U.S. National Library of Medicine's national Online Exhibitions and Digital Projects, provides access to the library's changing exhibitions as well as highlighting its extensive digitalization activities. The library, through its Web site at www.nlm.nih.gov/onlineexhibitions.html, also offers information, teaching suggestions, and resources for teachers. The U.S. National Institute of Health, through its health museum, provides online visuals concerning the historical development of medicine. The site offers online exhibits as well as resources for teachers: history.nih.gov/museum/virtual.html.

Film libraries operated by states and provinces, institutions, school districts, and not-for-profit organizations offer access to film materials. For example, the Texas Health Department maintains an audiovisual library devoted to health issues. These films cover a wide variety of topics, from driving safety to workplace safety. Many of these are appropriate for use in schools. Rental is free, but borrowing is limited by residence requirements. Nevertheless, a search of the online catalog offers suggestions for available films: www.dshs.state.tx.us/avlib/default.shtm. Check your state's health department to see if it has a similar service. Examples of not-for-profit film libraries are regional libraries operated by Planned Parenthood of America. The Christine H. Aubrey Resource Center for Sexuality serves Planned Parenthood's Texas Capital Region and offers hundreds of books, journals, and pamphlets on all aspects of reproductive health that are available for free use in homes and classrooms: www.planned parenthood.org/index.htm.

Commercial film companies provide health resources. Their catalogs offer access to their productions. Among others, these are produced and distributed by: Schlessinger Media (www.visualed.com/schlessingerdvd.htm); Great Plains National GPN Educational Media (www.shopgpn.com); Disney Educational Productions (dep.disney.go.com); Benchmark Media (www.benchmarkmedia.info); Visual Learning Company (www.visual learningco.com); and TMW Media Group (www.tmwmedia.com). WorldCat, through its advanced search protocol, can also provides access to commercially produced audiovisual items: www.worldcat.org/advancedsearch.

The Media That Matters Film Festival offers access to short films covering important current topics, including films that highlight events in local communities as well as events around the world. Teachers may use this source to identify short films that can be acquired for classroom discussion in the areas of health and safety. As the films are sponsored by advocacy groups supporting good health, this site offers access to additional information that can be used for resources as well as discussion: www .mediathatmattersfest.org.

The World Diabetes Foundation is dedicated to supporting prevention and treatment of diabetes in developing countries. The emphasis is on promoting awareness of diabetes, the prevention of diabetes and its complications, the education and training of patients and health care professionals, the enhancement of detection, and the treatment and monitoring of diabetes. The Web site offers online access to short films about diabetes: www.worlddiabetesfoundation.org.

SOURCES OF PAMPHLETS AND BROCHURES

As mentioned previously, many associations, such as the Medical Library Association, have pamphlets and brochures that relate specifically to health issues. Another good source for pamphlet materials is ETR Associates. This is a nonprofit organization founded in 1981 whose mission is to improve the health of families and individuals. Its publication program includes over 1,000 pamphlets, books, posters, flip charts, displays, curricula, and videos. Although these are not generally free, bulk orders are available for pamphlets and other small items: www.etr.org.

MATERIALS IN OTHER LANGUAGES AND CULTURAL CONTEXTS

The National Library of Medicine, the Department of Health and Human Resources, and other American government agencies list their non-English publication through their many Web sites. The Spencer Eccles Health Science Library at the University of Utah, through its 24 Languages Project, offers easy access to languages, including Arabic, Vietnamese, and Tagalog: library.med.utah.edu/24languages.

In the United States, the U.S. Food and Drug Administration as well as other governmental agencies at all levels offer health information in Spanish. For example, En Español: Publicaciones en Español is available from the FDA: www.fda.gov/AboutFDA/EnEspanol/default.htm. The National Network of Libraries of Medicine (NN/LIN) provides an extensive listing of foreign language consumer health materials (nnlm.gov/outreach/consumer/multi.html). For example, see www.gov.ns.ca/health/fls/health_fls.asp or www.sante.fr

In Canada, the French Language Health Services of the Ontario Ministry of Health and Long-Term Care provides access to French language materials and health information (www.health.gov.on.ca/french/publicf/programf/flhsf/flhs_mnf.html). Both French and Spanish materials can be used, especially with foreign language instructional units and issues discussed in Chapters 6 and 9.

In addition to language, materials that recognize the importance of culture and religion are often necessary, and some health care informational materials also address those issues. For a listing of cultural materials consult Culture Med, maintained by Jacquelyn Coughlan and available through the Web site of the State University of New York Institute of Technology: culturedmed.sunyit.edu/index.php/siteindex.

RESOURCES FOR THE SPECIAL CHILD AND PARENT NEEDS

Many advocacy and care groups exist for the support of children, parents, and caregivers of youth with special needs. A comprehensive and peer-reviewed list of support materials entitled *Knowledge Path: Children and Adolescents with Special Health Care Needs* is available through the Maternal & Child Health Library at George Washington

University. This document includes references and descriptions of health hotlines, Web sites, electronic publications, print materials, databases, electronic newsletters, foreign languages, and discussion groups. Search protocols are also included for locating specific subjects within various sites: www.mchlibrary.info/knowledgepaths/kp_cshcn.html.

REFLECTIONS

As stated in the introduction to this chapter, health information is so abundant that its identification and selection can be an overwhelming task. Nevertheless, school librarians and teachers can use much of this information to teach health information literacy skills in all areas of the curriculum. Because of their unique perspective, they can also influence what is produced and published in health care information that will be of special use to teachers. New technology also allows them to be involved in health care information dissemination through the design and promotion of health care information and current awareness services. Along with others who work with youth, teachers and school librarians will make a difference in the health and welfare of youth through well-designed and integrated curriculum instructions in all types of schools around the world.

NOTES

1. Robinson, Lyn. *Understanding Healthcare Information*. New York: Neal-Schuman, 2009.

2. Starr, Lea K. "Managing a CHIS: Selection (Evaluation) Tools. Choosing Health Books as a Consumer." caphis.mlanet.org/chis/selection.html. Accessed June 25, 2009.

3. Joint Committee on National Health Education Standards. *National Health Education Standards: Achieving Excellence*. 2nd ed. Atlanta: American Cancer Society, 2007, p. 100.

4. Joint Committee on National Health Education Standards.

5. Keselman, Alla and others. "Developing Informatics Tools and Strategies for Consumer-Centered Health Communication." *American Medical Information Association* 15 (2009): 473–483.

6. "Teen Health Resources." Compiled by. Sherri Vaughn and Judy Donlin, selector Librarians, Farming Community Library. www.farmlib.org/healthandmedicine/teenhealth.html. Accessed June 25, 2009.

7. The Boston LEAH Program (Leadership Education in Adolescent Health). www.bostonleah.org/youth.html. Accessed June 25, 2009.

6

Literature, the Arts, Performance Activities, and Languages

A BRIEF REVIEW AND A LOOK AHEAD

School librarians and classroom teachers are health educators simply by the role they play within the modern school. Teachers have daily contacts with students that are conducive to health literacy in that they follow carefully designed instructional tasks that can and often involve health literacy and information. School librarians do the same in their roles as collaborators with teachers and in the direct instruction of students that they do daily.

In Chapter 2, we discussed a number of curriculum and instruction concepts and models. We also discussed some prevailing curriculum constructs, such as the liberal educator curriculum, the scientific curriculum, the developmental curriculum (for children and youth), and the social/moral curriculum. Within that framework, we highlighted some of the most common ways of delivery health information and promoting health literary. These included demonstrations, lecturers and questioning, demonstrations as instruction, audiovisuals and interactive technology, field trips and visits (real and virtual), speaker programs and speaker opportunities, distant, online, and audiovisual transmissions, and commercial, community, and cable network television and radio.

Chapter 3 posed some of the major health issues that we face today, along with major standards for academic and health standard that are vital to presenting and designing health instructional experiences. Major problems considered included an overview of specific health problems faced by children and youth, dysfunctional family life and health, community risk to health, schools and the school environment, access to health information, promoting better health behaviors, health instruction units and teacher involvement, and consultants and consultation. More about some of these issues is covered in Chapter 10.

Chapter 4 considered the tools and skills needed for effective searching for information by using information technology, such as the Internet and commercial databases.

Chapter 5 addressed issues and sources for making sound collection decisions regarding a variety of information sources.

This chapter presents some instructional suggestions for a wide variety of curriculum areas focusing on health. These areas include literature, biography, art, music, and dance, highlighting their relationships to athletics and languages. These units consider approaches that are appropriate for a wide range of ages and grades. These units of instruction illustrate how all elements of the school community come into play when important aspects of health information and health literacy are considered.

BUILDING HEALTH UNITS AND RESOURCES THROUGHOUT THE CURRICULUM

The unit outlines suggested below are provided to help school librarians, working with their teachers, prepare information instruction in health. Basic ideas and resources are provided to help teachers and school librarians transform these ideas into more locally appropriate units based on identified needs in their schools.

Because students often have limited world views, it will be necessary to provide background and guidance to most of the units provided below. References and background materials are suggested for each unit.

PART I. LITERATURE, MUSIC, DRAMA, BIOGRAPHY

UNESCO (see Chapter 1) in its health education guidelines suggests that language and literature (and by extension music and biography) can be used to enhance health information and health literacy through communication. Communication skills include:

- Using the language correctly, through grammar and correct usage
- Listening, speaking, reading, and writing effectively
- Using language as a tool for thinking and doing: finding, interpreting, and working with information and ideas
- Writing used in observing, describing, and recording
- Promoting information literacy skills in finding, understanding, and using information

Reading and literature have also been highly regarded in society and culture. Artworks throughout time have often celebrated readings values. For example, the drawing shown in Figure 6.1 of a women reading to children during the depression years illustrated the importance given to reading and literature in society. We as teachers and school librarians can use this historic connection of literature and society to help integrate health into the literary and art curriculums of schools.

Instructional units in literature, drama, biography, music, art, and foreign languages can be used to introduce students to various health situations. Disease is one of the fundamental forces in society, and its influence is consequently reflected in literature and the fine arts. Biographies often describe the problems of creators of literature, drama, music, and art. The affect disease had on a musician's life or how the musician continued to create in spite of a disease offers excellent material for research assignments related to music classes. An understanding of how artists consider and are influenced by disease will help youth better deal with and understand its vast influence on personal lives.

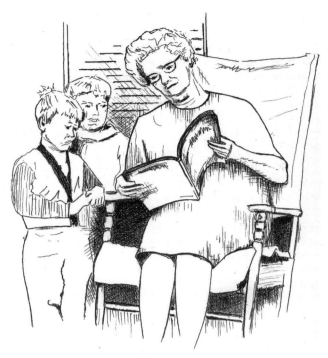

Figure 6.1.
Reading and literature are fundamental in society. Drawing of a woman reading to children. Line drawing by Richard H. Hendler based on a WPA photograph.

This chapter also discusses dance, its relation to sports, and the relationship of health to sports. The present focus on injuries to professional athletes and the effects this has on their futures as senior citizens is regularly in the news. The chapter ends with a discussion of foreign languages and how language study can be a useful vehicle for a holistic approach to health in the curriculum.

LITERATURE AND DRAMA

The use of literature and drama helps students place the effects of health and disease in a personal context through character study and plot development. Students should be introduced to the concept that literature and drama reflect life and that illnesses and disease—like all human experiences—have been used by writers throughout history to explore the human condition.

LITERARY CRITICISM USING MEDICAL FICTION

Definitions and Approaches to Literary Criticism

The following concepts are elements of literary criticism. Based on age and ability appropriateness, present these definitions to students and have them analyze these elements that are found in health and medical fiction.

Imagery

"[I]s a sensory impression used to create meaning in a story." Imagery is often based on visual narratives but can also use other senses, "such as sound, smell, touch, and taste." See bcs.bedfordstmartins.com/virtualit/fiction/elements.asp?e=7.

Plot

This is "the series of events that give a story its meaning and effect." The major elements of the plot are:

- **Conflict:** "The basic tension, predicament, or challenge that propels a story's plot"
- **Complications:** "Plot events that plunge the protagonist further into conflict"
- **Rising action:** "The part of a plot in which the drama intensifies, rising toward the climax"
- **Climax:** "The plot's most dramatic and revealing moment, usually the turning point of the story"
- **Falling action:** "The part of the plot after the climax, when the drama subsides and the conflict is resolved"

See bcs.bedfordstmartins.com/virtualit/fiction/elements.asp?e=1.

Theme

"http://www.plannedparenthood.org/index.htm [A] common thread or repeated idea that is incorporated throughout a literary work." Ask older students to identify one of their favorite novels with a health issue and discuss the major themes in the novel. See bcs.bedfordstmartins.com/virtualit/fiction/elements.asp?e=6.

Point of View

Point of view is the framing of the narrative. It is generally in the first person or the third person. More specifically, "point of view in fiction refers to the source and scope of the *narrative voice*." In the first-person point of view, the "I" is used, and it is the narrative voice of a character. "[A] character in the story does the narration. Third person point of view occurs when the narrator does not take part in the story. . . . [The] third-person omniscient, [is generally the author's] narrative voice [and the author's voice] can render information from anywhere, including the thoughts and feelings of any of the characters." See bcs.bedfordstmartins.com/virtualit/fiction/elements.asp?e=4.

Tone

Tone is the attitude that authors have for their readers and for the subjects of their writings. Using the examples given here, consider what tones the authors used. "Tone may be formal, informal, intimate, solemn, somber, playful, serious, ironic, condescending, or many other possible attitudes." See en.wikipedia.org/wiki/Tone (literature).

Setting

Is the "the time, place, physical details, and circumstances in which a situation occurs. Settings include the background, atmosphere or environment in which

characters live and move, and usually include physical characteristics of the surroundings."
See www.uncp.edu/home/canada/work/allam/general/glossary.htm.

Style

"[R]efers to the language conventions used to construct the story." This includes "diction, sentence structure, phrasing, dialogue, and other aspects of language to create style. . . . [A] story's style could be described as richly detailed, flowing, . . . [or sparse and minimal.]." See bcs.bedfordstmartins.com/virtualit/fiction/elements.asp?e=5.

Literary criticism also considers these elements:

- Morality: Concerned with what is good and evil
- Psychological: The integration of psychological theory into literary interpretation
- Sociological: The consideration of society and social ideas
- Formalistic: The relationship of literature and the aesthetic expression
- Archetypal (myth): Consideration of literature as cultural patters that permeates societies and assumes mystical qualities[1,2]

Learning Outcomes

The overall learning outcome is for students of all ages and abilities to identify and discuss basic literary analysis and to apply literary concepts to medical-related fiction and to relate that to their own lives.

Students will:

- Identify and discuss basic elements of literary criticism and apply critical analysis to their reading of medical fiction.
- Identify issues and problems found in literature and drama that reflect health issues.
- Critique and discuss how authors interpret health concepts, such as physical disfigurement and illnesses, in drama and musical theater, including musicals.

Questions and/or Activities (Adjust for Age and Abilities)

For Older Students

- Review as necessary the concept of literary analysis.
- Select a work of fiction (either short story, novella, graphic novel). See Appendix A for title suggestions. Have students analyze the fiction based on a selected number of literary characteristics, such as theme.
- Have students consider the ways that illnesses and accidents are used in fiction to develop a plot (e.g., personality of the main characters, psychological and sociological environments of the main characters, family circumstances).
- Have students read an appropriate novel and observe how diseases and/or accidents affect the lives of the major characters. Have students record their own feelings about how selected characters dealt with disease and/or accidents. Have students reflect on how they would react if they faced the same challenges.
- Have students select a character in a novel that they like and write a letter to that character discussing that character's role in the novel. If the character in the novel dies during the novel's

narrative, have students write a letter to a member of his or her family or a friend telling how you felt about the character.
- Some examples of novels that have young characters who suffer debilitating injuries:
- Robin Brancato. *Winning*. Bantam, 1978.
- Chris Crutcher. Staying Fat for Sarah Byrnes: An American Indian Odyssey. Paw Prints, 2008.
- Jeff Rus. *Paralyzed*. Orca Sports series. Orca Book Publishers, 2008.
- Cynthia Voigt. *Izzy, Willy-Nilly*. Paw Prints, 2008.

For Younger Students (Adjust for Age and Abilities)

- Introduce students to the basic concept of literary criticism (e.g., how to judge and appreciate fiction).
- Introduce the concepts of fiction and nonfiction.
- Ask students what kinds of illnesses or accidents an author might write about in fiction.
- Have students analyze an appropriate medical novel based on selected critical elements, such as how to describe a character or other elements from the previous lists and present them to students based on age and ability appropriateness.
- For preschool and primary students, in introducing the literary concept of describing character. Select from the following elements as appropriate:

    Character: A person, animal, or thing in a story
    Main character: The character in the story that is seen or heard from the most, with the story revolving around this character
    Minor character: One of the characters seen in the story other than the main character
    Static character: A character than changes the less from the beginning of the story
    Dynamic character: A character than changes the most from the way the character was presented at the beginning of the story

See www.scholastic.com.

Examples of books with strong characters based on survival theme:

Jon Agee. *Terrific*. Michael di Capua Books/Hyperion, 2005.
Kathi Appelt. *The Underneath*. Atheneum Books for Young Readers, 2008.
Jon Scieszka and Design Garage. *Uh-Oh, Max*. Starting to Read series. Aladdin Paperbacks, 2009.

The books listed in Appendix A designated for preschool and primary grades can be used for character analysis as appropriate for age and abilities. Some books listed for younger children can also be used with older students. All these books listed have elements suitable for literary analysis.

RESPONSE TO READING MEDICAL FICTION

Students read fiction for information, psychological and social meaning, and support. For older students, have them consider how they react to reading a story about illness. Do they base all their knowledge of the illness on how characters in the story respond to what they read or do they consider what they already know about the illness and respond to this prior knowledge within context of the story? This is the basic element of reader response theory and this can offer some insights into how students approach reading fiction.

Some research has suggested that reading fiction is a combination of what readers already know and what they learn from reading fiction. They then take both types of information and compartmentalize, taking some of this fictional information into their lives while not accepting other information coming from fiction. Fictional information penetrates judgments about beliefs, suggesting that this information is incorporated into the reader's life. Representations of fictional information retain features of compartmentalization. In other words, this research suggests that readers create hybrid representations of fictional information. Simplify this concept and then offer this explanation as to how they read fiction. Have students discuss how this related to their own reading of fiction.[3] Examples for reflection reading include *I Heard the Owl Call My Name* by Margaret Craven (Doubleday, 1973) for older students. *Nana Upstairs & Nana Downstairs* by Tomie daPaola (Paw Prints, 2009) offers reflective experiences for younger students.

LITERARY BIOGRAPHY AND DRAMA

Literary biography and drama take many approaches, one of which is to present history in terms of persons that have shaped and influenced the direction of history and social institutions. Closely related to this concept is presenting biography and drama as fine literature by using aspects of expert of literary excellence: character development, dynamic narrations, and appealing style. Fine literary biography and drama include authentic understandings and uses settings, times, and places to shape the live history. Good literary biography often integrates moral, psychological, and sociological interpretations into the biographical and dramatic narrative. Overall, the hallmarks of literary biography and drama are their appreciation of aesthetic structure of language and the building of a captivating literary narrative.

Literary drama employs many of the same elements used in general literary criticism, such as imagery, narration and narrator, plot, point of view, setting, style, theme, and tone. In drama, dialogue is the element that carries the plot, and diction offers ways that characters speak, helping to define themselves to the audience and to other characters. See en.wikipedia.org/wiki/Biography and highered.mcgraw-hill.com/sites/0072405228/student_view0/drama_glossary.html).

Beyond this, biographical literature and drama add to a personal understanding of the effects of health on human experiences. Explain to students that when a biography is written by the person who lives the life, it is an autobiography and/or personal narrative, but when it is written by someone else who provides context and interpretation to the person's life story, it is a biography. Obituaries and diaries are also a form of biographical narrative. The school librarian can explain where these resources are located in the library.

Learning Outcomes

Students will:

- Define biography and autobiography, personal narrative, diary writing, and obituaries and discuss how they are used by authors.
- Discuss how biography can help readers understand how illnesses and health affect personal lives.
- Critique literary drama and explain how drama offers ways to understand heath issues.

Questions and/or Activities (Adjust for Ages and Abilities)

For Older Students

Ask students to explain the differences between biography and autobiography.

- Ask students to discuss the differences between biography, autobiography, personal narratives, and keeping a diary.
- Explain that keeping a diary was a popular activity throughout history and that diaries have been kept by important people, such as U.S. presidents. Ask why it seems less popular today. Ask students to consider if electronic media, such as MySpace, Facebook, and Twitter, has some of the same elements of journal writing or keeping a diary.
- Ask student what can be learned about illnesses and accidents by reading biography or autobiographies.
- Have students read an appropriate biography where disease played a major part in the person's live. Have students write or discuss how the person managed to deal with the disease and how it influenced his or her accomplishments.
- Introduce obituaries and where they are found. Ask students why obituaries are important in the lives of individuals (e.g., notice of death but also celebrating and honoring the lives of people who are deceased). Direct students to the obituaries in the *New York Times* and have them discuss the characteristics of these obituaries in terms of biographical information and interpretations.

For Younger Students

Adaptations. Many of the suggestions made for older students are appropriate for younger students, provided adjustments are made for age and ability appropriateness. Make sure that students can demonstrate the differences between biography and autobiography. After having read about a person's experience with illness or injury in their life, make sure that students can describe either orally or in writing how reading about the person made them feel about the person.

Appendix A provides a list of novels and drama suitable for literary analysis and discussion. This list includes books and other materials suitable for both older and younger students.

PART 2. PERFORMANCE ACTIVITIES AND HEALTH: MUSIC, DANCE, ATHLETICS

Music, like drama and literature, also reflects health issues through thematic interpretations in music or in the lives of musicians, dancers, and athletes themselves. Introduce the concept that music is a part of human experience. As such, all music provides us with a broad understanding of human experiences. In many ways, athletics is a form of performance. We see this in how schools at all levels promote athletics and how the general public views these activities as entertainment. The rise of sports medicine is a direct outgrowth of needs from both amateur and professional athletics. Dance has much in common with both music and athletics in that similar health problems are experienced by them all. Taken together, music, dance, and athletics as performance offer ample opportunities to study health and wellness conditions.

CLASSICAL MUSICIANS AND THEIR HEALTH CHALLENGES

Classical musicians were often challenged by health problems. These include:

- Johann Sebastian Bach: loss of hearing
- Bela Bartok: leukemia [polycylhemia]
- Ludwig van Beethoven: total loss of hearing
- Leonard Bernstein: phenomena, probably complicated by emphysema
- Johannes Brahms: cancer
- Claude Debussy: colorectal cancer
- Antonin Dvorak: heart failure
- George Gershwin: brain tumor
- Frederic Handel: failing eyesight
- Nellie Melba: septicaemia
- Wolfgang Amadeus Mozart: rheumatic fever complications
- Niccolo Paganini: mercury poisoning from treatment for a sexually transmitted decease
- Jean Sibelius: brain hemorrhage
- Peter Tchaikovsky: cholera
- Giuseppe Verdi: stroke

Learning Outcomes

Students will:

- Identify and describe some of the major forms of classical music.
- Research and discuss some common illnesses that have affected classical musicians.
- Research and discuss how classical musicians met health changes and how those challenges affected their music.

Questions and/or Activities (Adjust for Age and Abilities)

For Older Students

- Have students of appropriate maturity and ability levels research and discuss these illnesses that affected well-known classical musicians:
- What is rheumatic fever? (Mozart)
- What is mercury poisoning? (Paganini)
- Why was mercury ever used to treat some forms of sexually transmitted diseases?
- Why are musicians susceptible to hearing losses? (Beethoven, Bach)
- What is septicaemia? (Melba)
- What is leukemia? What are some of its major forms? (Bartok)
- What does stroke mean in medical terminology? (Verdi)
- What does heart failure mean in medical terminology? (Dvorak)
- How might diet have an effect on colorectal cancer? (Debussy)
- What is a brain hemorrhage? Does age play a role in this brain hemorrhage? (Sibelius)
- What is a glioblasloma multiform brain tumor? Can it be caused by a head injury? (Gershwin)
- What is cholera? (Tchaikovsky)
- What are some modern day treatments for cholera? (Tchaikovsky)

For Younger Students

- Have students select these common illness listed below and then research and discuss their findings with other students:
- Rheumatic fever
- Cholera
- Leukemia
- Mercury poisoning
- Blindness
- Hearing loss

MUSICIANS (CLASSICAL), HEALTH, AND THEIR MUSIC

Much like literature and drama, classical music has used illness and health as major themes. Biography is a good way to introduce youth to classical music as well as to highlight health issues. It will often be necessary to provide some biographical information about a musician and outline some of the health problems that they faced and/or are now facing.

Learning Outcomes

Students will:

- Define various types of classical music. Students will discuss how classical musicians have used health and illnesses themes in their works.
- Discuss how music, like literature, helps people understand how illnesses and health affect personal lives.

Questions and/or Activities (Adjust for Age and Abilities)

For Older Students

- Have students read a brief summary of an opera that has a major disease or health theme. For more serious students, have them read about and listen to excerpts and/or the complete opera *La Traviata* by Giuseppe Verdi and/or *La Bohéme* by Giacomo Puccini. Have students identify the disease and write an explanation of how the disease influenced the behavior of selected characters, the plot construction, and the final outcome of the opera.
- Operas are famous for their drinking songs and consumption of alcohol, often leading to drunkenness and unhealthy living. Among others, these operas include:
- *La Traviata*: "Brindisi" by Giuseppe Verdi A *brindisi* is a song in which a company is exhorted to drink.
- *The Student Prince* (operetta): "Drink, Drink, Drink" by Sigmund Romberg (also known as "The Drinking Song"). A student drinking song sung in a German tavern.
- *Il Trovatore*: "Anvil Chorus" by Giuseppe Verdi. A Spanish Gypsy drinking song.
- *Carmen*: "Votre Toast" ("Toreador Song") by Georges Bizet. "Our Toast" is sung in celebration of the glories of bull fighting and bull fighters.
- *Don Giovanni*: "Nacht in Venedig" ("A Night in Venice"); "Solch Ein Wirtshaus Lob Ich Mir" ("Praise to the Traven I Give"); and "Finch'han dal Vino" ("Champagne Aria") by Johann Strauss II. These are songs about drinking and parties.

- Have students critique the roles that drinking and excessive partying have in operas and operettas. Divide the class into working groups, and have each group select an opera or operetta that has drinking or party scenes to study. The previous list as well as other drinking songs can be found on *Opera's Greatest Drinking Songs*, audio CD, RCA, 1995. Ask each working group to discuss what dramatic elements drinking and drinking songs contribute to the opera or operetta. We know that excessive drinking is not good health management, but drinking must have been an important structural element in plots and music.
- Have students analyze the attitudes about drinking displayed in the opera.
- Culture and social mores play significant roles in how people view drinking and health. How are these mores revealed in the operas? Could the opera being studied have been composed without such references to drinking and/or excessive partying?
- Have students prepare a presentation of their findings, such as an advertisement for the opera being staged locally, a review in the local paper, or an analysis of an interesting character or an interesting situation to share with a friend, or a write review of the drinking song. Sources for stories of operas can be found at The Metropolitan Opera (www.metoperafamily .org/metopera/history/stories/index.aspx), and synopses of operetta are available at The Guide to Light Opera & Operetta" (www.musicaltheatreguide.com/composers/romberg/ romberg.html).
- To provide background for the assignment, use the *Tales of Hoffman* (*Les Contes d'Hoffmann*) by Jacques Offenbach. Basically, the opera is concerned with the poet Hoffman's failure to continue to write great poetry because of his love obsessions. Hoffman's judgments about love are obscured by his psyche, which is complicated by alcoholism. The 2009 Metropolitan Opera's production emphasized Hoffman's alcoholism as revealed in Act I. Here, "a chorus of spirits of beer and wine sets the scene by singing 'I am wine/I am beer/We're man's best friends.' " By the end of the opera, we learn through his stories that Hoffman has lost his three loves because of his drunkenness and psychotic behaviors. He calls alcohol "the nothingness by which one forgets." A final chorus sings, "On est Grand par l'Amour," pointing out the moral that one is enriched by love and sadness. At the encouragement of his poetic muse, Hoffman returns with renewed fortitude to recover his genius as a poet.
- Summarize this story for students and emphasize how alcoholism was one of the opera's major themes. Ask students to consider if the current attitude about psychology, excessive drinking and alcoholism might have influenced the Met's 2009 interpretation.[4]
- Students may also research some of the illnesses and health issues suffered by some musicians listed below. After introducing musicians with health problems, have students research a life and describe how illness and health influenced their art:
  - **Johann Sebastian Bach:** Bach led a long and productive life, but he lost his hearing, probably from diabetes.
  - **Ludwig van Beethoven:** Beethoven also lost his hearing, but he continued to compose and conduct well after he lost all his hearing.
  - **Louis Hector Berlioz:** Berlioz was a well-known French musician and composer of operas. But he suffered from chronic illnesses and depression, which were fostered by feelings of loneliness.
  - **Wolfgang Amadeus Mozart:** A very popular composer during his life, but he died at an early age. His early death was probably caused by acute rheumatic fever that he experienced in childhood.
  - **Leonard Bernstein:** Bernstein was a popular, modern-day American composer who wrote for both the concert hall and the musical theater. His death was caused by pneumonia and a pleural tumor. He was also a smoker and suffered from emphysema.

○ **Richard Wagner:** Wagner was an extremely popular German opera composer of the latter nineteenth century. His operas today form the core of the operatic repertoire. He died of heart failure and suffered periods of depression because of the critical reception of some of his operas.

For Younger Students

• Select Bach (loss of hearing); Beethoven (total loss of hearing); Bernstein (pneumonia); Mozart (rheumatic fever complications); or another classical musician from the previous list and then explain that each experienced serious health challenges but still continued to write great music. Read excerpts from a biography and then play examples of his music. Have students discuss the nature of their personalities that still allowed them to create this fine music.

POPULAR MUSIC AND MUSICAL THEATER

Popular music is the medium of communication, recreation, and personal enjoyment of youth today. With this in mind, we can easily use music to promote health information and health literacy through biography and themes found in music. Ask students to read a biography of a popular musician who suffered or is suffering from a disease or is handicapped in some way and write a description of (or discuss) how his or her health conditions influenced or is still influencing his or her art. Entertainers who have struggled with health issues include: Elizabeth Newton Jones (cancer); Martha Davis (cancer); Johnny Ray (deafness); Peter Townshend (deafness due to music); and Ray Charles and Stevie Wonder (blindness). All these personalities provide opportunities for research.

Although not as numerous as themes in musical theater, health has been used to serve various health communities with adaptations for stage presentations.

Learning Outcomes

Students will:

• Identify and define the various types of popular music.
• Define and explain musical theater.
• Discuss what adaptation means in music and in musical theater.
• Discuss health issues that affect popular music and musical theater performers.

Questions and/or Activities (Adjust for Age and Abilities)

For Older Students

A recent production concerning deafness is an adaption of *West Side Story* entitled *Deaf Side Story: Deaf Sharks, Hearing Jets, and a Classical American Musical* (with deaf performers signing the script) by Mark Rigney (Gallaudet University Press, 2003). The original casting was by the Illinois School for the Deaf. In similar fashion, *Grease* was recently performed by the Texas School for the Deaf. In this production, interpreters read the script to correspond with the action on stage.

• Have students read these plays and discuss the difficulties that the actors, directors, and writers faced (or might have faced) in staging theses productions.

- Have students research the deaf theater movements, using as a springboard the National Theatre of the Deaf (www.ntd.org) and Stephen C. Baldwin's *Pictures in the Air: The Story of the National Theater of the Deaf* (Gallaudet University Press, 1994).

For Younger Students

- Introduce the basic constructs of drama (e.g., theme, plot, actors, actions, problems to be solved, conclusion). Have students discuss, create, and perform small scenarios based on these or similar concepts:
  - Native Americans in the United States, First Nations people in Canada, and other native peoples used medical cures found in plants. Select some of the more interesting and common plant medicines. Describe these to the students, and have students develop skits about how native peoples found herbs and other ingredients and made medicines from them. Have students form work groups and then pick one plant that they have researched and which perhaps grows locally. Ask each group to create a dramatic skit about the plant: where it grows and how it was used as a medical remedy. The plants might include those with fun names, such as: skunk cabbage, horsemint, wormwood, broom snakeweed, boneset, catnip, dogbane, milkweed, devil's club, dogwood, feverwort, witch hazel, saltbush, pokeweed, bloodroot, and persimmon. To select appropriate plants and diseases, read the descriptive information about the cures at Native American Herbal Remedies (www.powersource.com/cherokee/herbal.html).

HEALTH RELATIONSHIPS AND ISSUES SHARED BY MUSICIANS, ATHLETES, AND DANCERS

Musicians and people involved in sports and dance often suffer similar health conditions based on their musical and dance artistry and sport activities. Nevertheless, students often do not see these relationships. The following instructional suggestions are provided to help students learn health issues and to also bridge the gap between music, dance, and sports as performance and recreation. Common conditions affect the muscles, bone joints, and voice and vocal control and also influence movement and hearing. Explain these injuries to students, and note that they often result from incorrect posture, non-ergonomic techniques, excessive force, overuse, stress, and insufficient rest. Explain that these other health matters often lead to chronic injuries (ongoing) that can cause great pain, disability, and the end of careers.

Select some of the following medical terms (based on age and grade appropriateness) and describe these conditions to students:

- Bursitis
- Carpal tunnel syndrome
- Hearing loss
- Performance stress
- Tendinitis
- Tenosynovitis

Learning Outcomes

Students will:

- Identify and discuss major illnesses and injuries that affect musicians and dancers.
- Discuss how medicine and exercise help to heal and prevent injuries.

Questions and/or Activities (Adjust for Age and Abilities)

For Older Students (Grades 6–12)

- Have students select some injuries and health issues listed previously that musicians, athletes, and dancers of all types face. Have students write and/or discuss their selections.
- Have students read and research about the proper health management techniques that a musician should follow.
- Ask students to select a musical instrument and research, write, and discuss selected injuries that are or can be associated with these types of instruments.

For Younger Students (Grades K–5)

- Select some of the common health/medical problems listed previously that affect musicians, dancers, and athletes and then describe them to the students.
- Have students discuss how they are common to athletes, dancers, and musicians.
- Ask students if they know anyone who has suffered an injury as a musician, dancer, or athlete.
- Have them describe the injury, and ask them describe it and tell how it was cured or medicated.

MUSICIANS: HEALTH ISSUES AFFECTING THE VOICE AND HEARING

Voice maintenance is a problem for both classical and popular singers. Vocal health problems include how to control tone, projection, breathing, and vocal strength as well as how to maintain the quality of the voice over time. A particular problem for singers is the development of nodules on the vocal cords. Introduce students to nodules of the vocal cords as a health problem and describe it in general terms.

Musicians, especially rock musicians, often suffer from losing their hearing and/or suffering a reduction in hearing because of the loudness of the music they perform. Both voice and hearing losses offer opportunities for health information instruction.

Learning Outcomes

Students will:

- Identify voice and other health problems that affect popular singers.
- Identify selected medical terms associated with voice and singing problems.
- Discuss how singers can improve their health through better health care and behavior.

Questions and/or Activities (Adjust for Age and Abilities)

For Older Students (Grades 6–12)

- Have students define vocal fold nodules and research the biographies of popular singers who have developed this problem and how this health condition influenced their careers. Some popular singers who have experienced this problem include: Lucinda Williams, Julie Andrews, Robert Plant, Bonnie Tyler, Amanda Parker, Davey Havok, Freddie Mercury, Whitney Houston, Belle Midler, Lee Ryan, Elton John, Madonna, and Joni Mitchell. Because published books are not always available on individuals, students may need to use the Internet to find recent popular singers.

- Have students select a style of modern popular music. Ask them to research hearing and voice problems associated with this music and then discuss how performers can better protect themselves and their careers from voice decline and hearing lose. Suggest Wikipedia as a source, as it provides a summary of vocal fold modules (en.wikipedia.org/wiki/Vocal _fold_nodule).

For Younger Students

- Explain in basic terms the fold module condition. Introduce students to Julie Andrews. Explain her nodule problem. Explain how over her career, Andrews developed nodules and then turned more to acting and writing children's books. Remind them that she performed in the movie *Princess Diaries* (2001).
- Explain how Andrews became famous as a singer. Be sure to explain that she became known for her role in the movie *The Sound of Music* based on the career of the von Trapp Family Singers. As background, read sections from the *Story of the Trapp Family Singers* by Maria Augusta Trapp (HarperCollins, 2001); also share with students some of Andrews's children's books, such as *Mandy* (HarperCollins, 2006) and *The Last of the Really Great Whangdoodles* (HaperCollins, 1989).
- Introduce the basic physiology of the ear and how the ear is susceptible to damage from loud music.
- Have students discuss and write how musicians can protect themselves from this type of health injury.

HEALTH ISSUES AFFECTING DANCERS AND ATHLETES

Dance is both an art and athletic experience. Athletic requirements in dance call for the proper use of muscles, balanced and coordination, strength and endurance, stress and anxiety management, weight control, and diet and nutrition. Injuries can include inflammation of the fascia (lining tissue under the skin that covers a surface of underlying tissues), stress fractures, knee injuries, ankles and joint problems, hamstring injuries, hip injuries, and back problems. Make sure that students understand that these problems affect all types of dancers. Dance offers many layers of health instruction. The emphasis should be on relating dance to conditioning and to athletics.

BIOGRAPHIES OF DANCERS AND ATHLETES

Dancers and athletes generally experience health issues at some time during their careers. Reading biographies of these people will undoubtedly help students understand how everyone must take special care of their health and bodies. A list of biographies of both dancers and athletes is provided in Appendix A.

Learning Outcomes

Students will:

- Explain how dance and athletics are related in terms of injury and care of the body.
- Describe health and body care that both dancers and athletes should follow.

Questions and/or Activities (Adjust for Age and Abilities)

For Older Students (Grades 6–12)

- Have students read about injuries and health issues that all types of dancers face. Have students write and discuss how these compare with sports injuries.
- Have students read about the proper health management that a dancer should follow. Ask students to read about a dancing tradition of their choosing and then write and/or discuss selected injuries that are often associated with this type of dancing.
- Ask students (depending on age and development) to read a biography of a famous athlete, followed by writing and/or discussing how both dancers and athletes share common health problems and issues.

For Younger Students (Grades 1–5)

- Select some of the medical problems that affect both dancers and athletes, describe them to the students, and then have students discuss how they are common to both athletes and dancers.
- Ask students if they know anyone who has suffered an injury as either a dancer or athlete.
- Have them describe the injury, and ask them describe it and tell how it was cured or medicated.
- Have students select a biography of a dancer or an athlete. Describe the health problems they experienced and how the person worked with and/or adjusted to the problem.

PART 3. ART AND HEALTH

Art is a meaningful way to introduce health literacy into the lives of students. The art health movement has expanded greatly in the last few decades, being embraced in various ways by the health care industry and providers. Art in many forms is found in hospitals, health care units, and in the direct care of patients. Art as a part of performances, such as drama and dance, is also a part of health care.

BIOGRAPHIES OF ARTISTS

The biographies of artists often reveal health issues. Some artists were victims of the age in which they lived in that medicine and cures were not available to them. Others were victims of their own making in that they did not make good decisions about their own health.

With this in mind, have students—based on age and abilities—research some of the health issues faced by artists. Ask students to consider why so many of these artists suffered from heart failure and pneumonia. First, have students research and understand a medical explanation of the disease of the artist then ask students to answer such questions based on the medical definition and consider whether the health problem was related to the times in which the artists lived:

- John Audubon: declining health and senility
- Paul Cézanne: pneumonia
- Salvador Dalí: declining health and emotional problems, heart
- Frida Kahlo: pulmonary embolism
- Keith Haring: AIDS-related complications
- Roy Lichtenstein: pneumonia

- Daniel Maclise: acute pneumonia
- Jackson Pollock: fatal car accident caused by his longstanding alcoholism
- Andy Warhol: post-operative cardiac arrhythmia

An extensive list of artists can be found at www.dropbears.com/a/art/biography.

ART IN HEALTH CARE AND EVIDENCE-BASED RESEARCH

Some of the various forms of art as health care support include permanent as well as temporary collections and exhibits; healing gardens; murals and panels; nature photography; digital art; and art in patients' rooms and reception areas. Art carts delivered to rooms and other areas where patients are found allow patients to take an active role in their care as they make choices from the carts.

We often ask the question: How does art help in health and healing? Although research is sparse, evidence suggests that well-selected and appropriate art offers comfort to both those that are ill and to their families and caregivers. Some interesting findings offered by evidence-based research regarding art indicate that patients, families, and others prefer images of gentle waterfalls with vegetation and representational nature paintings containing human figures and harmless animals such as deer (Figure 6.2).

Research in the art preferences of schoolchildren and hospitalized pediatric patients across four age groups—5–7, 8–10, 11–13, and 14–17—suggested that irrespective of age or gender, the great majority of hospitalized pediatric patients and schoolchildren were similar in preferring nature art, such as a forest setting with a lake and deer, over abstract or cartoon-like images. Research into the reaction of emotionally challenging art by psychiatric patients:

[S]howed negative reactions to artworks that were ambiguous, surreal, or could be interpreted in multiple ways. The same patients, however, reported having positive feelings and associations with respect to nature artwork.

In another study, cancer patients showed similar reaction to a sculpture garden created especially for them. The art featured "straight-edged and abstract forms, many having pointed or piercing features." Some 22 percent of the patients rated the work negatively and many found the "work ambiguous" ("doesn't make any sense"), and some patients interpreted the sculptures as frightening and asked for a room change so they would not need to look out at the artworks.[5]

THE SOCIETY FOR THE ARTS IN HEALTH CARE

A leading center for the promotion of art in health care is the Society for the Arts in Health Care, founded in 1991 and located in Washington, D.C. Its mission is:

- Demonstrating the valuable roles the arts can play in enhancing the healing process
- Advocating for the integration of the arts into the environment and delivery of care within health care facilities
- Assisting in the professional development and management of arts programming for health care populations
- Providing resources and education to health care and arts professionals

Figure 6.2.
Research shows that landscape art and other pleasing images help promote healing.
Private collection. Used by permission.

- Encouraging and supporting research and investigation into the beneficial effects of the arts in health care

The society also offers advice and materials to promote art as a viable component of health care and health literacy.[6]

USING ART TO PROMOTE HEALTH AWARENESS AND LITERACY

One of the overriding issues found in art curricula is the impact that art has on human experiences. The Brownsburg Community School Corporation in Indiana as well as other schools in Indiana express the concept in this way based on Indiana Academic Art Standards: "Students understand the significance of visual art in relation to historical, social, political, spiritual, environmental, technological, and economic issues."[7]

Such concepts are found throughout the art curricula and are helpful in using art to advance health literacy and information. We must help students learn how to view the environment as art and as a conveyor of health information. Students should be encouraged to appreciate their roles in helping make the environment a healthy place to live, play, and work.

Learning Outcomes

Students will:

- Describe ways that art can be used to help persons who are ill or in emotional stress.
- Discuss in details safety precautions that must be taken when using art supplies and technologies.
- Explain how art can be used to promote better health attitudes and behaviors.
- Discuss art as a means of celebrating the values of health care.
- Define medical anatomy and explain its relationships to art.

Questions and/or Activities (Adjust for Age and Abilities)

For Older Students

- Help students recognize the role of art in healing by introducing them to the art health movement.
- Ask students to investigate some of the health factors that must be applied by the artist in using art technologies and supplies.
- Have students study the role of medically themed art as a part of history and culture.
- Ask students to read and discuss the concepts of art in health care, discussing the rationale for this concept.
- Encourage students to investigate health concerns when using the technologies of art, such as oil-based paint, clearing fluids, air control, and other health challenges.
- Direct students to identify and discuss the lives of some well-known persons associated with the advancement of health, such as Charles Drew, Walter Reed, and Clara Barton, and ask students to find portraits or pictures of these people to aid discussions.
- Have students explore works of art that have medical themes, and have students place these in the historical context of their creations (e.g., have students look at dress, environment, visible symbols of medicine, medical procedures). One of the most famous of all time is Rembrandt's "The Anatomy Lesson."
- Ask students to consider art as cultural issues, such as tattoos and body piercing and health issues that might be connected with such practices.
- Have students research art as a means of promoting health issues, and have them as a group design and/or produce an art object to promote awareness of a specific disease to an audience.
- As a group, have students discuss the elements of the designs, which might help promote better awareness of the disease.
- Introduce students to Robert Thom's artistic interpretation of medicine through his painting series, "History of Medicine and History of Pharmacy," published as *Parke-Davis's Pictorial Annals of Medicine and Pharmacy* (Warner-Lambert Co., 1999).
- Use these artworks to guide students to an understanding of the progression of medicine through time. Unfortunately, Thom's works are not widely available in published forms, but they can be located on the Internet and through commercial art dealers, museums, and medical institutions. For example, many of his works are available on the Internet via an image search on Google.
- For serious and mature art students, introduce them to the history of artistic anatomy and medical illustrating through such publications as Benjamin A. Rifkin and Michael J. Ackerman's *Human Anatomy: From the Renaissance to the Digital Age* (Abrams, 2006). A useful instructional guide to artistic anatomy and medical illustrating is Jeno Barcsay's *Anatomy for the Artist: Drawings and Text*. This includes information on how to draw the muscular system and shows relationships among muscles, movements, and body structure.
- For advance art and science students, introduce them to *Gray's Anatomy* (various editions and editors), and help them understand its importance as a work of medical art and medical information.
- For serious and mature students who are interested in art and medicine, introduce students to the resources exhibited at the U.S. Library of Medicine at www.nlm.nih.gov/projects/bydate.html. American Memory at the Library of Congress also has photographic and other items dealing with health and medicine. It will be necessary for users to enter a search terms related to health or medicine to retrieve appropriate items (memory.loc.gov/ammem/index.html). Medical history in art (including the military) can be found at the Office of Medical History, Office of the Surgeon General at http://history.amedd.army.mil.

For Younger Students

Plan instruction that will encourage students to:

- Explain health in art through medical symbols.
- Demonstrate health precautions that must be taken when using art supplies and technologies.
- Discuss health care workers represented in art.
- Assess the concept of anatomy and how art is an essential part of presenting anatomical concepts.
- Identify medical art and directional systems found in their towns and neighborhoods, such as the Red Cross and Red Crescent, a physician's logo, directional signs to hospitals, street and highway emergency routes, etc.
- Discuss why they must be careful in using tools and technologies of art, such as paints and sharp instruments, and the importance of order and cleanliness when using art supplies and technologies.
- Explain why people who are ill appreciate nature scenes in art (because it is relaxing and calming).
- Create (or discuss a design) of art they would take to an ill friend or relative.
- Discuss why they feel their art might help their friend or relative feel better.
- Define anatomy and help students consider this definition in terms appropriate for young children
- Introduce students to the concept of drawing life forms, such as people, animals, and plants. Have students draw a realistic illustration of a pet, a favorite animal, a plant, or a person.

FOREIGN LANGUAGES AND HEALTH INFORMATION

Foreign languages have always played a part in helping students understand the world they live in. Today, it is becoming clear that the integration of national cultures has increased the need for language skills. Literature produced within a language and a specific culture (e.g., American English and British English cultures) helps in understanding the culture from which a literary tradition derives it power and nuances. The cultural aspects of foreign language study are further discussed in Chapters 7 and 9.

Aside from culture:

[F]oreign "language literature and literature-based instruction provide a rich source of language vocabulary and syntax in a way that oral language alone cannot. A thematic organization of [foreign language literature] offers ways to extend linguistic support and to offer a variety of reasons to read, write, and talk."[8]

The following lessons suggestions use both culture and foreign language literature to help students understand how health and safety are often found in foreign language literature. Folklore, useful symbols found in life such as road signs, classical and popular literature in the language—such as novels, newspapers, magazines, nonfiction books, and cinema—also encourages cultural literacy. The sample languages we use to suggest learning activities are French, German, Russian, and Spanish. We feel that other languages can fit within the activities we suggest.

Learning Outcomes (For All Language Levels)

Students will:

- Demonstrate increases in their use of health and safety vocabulary from reading foreign language literature.

- Demonstrate awareness that foreign language literature reveals how health is valued in cultures and in various historical time periods.
- Analyze foreign language literature based on narrative literary analysis.
- Apply foreign language words to common health, medical, and safety symbols and signs.
- Assess how foreign language literature helps in understanding common medical and safety rules found in other cultures.
- Identify and interpret health and safety issues and themes found in foreign language literary works and popular media.
- Create personal responses to health and safety issues found in foreign language literature and media through writing, speech, or visual representation.
- Discuss how foreign language literature reveals gender, ethnicity, and class in terms of health and safety issues.

Questions and/or Activities (Adjust for Age and Abilities) (For All Language Levels)

The following ability levels and some of the exercises are based on North Dakota foreign language standards.[9]

Novice Levels (Grades K–4, 5–8, or Any Two Years in High School)

Developing Vocabulary and Health Skills

- Depending on abilities and age levels, introduce students to the U.S. Department of Agriculture (USDA) food pyramid available at www.mypyramid.gov. Have students construct a booklet of pictures of healthy food based on the pyramid. Have them label the pictures with the correct target language (e.g., foreign language) word for the food item. After that, have the students prepare a shopping list of items they would want to buy at the supermarket.
- Have students identify health workers in their communities that need to have a speaking knowledge of a foreign language in their work. Create career posters, collages, or mobiles of the personnel that they have identified.
- Compile words that relate to health in their native languages and then identify cognates and/or borrowed words in the target language.
- Research and then discuss how religious beliefs and practices of the target foreign language's culture influences how health is practiced in the culture of the target language.
- Identify ways that are commonly used to express health issues in their own language and then find corresponding words or phrases in the target language to express those issues.

The following are common traffic signs. Have students label these according to words in the target language and then prepare collages of these symbols labeled with the target language words:

- Handicap Parking Signs
- Parking Signs
- Regulatory Traffic Control
- Road Work Construction
- School Zone
- Watch for Children Playing
- Caution
- Slippery When Wet
- Left Turn Only
- Barricade Ahead
- Men Working
- No Parking at Anytime
- Divided Highway
- No Right Turn on Red

- *Medical Words*. Have students compare the following words in their own language with words for the medical terms in the target language. Other terms are available at the National Library of Medicine (www.nlm.nih.gov/medlineplus/all_healthtopics.html).

• Anxiety	• Diabetes
• Abdominal pain	• Emergency
• Acne	• Pain
• Bacterial infection	• Paralysis
• Calcium	• Sodium (dietary)
• Cavities in teeth	• Warts
• Deafness	• Wounds
• Depression	

Intermediate Language Level (Grades 7–12 and Advanced Programs K–8)

Literature Analysis, Vocabulary Development, and Health

Understanding Folklore in Culture

- Have students name and talk about folktales that they remember from their childhood or, if younger, that they enjoy now.
- Divide students into small groups and have them answer these questions: Why do we have folktales? How have folktales influenced our behavior and attitudes? Where do folktales come from? Do you remember any folktales that include medicine and health? Name them.

Folklore and Mythology

- Select a folktale written in a foreign language (or in English depending on abilities of the class) that has a health theme. Remember that some folktales have levels of violence and sexual references that some would find unacceptable today. After sharing the folktale(s) with the class, ask students to speculate why such ideas about death, revenge, illnesses, and accidents that are often found in folklore were so prevalent in folktales from long ago. Some examples:
  - *The Sick Lion* (Aesop) at www.elook.org/literature/aesop/fables/423.html.
  - *Is Lion Sick?* by Gina Nuttall; QEB, 2005; primary grades.
  - *The Sick Lion: And the Hare and the Tortoise* (Aesop); Award Publications Ltd., July 2001; primary grades.
  - *Snow White* (*Blancanieves*) by Miquel Desclot and Ignasi Blanch; Chronicle Books, 2008; bilingual for elementary school. A more authentic version of the tale is found at en.wikipedia.org/wiki/Snow_White.
  - Hansel and Gretel (Grimm Brothers); *Hansel and Gretel* by Cynthia Rylant and Jen Corace; Hyperion Books for Children, 2008; elementary. A version of Hansel and Gretel is available at www.ivyjoy.com/fables/hansel.html.
  - Additional Aesop fables can be found at eLook.org (www.elook.org/literature/aesop/fables). Full-text versions of the Grimm Brothers' folktales are available at www.pitt.edu/~dash/grimmtales.html.
- Read a folktale to the students, making sure they can identify the following: main characters and their characteristics; important events; central theme; story development; and climax. Make sure students can identify health or abuse issues contained in the story and how it influenced the plot and tone of the story. The selected folktale can deal with such health issues as

illnesses and diseases, poverty and health, death, magic cures; danger and violence; and child abuse. After the story, divide the class into groups, and have each group prepare a story map of their interpretation of the story and display it in class. Have students take a gallery walk and compare interpretations among the groups.

Motifs in Folklore

Many kinds of fruit are found in folklore motifs. A list of more folklore motifs available for study is An Index of Folk Motifs (inquiryunlimited.org/x1/etoc/dewey/dewey398motifsindex.html). For this discussion, we have selected to highlight the apple as a motif:

- Explain that apples are a healthy fruit and that the apple motif is found in folklore from around the world. As background, explain that apples are health food because they help with:[10]
  - **Diet:** Energy-boosting and fat-free
  - **Heart:** Helps fight the damaging effects of LDL (bad) cholesterol
  - **Digestion:** Provides fiber for digestion
  - **Lungs:** Strengthens lungs
  - **Bones:** Can strengthen bones
- Provide some of the names given to the apple that are found in folklore: golden (gold); magical (magic); luxurious (luxury); pleasurable (pleasure); loving (love); and jealously (jealous). Ask students to translate these English words into appropriate words from the target language.

Idioms and Proverbs

Idioms and proverbs are found in all languages and cultures, but they are not easy to translate, and they often cannot be translated literally. Idioms and proverbs also have different meanings depending on the context. Help students build their vocabulary skills as well as learn how idioms and proverbs are culturally and/or context specific. The apple provides a means of introducing the concepts of proverbs and idioms as well as demonstrating that the apple is a healthy food. Provide some of the stories, proverbs, and idiomatic expressions that are attached to the apple in folklore.[11,12]

Make sure that students can define idioms and idiomatic expressions. Ask students to analyze the meanings of some of the following proverbs or idioms. Depending on the ability of the students, ask students to find equivalent expressions in the target language for some of the following proverbs and idioms. Challenge students to apply as many of these to health situations, realizing that some may not be relevant. For example, "American as apple pie" may not have an obvious connection to health, but "Everything round isn't an apple (Armenian) could imply that on the surface, a health situation may seem obvious, but that may not be the case on further examination:

- American as apple pie
- An attractive apple sometimes hides a worm within. (German)
- An apple a day keeps the doctor away. (English)
- The apple does not fall far from the tree. (German)
- The apple never falls far from the tree. (English)
- An apple thrown into the air will turn a thousand times before it reaches the ground. (Persian)
- An apple that ripens late keeps longest. (Serbian)
- Apple of his eye
- Bad apple floats on top. (Yiddish)
- Best thing since little apples

- Bite into a bitter apple first, and the good one will taste all the sweeter. (German)
- Comparing apples to oranges
- Don't look for apples under poplar trees. (Slavic)
- Don't upset the apple cart.
- Everything round isn't an apple. (Armenian)
- Handsome apples are sometimes sour. (Dutch)
- How could the apple be but as the apple tree? (Irish)
- Mom and apple pie
- Never look for a worm in the apple of your eye. (French)
- One bad apple spoils the bunch.
- One bad apple will spoil the whole barrel. (English)
- One rotten apple spoils the whole barrel.
- Rotten apple spoils his companion (Poor Richard)
- Sometimes, it is better to give your apple away than to eat it yourself. (Italian)
- Sour as a green apple
- Sweet as apple pie
- Who has tasted a sour apple will have the more relish for a sweet one. (Dutch)

Apple Stories from Mythology and Folklore

Share these stories with students:

- People in Medieval England who wanted a nice apple harvest would "select the largest apple tree in the orchard, and hang cider-soaked pieces of toast on its branches to attract robins. To those villagers, robins were considered the good spirits of the tree." Identify Medieval England.
- Golden apples were given to Hera as a wedding gift at her marriage to Zeus. Identify Hera and Zeus.
- The prophet Mohammed inhaled the fragrance of an apple brought to him by an angel just before his last breath of life. Identify the prophet Mohammed.
- Eve took a bite into an apple that she plucked off the forbidden tree of knowledge of good and evil in the Garden of Eden. Identify Eve and the Garden of Eden.
- Atalanta married the suitor who distracted her in a race with golden apples. Identify Atalanta.
- Snow White bit a poisoned apple. Identify Snow White and the Grimm Brothers, who collected Snow White folklore.[13]
- Read or have students read some of the following folktales and have them research the origins of the tale. Have students identify and describe some of the folktales attributes (by using adjectives) from the target language. These folktales can be used by older students for literary analysis and vocabulary-building in the target language:

    The Apple of Youth and Other Russian Folk Stories. By John Yeoman and Barbara Swiderska. 1967. Grades 4–6. Four traditional Russian tales entitled "Antipka and His Bad Tempered Wife," "The Helpful Mouse," "The Two Brothers," and "The Apple of Youth and the Water of Life."

    Blanche-Neige et les Sept Nains. By Fran Hunia. Scholastic-TAB, 1984. Grades 4–8. A princess takes refuge from her wicked stepmother, the queen, in the cottage of seven dwarfs, but the queen pursues her with a poisoned apple. French translation of *Snow White and the Seven Dwarfs*. Adaptation of *Schneewittchen*.

    The Farmer's Wife. By Idries Shah and Rose Mary Santiago. Hoopoe Books, 1998. Primary grades. A cumulative Sufi teaching tale of a farmer's wife, who is trying to retrieve an apple from a hole in the ground.

The Crystal Apple: A Russian Tale. By Beverly Brodsky. Viking Press, 1974. Grades 4–8. Three sisters receive gifts from their father, but Marusha's crystal apple proves to be a greater gift than she had imagined.

That Apple is Mine. By Katya Arnold and V. Suteev. Holiday House, 2000. Primary grades. In this retelling of a Russian folk tale, Rabbit, Crow, and Hedgehog fight over ownership of an apple, until Bear persuades them to share.

The Magic Apple: A Middle Eastern Folktale. By Rob Cleveland and Baird Hoffmire. Paw Prints, 2006. Grades K-3.In their travels, three brothers find a magic spyglass, a flying carpet, and a magic apple, which they use to help save a sick princess.

Snow White and the Seven Dwarfs. By Raymond Sibley, Jacob Grimm, and Martin Aitchison. Ladybird Favorite Tales series. Ladybird Books USA, 1996. Grades 4–8. A jealous stepmother orders Snow White to be killed, but she finds a safe haven with seven dwarfs, survives a poison apple offered to her by her disguised stepmother, and is rescued by the handsome prince.

Strudel, Strudel, Strudel. By Steve Sanfield and Emily Lisker. Orchard Books, 1995. Grades 4–8. Explains why teachers living in Chelm may not live on the top of a hill, own a trunk with wheels, nor eat apple strudel.

William Tell and His Son. By Bettina Hürlimann and Paul Nussbaumer. Brace & World, 1965. Grades 4–8. Translation of *Der Knabe des Tell*. Relates the story of the Swiss farmer, William Tell, who—as punishment for his patriotic activities—was required to shoot an apple off his son's head.

Fiction in Foreign Languages for Immediate Level Students

Fiction in foreign languages offers ways of understanding the values and expectations of foreign cultures. To help students better understand fiction in a foreign language, ask immediate level students these questions:

- What are the elements we expect to find in fiction written in a foreign language? Ask students to discuss how an author might write a story in the target language about an illness.
- Be sure that students apply these terms: logical plot (e.g., conflict, resolution, struggle, reconciliation, separation, reunion), characters and their actions and development, climax, and conclusion.[14]

Pre-Advanced Level (Grades 9–12) or Advanced Level (K–12)

Literacy Analysis, Vocabulary, and Health

- For vocabulary and reading development, have students search for information written in the target language and meant to be read by native speakers of the language. Have students critique the items they select for readability and the use of appropriate words for the intended audience. Sources for this type of materials include the U.S. Department of Agriculture, which has numerous publications in a wide variety of languages. The best way to access these is to conduct a subject search on the home page and then select the type of information needed from what is retrieved. Because the department has so many publications and references to other sources, the search is not always transparent. Subjects are often subordinated in technical terms with long listings. One can always insert a specific language and follow directions to subjects in the target language. For example, information on food stamps will be retrieved as Food Stamp Program following this linkage www.fns.usda.gov/snap/outreach/translations.htm.

Other U.S. government health online resources include the National Network of Libraries of Medicine (NN/LIN) (nnlm.gov/outreach/consumer/multi.html); the Centers for Disease Control (www.cdc.gov/Other/languages); and the U.S. Food and Drug Administration, "En Español: Publicaciones en Español" (www.fda.gov/AboutFDA/EnEspanol/default.htm). The Spencer Eccles Health Library at the University of Utah offers the 24 Languages Project, which as mentioned in an earlier chapter includes Arabic, Vietnamese, and Tagalog (library.med.utah.edu/24languages). The French Language Health Services, of the Ontario Ministry of Health and Long-Term Care, offers access to French language materials and health information (www.health.gov.on.ca/french/publicf/programf/flhsf/flhs_mnf.html).

- Another approach to building vocabulary is to have students select a website in the target language and then have them evaluate how accessible the website is for consumer health information. For example: Spanish—Ministerio de Sanidad y Politica Social (www.msc.es/en/home.htm); French—Nova Scotia Canada (www.gov.ns.ca/health/fls/health_fls.asp); Ministère-de-la-Santé et des Sports (France) www.sante-sports.gouv.fr); German—Bundesministerium für Gesundheit und Soziale Sicherung (www.bmg.bund.de); Russian—Federal State Institution, Central Research Institute for Health Information and the Ministry of Health and Social Development of Russia (FGU, ЦНОЗ MHSD RF) (www.mednet .ru). These experiences can be used at the intermediate level with appropriate selection of materials.

Fiction for Pre-Advanced Level Students

Examples of novels originally published in a foreign language are available in Appendix A. Based on abilities, have students:

- Select and read from these or similar novels in the target language and discuss health and safety issues presented in the novels. If students are not able to read with sufficient comprehension, have them read an English translation of the novel. The novel selected can deal with such health issues as illnesses and diseases, poverty and health, death, danger and violence, child abuse, and health in society. Have students discuss and analyze these issues:
- Describe the health themes and how they influence the plot.
- Identify important events, central themes, story developments, and climaxes.
- Describe the main characters and their relationships to health issues.
- Describe the historical period of the novel, and comment on ideas about health care prevalent during the time of the novel.
- Have students display their understanding of literary narrative by selecting a character and choosing: proper nouns that identify the character; the character's actions by selecting verbs that best describe the character; and the character's attributes by selecting adjectives that fit the character's actions.[15]
- Have students select a character from the reading and then prepare a character sketch of the persons. Have students share the sketch with the class through a brief discussion of why the character appealed or did not appeal to them.

Other aspects of literacy criticism that are appropriate for foreign languages are listed in the literature portion of this chapter.

Selected Foreign Language Literature

For students who have limited or average reading and comprehension abilities, have them select an author that writes in the target language, research that author, and write a brief biographical sketch in the target language (or English), highlighting any health issues that the author might have experienced. Wikipedia includes listings of author from many language groups, including:

- **French:** en.wikipedia.org/wiki/Category:French_fiction_writers
- **German:** en.wikipedia.org/wiki/List_of_German-language_authors
- **Russian:** en.wikipedia.org/wiki/List_of_Russian_language_novelists
- **Spanish:** en.wikipedia.org/wiki/List_of_Spanish_language_authors

As these listings are extensive, teachers and librarians will need to first research the lists and select those authors that are appropriate for this activity.

Advanced Students

For students with more advanced reading skills, have them select a novel in the target language and develop a book talk, a poster board, an advertisement for the book, or other types of presentations to present to the class. Examples of novels for advanced levels students are listed in Appendix A.

Less Advanced Students

Have students read English translations of young adult novels (and nonfiction) published originally in the target language (or in another language and translated into the target language) and then prepare a presentation in the target language (or English if preferred) describing the books. As with more advanced students, these presentations can include a book talk, a poster board, an advertisement for the book, or other types of presentations. Examples of novels (and a few nonfiction) books are listed in Appendix A.

Adaptations for Intermediate or Pre-Advanced Levels

1. For students who are at the intermediate or pre-advanced levels and who do not have the reading ability in the target language to read novels or other materials written in the language, have these students study the target language as used in their own country or worldwide and research how health needs are met. Some examples:
   - **French in Louisiana.** Cajun and Creole French dialects are spoken in Louisiana. What are the special health needs of these speakers, and how are they addressed by the prevailing health systems available to them?
   - **French in Canada.** How different is the French in Quebec from other parts of Canada? Research the Canadian national health systems to see how French-speaking Canadians are served.
   - **Spanish.** Various Spanish language groups exist in the United States and elsewhere. What provisions are made by the health systems in these varied locations to serve Spanish speakers' needs?
   - **German in Pennsylvania and parts of Canada.** Although Pennsylvania German is spoken by few in modern Pennsylvania, it is still a living language. For example, the Amish is a German-speaking group that has a very distinct living and religious style. They are located both in the United States, Canada, and Mexico. How are Amish as well as other Pennsylvania German speakers' health needs met?

- **Russian in the United States and Canada.** Since the fall of the former Soviet Union, many Russian-speaking people have come to major cities in the United States and Canada. Because Russia is not widely spoken in these countries, how are their health needs met?
2. Have students refer to national health sites for all these language groups cited here to begin their research:

French Language in Quebec, Canada

- www.republiquelibre.org/cousture/FRANC2.HTM
- faculty.marianopolis.edu/c.belanger/quebecHistory/readings/langlaws.htm
- www.thecanadianencyclopedia.com/index.cfm?PgNm=TCE&Params=A1ARTA0003063

French Dialects in Louisiana

- www.codofil.org/english/lafrenchlanguage.html
- www.codofil.org/bilingual/ressources%20maitresses.html
- en.wikipedia.org/wiki/Cajun_French
- en.wikipedia.org/wiki/Louisiana_Creole_French

French in France

- en.wikipedia.org/wiki/Languages_of_France
- www.france-property-and-information.com/dialects_of_the_french_language.htm

German

- en.wikipedia.org/wiki/German_language

Pennsylvania German Dialect

- en.wikipedia.org/wiki/Pennsylvania_German_language
- en.wikipedia.org/wiki/Pennsylvania_German_language#Comparion_to_Standard_German

Russian in the United States and Canada

- en.wikipedia.org/wiki/Russian_language

Spanish

- en.wikipedia.org/wiki/Spanish_language (see links to Geographic areas)

Have students compare the health care systems and/or needs that serve people in a selected target language area and then prepare a presentation. The presentation can be in the form of a written news release, a broadcast, or a poster. Make sure that the presentation includes an introduction to language as used in the target area and is addressed to an audience that knows little about the language.

Together with this introduction, make sure that health care situations in the targeted area are explained. For example, how are various dialectics of the language addressed in terms of health care for speakers of those languages? If the dialect is in a language that is not the major language, how are services provided and health care needs met for those who speak the dialect or the language.

History of words in a language can help students understand the relationships between history, culture, and medicine. Introduce the concept of etymology as the study of the historical development of words in languages. Make sure that students understand that dictionaries often include information about the origins of words coming from languages, such as old French (OF), old English (OE), Middle English (ME), etc.

Introduce the concept of medical etymology; that is, medical terms often originate from older forms of languages as well as from more current situations, such as Down syndrome. To help students with this concept, have them study the language origins of medical terms. Like many words, medical terms are formed from word roots, prefixes, suffixes, and combining vowels/forms. For example: Root is the foundation of the word that is often combined with a prefix or a suffix. A prefix precedes the root word, and a suffix follows the root. A suffix modifies the root, and it can be a noun, verb, or adjective. A combining form is needed to tie the concepts together. This is a vowel, such as "o," and it is attached to the root word. When analyzing medical terms, look at the suffix first, then the root, and lastly the prefix.

Example: pericarditis, the inflammation around the heart
• **Prefix:** peri- = around
• **Root:** cardi = heart
• **Suffix:** -itis = inflammation

Most medical terms are based on Greek and Latin words, but many more modern words come from German, English, and French words. Generally, surgical and diagnostic words are Greek in origin, and anatomical words come from Latin.[16]

Introduce students to medical dictionaries, such as *Dorland's Illustrated Medical Dictionary* (31st ed. Saunders, 2007), the *English Oxford Dictionary* (print or online) or other good medical dictionaries that provide etymological information. Using such dictionaries, have students research the origin of commonly used medical words or words associated with categories of illnesses.

Individual Words

• Alzheimer's disease
• Arrhythmia
• Arthritis
• Asthma
• Cardiac
• Cholera
• Diabetes
• E. coli
• Glioblasloma
• Heart failure
• Hemorrhage
• Hepatitis
• Inflammation
• Influenza
• Leukemia
• Meningitis
• Nuclei
• Pathology
• Obesity
• Pneumonia
• Pulmonary embolism
• Rheumatic fever
• Salmonella
• Senility
• Septicaemia
• Stroke
• Thrombosis
• Tuberculosis
• Typhus

Types of Disease Categories

- Autoimmune conditions
- Back conditions
- Bacterial infections
- Chromosome conditions
- Dental conditions
- Diabetes
- Digestive conditions
- Ear conditions
- Foot conditions
- Gall bladder conditions
- Genetic conditions
- Gynecological conditions
- Hearing disorders
- Immune disorders
- Kidney conditions
- Lung conditions
- Liver conditions
- Parasitic infections
- Pancreas conditions
- Obstetrical conditions
- Pregnancy conditions
- Prion diseases
- Spinal disorders
- Thyroid disorders
- Viral infections
- Worm condition[17]

Have students do one of the following:

- Select a disease category, and using appropriate dictionaries and other sources for background information, prepare a brief report (oral report, poster board, news report, etc.) on the historical development of words commonly related to the chosen disease category.
- Research the history of individual words and compare their language origins. Prepare a brief report (oral report, poster board, news report, etc.).

The online version of the *Oxford English Dictionary* has excellent information on etymology. This information includes time charts, pronunciations, and quotations that can be used with either choice.

RESOURCES

In addition to foreign language and folklore resources just discussed, annotated items that support learning activities discussed in this chapter are available in Appendix A. Grade and age designations are provided.

REFLECTIONS

Literature, art, and performance activities (e.g., dance, music, athletics) are found everywhere in society. Language and culture underpins all these human attributes. All cultures from the beginning of human experience have expressed themselves artistically and in forms of literature, music, drama, dance, sports, and language. Because the arts, sports, and languages are so identified with human life and human expression, they present a wealth of opportunities to introduce and teach healthy lifestyles and behaviors to youth.

NOTES

1. "Literary Criticism and Theory." staff2.esuhsd.org/danielle/APLit/Lit%20Crit/Literary_Criticism%20and%20Theory.pdf. Accessed Dec. 14, 2009.

2. "Literary Criticism." www.textetc.com/criticism.html. Accessed Dec. 14, 2009.

3. Gerrig, R. J. and D. A. Prentice. "The Representation of Fictional Information Acquired Through Fictional Worlds Is Incorporated into Real-World Knowledge," *Psychological Science* 2 (5), 1991, pp. 336–340.

4. Sources for Hoffman: arts.jrank.org/pages/9247/Contes-d'Hoffmann-Les-('The-Tales-Hoffmann').html; www.semissourian.com/story/1596013.html; www.news times.com/news/article/Wildly-imaginative-Tales-of-Hoffmann-at-Met-280365.php; and www.thelmagazine.com/TheMeasure/archives/2009/12/11/offenbachs-tales-of -hoffman-spectacle-singing-comedy-crying).

5. Ulrich, R. S. "Effects of Health Facility Interior Design on Wellness: Theory and Recent Scientific Research," *Journal of Health Care Design*, 3 (1991): 97–109. Reprinted in: Marberry, S. O., ed., 1995. *Innovations in Healthcare Design*, pp. 88–104. New York: Van Nostrand Reinhold, 1995.

6. Society for the Arts in Health Care. www.thesah.org/template/index.cfm. Accessed Feb. 20, 2009.

7. "Indiana Academic Art Standards." www.ipfw.edu/vpa/CAA/Visual%20Art% 20Standards%20Web%208-15-05%5B1%5D.pdf. Accessed Sept. 23, 2009.

8. "Value of Literature-Based Instruction for All Students." www.eduplace.com/ rdg/res/literacy/meet4.html. Quoting Allen, V. G. "Teaching Bilingual and ESL Children." In J. Flood, J. M. Jensen, D. Lapp, and J. Squire, eds. *Handbook on Research on Teaching the English Language Arts*, pp. 356–364. New York: Macmillan Publishing Company, 1991.

9. North Dakota Department of Public Instruction. *North Dakota Standards and Benchmarks Content Standards: Foreign Language.* Bismarck, ND: The Department, 2001. www.dpi.state.nd.us/standard/content/foreign.pdf. Accessed Dec. 4, 2009.

10. "Local Virginia Apples." www.virginiaapples.org/facts/5reasons.html. Referenced from University of Illinois Extension. "Apples and More." urbanext.illinois.edu/ apples/nutrition.cfm. Accessed Dec. 6, 2009.

11. "A Crop of Clichés from the Garden: Farming, Gardening and the Outdoor Life, Short Quotes, Sayings, Epigrams, Adages, Brief Thoughts, Catchy Ideas." www.gardendigest.com/cliche.htm. Accessed Dec. 6, 2009.

12. Bookrages. www.bookrags.com/tandf/apple-5-tf. Accessed Dec. 6, 2009.

13. I Really Like Food. "Folklore of the Apple." Posted August 12, 2009. www.ireallylikefood.com/709585065/folklore-of-the-appl. Accessed Dec. 5, 2009.

14. Tyson, Lois. *Critical Theory Today: A User-Friendly Guide.* New York: Garland Publishing, Inc. 1999.

15. Tyson.

16. "Basic Concepts of Medical Terminology." nnlm.gov/psr/training/class_materials/ docs/Medical_Terminology_Modulev2.doc. Accessed Dec. 28, 2009.

17. "What Is All Disease Categories?" www.wrongdiagnosis.com/a/all/ subtypes.htm#typeslist. Accessed Dec. 29, 2009.

7

Connections to Good Health: Social and Behavioral Sciences, and Languages

WHAT ARE THE CONNECTIONS TO HEALTH?

Collectively, social and behavioral sciences offer a wealth of ideas and resources for teaching health care as well as providing health care information and building sound foundations for health information literacy. Broadly speaking, social sciences include history, government and civics, economics, social and government policy, public health, geography, anthropology, and sociology. Social sciences investigate the structure of social systems and how those systems interact and influence how we organize our social lives.[1] Although they share some similarities with social sciences, behavioral sciences are different in that they investigate processes and communication strategies between groups in a social system.

INSTRUCTIONAL THEMES, SKILL SETS, AND LEARNING OUTCOMES IN THE SOCIAL SCIENCES

The important guidelines by UNESCO as well as other groups offer directives and themes, skill sets, and learning outcomes for the social sciences and health instructions. Some themes are:

Theme 1. Living Together and Social Dependency

- Food and food culture
- Child growth and development
- Community health and hygiene
- Disease and infection prevention
- Prevention and control of epidemics
- Importance of immunization

Theme 2. Living in, Preserving, and Protecting the Environment

- Pollution and its effects on community life and health
- Soil conservation and its relationship to food and community life
- Water management and distribution and its effects on health and community well-being (Figure 7.1)

Theme 3. Rights and Duties of Citizenship

- Knowledge and actions concerning good health behaviors
- Knowledge of major health providers and emergency assistance in communities

Theme 4. Responsibility to Respect Diversity and Those in Adversity

- Consideration of the social and economic connection of poverty and health
- Building of constructive attitudes about persons with disabilities children in society as well as concern for those in challenging situations, such as those facing wars and displacements as well as AIDS and the social effects of AIDS, such as AIDS orphans (Figure 7.2).

Theme 5. Health in a Social and Cultural Context

- Evaluate the effects of disease on history and community life
- Consider medical advancements and cures and their wide-spread influence on modern life

Figure 7.1.
Social message from the United States during World War I—"Uncle Sam Says 'Garden to Cut Food Cost.' " Courtesy of the U.S. Department of Agriculture.

- Study of medical biography, medical sociology, social geography and demographics, social anthropology, medical folklore, and folk culture
- Apply basic research skills, such as interviewing, observation, and surveys, to health topics

Useful Skill Set

UNESCO suggests several skill sets that educators can integrate into social science instruction. These include:

- **Constructing, Designing, and Using Maps**

Map ideas include making a plan to lay out a vegetable garden, making a "health map" of a neighborhood, and locating district health services on a local map.

- **Developing Community Surveys**

These can include surveying local people about treatments and attitudes, their knowledge about health care facilities, and their awareness about the prevention of diseases and accidents.

- **Developing Skills in Listening and Understanding Differences in Views and Lifestyle**

These skills include learning how to listen without judgment to people as they express their views and knowledge; learning how to show empathy while listening; gaining knowledge about how to listen and remember and how to ask questions for clarification; and knowing how to politely end a conversation. UNESCO suggests that listening can involve encouraging people to talk about food and eating customs and practices, health practices, and folk medicine. Listening skills can also be used in helping students become actively involved in health campaigns as well as helping people talk about disabilities and how society views those with disabilities.

Figure 7.2.
Crippled children playing on roof. Henry Street, New York City, ca. 1909. Library of Congress, George Grantham Bain Collection. Courtesy of the Library of Congress.

THE SOCIAL BASE FOR FOREIGN LANGUAGES AND HEALTH EDUCATION: A RATIONALE

In this chapter, we approach foreign languages information from a culture prospective much as we did in Chapter 6. The National Standards for Foreign Language Education (NSFLE)[2] imply—along with other reasons—that in studying languages, students can be helped to understand that culture plays an essential role in how people view health and health care. Ideas about culture are reflected in the NSFLE standards below:

Cultures: Gain knowledge and understanding of other cultures.

- Students demonstrate an understanding of the relationship between the practices and perspectives of the culture studied.
- Students demonstrate an understanding of the relationship between the products and perspectives of the culture studied.

Connections: Connect with other disciplines and acquire information.

- Students reinforce and further their knowledge of other disciplines through the foreign language.
- Students acquire information and recognize the distinctive viewpoints that are only available through the foreign language and its culture.

Comparisons: Develop insight into the nature of language and culture.

- Students demonstrate understanding of the nature of language through comparisons of the language studied and their own.
- Students demonstrate understanding of the concept of culture through comparisons of the cultures studied and their own.

Communities: Participate in multilingual communities at home and around the world.

- Students use the language both within and beyond the school setting.
- Students show evidence of becoming life-long learners by using the language for personal enjoyment and enrichment.

These objectives are addressed in this book and in this chapter in several ways. We suggest that cultural studies through foreign languages are especially useful in understanding the roles that history, sociology, and geography play in informing students about health. Many of the topics in Chapter 7 can be studied in foreign language curriculums to illustrate how globalization interconnects the world and cultures, impacting health care and health information (Chapter 10). Issues involved in improving health within local communities, including multilingual communities are discussed in Chapter 9, while Chapter 6 addressed the literary aspects of foreign language studies.

ROLE OF GOVERNMENT IN HEALTH

Good health is a fundamental social issue. Health management is generally considered a responsibility of everyone, including governments and organizations. As society

Figure 7.3.
Government school lunch programs. Courtesy National Library of Medicine and U.S. Department of Agriculture.

becomes more complex and diversified, problems associated with providing adequate health care to citizens at all levels of society energize both humanitarian and political issues (Figure 7.3). The options that governments take range from providing total health care to governments that provide none. These options are often based on philosophical theories about the role of governments in society as well as how health care costs are to be managed. Although varied in range, most developed countries provide some level of government health support for citizens.

THEMATIC AND HOLISTIC HEALTH INSTRUCTION

Instructional approaches can be constructed based on the themes suggested previously in this chapter. They are broad yet reflect principles of an holistic approach to health education.

Learning Outcomes

Students will:

- Define community and identify factors that contribute to healthy communities.
- Identify and demonstrate how to communicate with important health support systems in their communities.
- Describe how to help prevent diseases.
- Select and describe important ways that families and friends can be healthy.

- Locate information resources in their communities that will promote healthy living.
- Analyze cultural and social forces that prevent good health.
- Classify and integrate historical and geographical forces that have produced poor or unhealthy conditions throughout history.
- Define government and discuss, analyze, and generate a model for government policies that promote good health.
- Describe and analyze examples of medical discoveries that have impacted society.
- Find and report on biographies of people who have promoted good health through their works in public health, community development, science, and other fields.
- Deduce reasons why medical and scientific discovers are sometime used against groups of people.

Learning Activities and/or Questions (Adjust for Age and Abilities)

For Older Students (Grades 5–12)

- How do governments promote health as a civic and personal responsibility?
An obligation in relation to:
  - Education and information about health and healthy lifestyles
  - Concern for other people's welfare
  - Observing expected rules of conduct and behavior
  - Concern for social conditions that impact community and personal health
  - Maintaining positive living and working relationships
  - Forming and following a pattern of personal hygiene
- How do governments provide or not provide social support systems relating to the:
  - Need for health insurance and regulations
  - Role of regulations concerning food and food production
  - Water issues at all levels of governments (e.g., clean water)
  - Protection of the environment with law, rules and regulations
  - Promotion of health screenings
  - Enforcement of health ordinances, rules, laws, and regulations
  - Safety conditions in homes and workplaces
  - Identification and monitoring of sex offenders
  - Child neglect and child sexual and physical abuse
  - Systematic programs for disease prevention and control
  - Food and feeding programs for hunger and malnutrition prevention
  - Programs for the handicapped and disabled
  - Promotion and enforcement of sanitation laws and regulations
  - Promotion of recreation and physical activities
  - Workplace safety and hygiene
- What are economics factors of health faced by governments relating to:
  - Health cost management
  - Factors in rising health cost
  - Health expenditure and financing health expenditure per capita according to selected states or provinces
  - Health expenditure in relation to gross domestic product (GDP)
  - Health expenditure by function
  - Pharmaceutical expenditure

- ○ Financing for health care
- ○ Health insurance coverage (public and private)
- ○ Single-payer systems (provide definitions and examples)
- ○ Socialized medicine (provide definitions and examples)
- ○ Market-oriented health care (provide definition and examples)
- ○ Profits and government controls
- What is the role of governments in promoting ethics in health in relation to:
  - ○ Scarcity of resources and health resource distribution
  - ○ Rationing of health care
  - ○ Protecting the public from medical abuse and fraud
  - ○ Physician-assisted death
  - ○ Care of the elderly
  - ○ Care of the disabled and handicapped
  - ○ Domestic violence
  - ○ Abortion
  - ○ Medical competency and certification
  - ○ Human cloning
  - ○ Assisted reproduction
  - ○ Protecting of human research subjects

SOCIAL AND HISTORICAL ASPECTS OF ILLNESS

A number of themes relating to health can be developed within the context of the social sciences, including history.

For Older Students (Grades 5–12)

Theme 1. Disease and History

Diseases have always influenced human history and offer students opportunities to learn history and the roles that health and disease have and continue to play in human development.

- What are epidemics? Have student research famous diseases and epidemics that have had catastrophic effects on culture and society. These can include the black plague, yellow fever, smallpox as more modern diseases, such as AIDS, the 1918 influenza, Ebola, cholera, and malaria.
- Ask students to research and discuss diseases that were introduced to native populations by European exploration. Have students research diseases that were introduced to Europeans through their exploration of other parts of the world.
- What are famines? What are some of the famous famines that have occurred throughout history (e.g., potato famine in Ireland)?
- What are some modern-day famines? Have students research and discuss famines of the twentieth and twenty-first centuries.
- How do political and social conflicts often cause famines? Have older students consider the political backgrounds that often foster and cause famines.
- Research some diseases of animals and discuss how these diseases have affected and continue to affect people.

- What are some health treatments that were discovered in ancient times that we still use today? Encourage students to research ancient medical treatments and discoveries and how they might be still continued today. Such discoveries can include surgery, use of alcohol, pain relievers, and herbs.
- Research and discuss prevalent illnesses that have historically occurred more frequently among minorities groups, especially native groups (e.g., Native Americans and African Americans in the United States, First Nations in Canada, and Aborigines in Australia). What are some of the major reasons for these illnesses? How have governments addressed these problems?
- Foreign language students can select a country and time period and research diseases that have influenced that country socially, culturally, and politically.

Theme 2. Disease in Culture (Medical Discoveries)

Medical discoveries for diseases and the prevention of disease offer a wealth of ideas for introducing health information to students. Have students research these diseases and how cures or treatments were discovered for them:

Scurvy and its cure
Discovery of what caused the 1918 flu pandemic
Rickets and its cure
Pellagra
Smoking and lung cancer
Discover of the structure of DNA
Heart disease and the use of aspirin
Childbed fever
First effective cure for syphilis
Discovery of the cause of AIDS and its treatment

- Have students research biographies of scientists that are associated with disease, cures, treatments, and medical research:

James Lind: scurvy
Paul Ehrlich: syphilis
Edward Mellanby: rickets
Joseph Goldberger and Conrad Elvehjem: pellagra
Rich Doll and Austin Bradford: lung cancer and smoking
James D. Watson, Francis Crick, Rosalind Franklin and Maurice Wilkins: DNA structure
Tgnoz Semmelweis: childbed fever
Joseph Lister: antisepsis theory
Louis Pasteur: microorganism and disease
Charles Darwin: genetics and evolutionary theory
Gregor Mendel: genetics
Claude Bernard: Scientific methods used in medical research
Charles Drew: Blood plasma

- Foreign language students can select a country and time period and research the medical biography of that country to find persons that have made contribution to health (e.g., Claude Bernard, Madam Currie).

Theme 3. Medical Sociology and Anthropology

Introduce the concept of medical sociology and medical anthropology. The National Library of Medicine defines medical sociology as:

[C]oncerned with the relationship between social factors and health and with the application of socio-logical theory and research techniques to questions related to health and the health care system.[3]

Several specific topics within this definition will be of interest to students. Have students research some of these issues:

- What are the influences of ethnicity, gender, age, or socioeconomic status on health?
- Do minorities generally have convenient access to health providers?
- How are people provided or denied access to quality health care (e.g., lack of health insurance or national health plans and coverage, living in isolated areas)?
- What are some well-known health and risk-taking behaviors (e.g., smoking, drug use)?
- What are some social constructs (e.g., environments) of illness (e.g., poverty, lack of education)?
- What are some of the health beliefs and perceptions among specific groups of people?
- How is health affected by social and cultural changes?
- What are some of the expected roles of health institutions and health professionals in society?
- What are some of the social implications of biomedical innovations (e.g., generic engineering)?
- What is the role of education in health care and information?
- What role does mass communication play in health care and health information?
- Foreign language students can select a country and research some of the prevailing social issues that that country presently faces regarding medical and health issues.

Medical anthropology is the study of "ways in which cultures define, experience, and manage health and illness" (National Library of Medicine). Using this definition, have students research and discuss some of these issues:

- What are some medical belief systems of various groups of people (e.g., medical astrology)?
- What are some healing practices followed by various groups of people (e.g., herbalism)?
- What are some prevailing belief systems and customs surrounding birth, death, and diet?
- How are health and illnesses expressed in speech and language, including dialects and region-alisms (e.g., what might "I am stove up" mean)?
- How different is maternal and child health in selected populations, regions, and countries?
- How is dieting and nutrition affected by culture and society?
- How do we in this country promote human development in relation to health and disease?
- What is government health policy? Give some examples of government health policies in your city, state, province, or country.
- Foreign language students can select any of the previously mentioned issues and research how they apply to a country of their choice. For example, research government health policies in one country and compare it with another (e.g., compare France to Spain).

Theme 4. Geography and Health (Medical Geography)

Medical geography combines geography and medicine in relation to health care. It considers the effects that environments and climates have on health both currently and in the historical past. Diseases that are generally associated with geography include malaria, cholera, and dental diseases.[4]

- What is cholera? How was the cause of cholera discovered?
- How was fluoride discovered to help prevent tooth decay?
- What was the "little ice age"? Discuss how it affected health and culture of Europe and the Northern Hemisphere for 500 years.
- What is the story behind the cold summer of 1815? Consider how this cold summer affected health.
- What is the geography of malaria? Why does it occur most frequently in some regions and not others?
- What is lead poisoning? Why does it seem to be affecting children today? How is it related to location and the time periods of home construction?
- Define health demographics. How can they be used to illustrate the geography of health?
- How is childhood diabetes associated with location and geography? How can medical geography be used to locate and inform high-risk populations, such as those with a high percent of childhood diabetes, to become better informed about prevention and health management?
- Foreign language student can select a country and research a disease and the demographics of that disease in that country (e.g., childhood diabetes in Mexico)

Theme 5. Psychological Health

Students should be encouraged to consider psychological health as a fundamental part of good health management. Psychological health involves many aspects of good healthy living and lifestyles. Have students—based on age appropriateness—consider these questions:

- What makes for good psychological health? Encourage students to consider these factors:
  ○ Being productive
  ○ Having good interpersonal relationships
  ○ Behaving compassionately toward others
- What roles do environmental, social, and cultural factors play in psychological health?
- How do social and cultural factors contribute to disease or its prevention?
- How can everyone promote better psychological health in themselves and others by changing bad beliefs, attitudes, and behaviors regarding disease and health?
- What do you know about these conditions? Research and discuss how these conditions affect psychological health:
  ○ Alcoholism and drug abuse
  ○ Depression
  ○ Diabetes
  ○ Environmental conditions
  ○ Gambling
  ○ Generalized anxiety disorder
  ○ Anxiety about health
  ○ Insomnia
  ○ Obsessive-compulsive disorder
  ○ Relationship with parents
  ○ Perfectionism

- ○ Phobias
- ○ Physical activity
- ○ Behavior and conduct disorder
- What is intelligence testing or IQ? Who is generally credited with its creation? How does it relate to health?
- What is eugenics as practiced in the early twentieth century in the United States? How is it related to intelligence, race, national origins, and health?
- Explain how economic and social conditions helped promote the idea that eugenics would correct many of the problems that the world faced at that time? How did the Nazis in Germany practice eugenics?
- What are some of the factors that cause teenagers to have psychological and other health problems?
- How do governments help people who face psychological health issues?
- How can everyone promote better psychological health in themselves and others by changing bad beliefs, attitudes, and behaviors regarding disease and health?

Foreign language students can select a country and research issues that the medical communities in that country have identified as major behavior and psychological problems.

For Younger Students (K–4)

Social Responsibility and Health (Includes Thematic and Holistic Health Concepts)

Social learning for younger students generally focuses on community and the role that all citizens play in a democratic society. The close relationship between social learning, community, and health suggests an active role for school librarians and teachers.

American national social studies standards for government and civics instruction focus on helping young students (K–4) understand the role of community, community responsibility, and community leadership, and teaching health information skills directed at helping young students better understand their communities and their roles and responsibilities for living in specific communities. These same questions/activities can be used with foreign language students within language cultures and groups. Questions and instructional approaches that relate to social responsibility and health include:

- Do I eat wisely?
- Do I eat enough or do I eat too much?
- What is malnutrition? How can we recognize it?
- What are some special foods I enjoy? Why do I enjoy eating those? Are they healthy for me?
- What kinds of foods can you grow in your neighbourhood, village, town, or city?
- Have students keep a food diary, writing what they eat and when. For young students who cannot yet write, supply images and have then keep a diary of pictures they can draw that represents what they eat. Discuss the diaries with the students.
- Have older students map and discuss where major types of food are grown in their country and where they live as well as in other parts of the world.
- Introduce the concept of famine. Have older students (e.g., grades 3–6) consider why people in some countries have plenty to eat and others often suffer famine.

- Have students consider how they can help their community by eating well and being responsible for their safety and the safety of others.
- Ask students to identify and name the major health providers in the communities.
- Ask students to identify a health or safety emergency and how to call for help.
- All students are familiar with milk. Have students talk about how milk is made safe to drink. Introduce the concept of pasteurization as used to protect milk. Help students understand the difference between pasteurization and sterilization.
- Introduce Louis Pasteur as the scientist who discovered pasteurization as a process that promotes the safety of children.
- Introduce the concept of vaccination in the prevention of diseases. Suggest that students discuss some of the diseases that vaccinations help prevent or contain, such as smallpox, mumps, polio, rabies, measles, German measles, chicken pox, and whooping cough.
- Discuss how smallpox was almost completely eliminated from people through vaccinations campaigns all over the world. Note: "The disease is now eradicated after a successful worldwide vaccination program. The last case of smallpox in the United States was in 1949. The last naturally occurring case in the world was in Somalia in 1977. After the disease was eliminated from the world, routine vaccination against smallpox among the general public was stopped because it was no longer necessary for prevention."[5]

Other questions such as these can be framed to consider safety and safe ways of living. Personal hygiene, disease and disease prevention, how children grow and develop, and environmental protection are topics that can be discussed within social and historical contexts. Younger foreign language students can select countries and conduct basic research on how some of the previous issues occur in their selected countries. Have students:

- Identify health symbols that are used to identify hospitals, pharmacies, emergency routes, hazardous materials and waste, etc., used in the selected foreign countries.
- Identify how to reach help when emergencies occur in the selected foreign countries (e.g., 911, 311). See Chapter 6 for additional suggestions.

RESOURCES

Suggested resources for instruction in these various topics are provided in Appendix A. They have been selected for subject and grade coverage and to enhance classroom discussions, activities, and projects.

REFLECTIONS

This chapter is based on the assumption that health education and health literacy are fundamental parts of everyday society and culture and that health literacy is an essential part of all instruction in the modern school, including the social sciences. School librarians and teachers play significant roles in promoting healthy lifestyles based on a systematic understanding of how health influences the world in which we all live. Students need to know how to contribute to and sustain a healthy world by understanding its social, historical, geographical, linguistic, and cultural impacts.

NOTES

1. Klemke, E. D., R. Hollinger, and A. D. Kline, ed. *Introductory Readings in the Philosophy of Science*. New York: Prometheus Books, 1980.

2. *National Standards for Foreign Language Education. A Collaborative Project of ACTFL, AATF, AATG, AATI, AATSP, ACL, ACTR, CLASS and NCJLT-ATJ*. www.actfl.org/i4a/pages/index.cfm?pageid=3392. Accessed Dec. 4, 2009.

3. National Library of Medicine. "Collection Development Manual." www.nlm .nih.gov/tsd/acquisitions/cdm/subjects59.html. Accessed Sept. 25, 2005.

4. Medical Geography. www.medterms.com/script/main/art.asp?articlekey=18879. Accessed Sept. 25, 2005.

5. U.S. Centers for Disease Control. "Smallpox Fact Sheet: Smallpox Disease Overview." www.bt.cdc.gov/agent/smallpox/overview/disease-facts.asp. Accessed Sept. 22, 2009.

8

Connections: Health, Physical Education, Science, and Mathematics

WHAT IS THE CONNECTION?

Formal physical education instruction has traditionally played a fundamental role in bringing health information to students throughout the world. This is based on the long-standing recognition that health is important to learning and that schools can play an important role in educating youth about healthy living. The roles that schools have played in health education are well- documented and are discussed in Chapter 1. We must never forget that because public school education reaches a huge number of youth throughout the world, schools and their curricula, including physical education and formal health classes—reinforced by other curricula—will always serve as an important vehicle for providing health information to youth. Later, we will discuss how well science and math instruction integrate with physical education and health.

OVERVIEW OF PHYSICAL EDUCATION HISTORY

Society generally recognizes that among the first cultures to institutionalize sports were the ancient Greeks. The first Olympiad of the ancient Greek world was held in 776 BCE. Not only were physical games and competition a part of ancient Greek society, but they surrounded all elements of that society (at least for the privileged classes), including philosophy, religion, medicine, and views of mental health. The ideas of health rested on these basic concepts: "balance, harmony, proportion, equilibrium, regularity and proper mixture of blending (temperament)."[1]

In Greek life, health resided at the top of a hierarchy of values, followed by prosperity, pleasure, and owing no debts. Health was viewed as necessary so that all other important aspects of life could be enjoyed, including family and children. Moderation and moral behavior in all parts of life were also a part of the Greeks' ideas about

Figure 8.1.
A coeducation physical exercise class, ca. 1909, Washington, D.C. Courtesy of the
Library of Congress.

good health behaviors.[2] Some of these values still affect our modern views of health
and life.

The nineteenth century witnessed an expansion of physical education into schools,
especially in Europe. In 1814, Denmark started to require physical education. By 1820,
some American schools had begun to integrate physical education into their curricula.
Generally, these include games and exercises (Figure 8.1). In 1866, California became
the first American state to require physical education in its schools.[3]

Charles Beck was the first physical education teacher in the United States. He mod-
eled his program on the German system that emphasized gymnastics. Dio Lewis,
deploring the health of Americans of the day, advanced physical education and its
instructional pedagogy when he established the Normal Institute of Physical Education
in Boston in 1861.[4] Today many school systems throughout the world require some
degree of formal physical education, including colleges and universities.[5] Almost all
governments are involved to some extent in health education in schools.

In 1984, the Centers for Disease Control and Prevention (CDC) in the United
States conducted an extensive study of 30,000 students in fourth through seventh
grades in 1,071 classrooms in 20 states to determine the effectiveness of formal
health and fitness programs. Data indicated that students in formal health education
increased their knowledge of health issues, developed better attitudes about health,
acquired better health behaviors and skills, and were able to better perform those
than students who did not receive similar instruction. According to the data, time
exposed to health instruction plays a significant role in instructional effectives. The
study reported that 50 hours of instruction is required to reach a stable level of health
information.[6]

COMPREHENSIVE PHYSICAL EDUCATION AND HEALTH
PROGRAMS: AN INTRODUCTION

In recent years in the United States, the CDC, through its Healthy Youth! program,
has become active in promoting compressive health and physical education.[7] In 1999,

the New Jersey State Department of Education moved to support a "comprehensive health education and physical education" based on CDC principles (see Chapter 1). The New Jersey program design reflects these values:

- **Empower** students to make informed decisions about issues that impact their present health, the health of their family and friends, and the health of society at large.
- **Enable** students to enact health-enhancing behaviors before damaging patterns are have become firmly established.
- **Enhance** students' ability to become cautious and competent consumers.
- **Strengthen** students' ability to recognize, analyze, and react to unhealthy or dangerous situations in a safe and appropriate manner.
- **Strengthen** students' ability to focus on learning, academic achievement, and preparation for the world of work.
- **Empower** students to navigate through and around conflicting messages, risky behaviors, and mounting pressures and to develop dependable support systems.
- **Assist** students to recognize, understand, and address immediate or chronic health problems in order to prevent long-term health problems.
- **Empower** students to choose lifetime physical activities that they enjoy and in which they have confidence.
- **Enable** students to participate in lifetime activities that promote, support and maintain wellness.[8]

The department stated the rationale for these values as: "Good health is necessary for effective learning. Feeling physically and mentally healthy is essential as students face intense competition, peer and media pressure, and the stresses of daily physical, emotional, social, intellectual, and work-related activities."[9] The relationship with health and physical education is well-developed in New Jersey's Comprehensive Health and Physical Education curriculum. The curriculum standards for grade 8 illustrate this relationship. Along with major attention given to health issues, the curriculum addresses these physical education issues: motor skills; movement concepts; strategy (offensive, defensive, and cooperative strategies and their appropriate applications); sportsmanship, rules, and safety; sport psychology; fitness and physical activity; training; and achieving and assessing fitness.[10]

THE VALUES OF COMPREHENSIVE PHYSICAL EDUCATION

Current values of physical education in connection with health education reflect many of the CDC principles, in their evolution over the years. This is displayed in New Jersey's statement to "Empower students to choose lifetime physical activities that they enjoy and [in which they have] confidence."[11]

This value is again seen in physical education moving away from large group instruction to small groups supported with adequate equipment to promote participation. Good programs now encourage the success of all students in activities, lessening the role of the athletic leader. Modern approaches reduce the role of competition and grades in favor of teachers as guides, promoting cooperation among participants, and self-improvement. Self improvement is encouraged through self-evaluation, peer assessments, and skill rubrics.[12]

Physical education has had its detractors over the years. Often, these negatives attacks are attached to claims that they take time away from academic subjects and that instructional programs are elitist, as they encourage high attainment of athletic skills. The counter argument is that physical education "promotes comradeship, excitement and good health and other intrinsic and extrinsic gains."[13]

Like most areas in modern society, comprehensive physical education and health instruction are concerned with gender and race discrimination, individual lifestyles, family lifestyles and compositions, athletes as role models (and the means that mass media uses to present these models to youth), aggression and violence in society, and the role that athletics plays in endorsing these actions. Social and political issues also are also a part of modern physical education. These include environmental issues: health and injury, affordable health care, ethnicity, sporting conduct and ethical behaviors, social mobility, life changes for individuals, social planning that ensures safe participating areas for sports, and the political and economic use of sports in modern life. The Sport in History: Promises and Problems conferences address these problems within a scholarly format. [14]

Comprehensive health and physical education programs often face problems (e.g., the filtering and/or censorship of information is a common). Sexual health is an important aspect of compressive health and physical education, and cultural conflicts often lay a role in how sexual health information in is delivered. In recent years, the U.S. government has endorsed an abstinence-only approach to instruction, while Canada allows for a more comprehensive sexual education program. Depending on local preferences, sexual health education can be emphasized in either health or physical education instructional units.[15,16]

SCIENCE AND MATHEMATICS: PROVIDING DIRECTIONS FOR PHYSICAL AND HEALTH EDUCATION

Science, including mathematics, has contributed greatly to the advancement of physical education within the twentieth and 21th twenty-first centuries. Based on the training provided to teachers of physical education, we can easily see the influence of science on the modern curriculum. Biology provides an understanding of human structure and functions as well as human growth and development and how to adapt to different human circumstances. Kinesiology provides insight into the mechanics and anatomy in relation to human movement. Nutrition and its relationship to both sports performance and general health promote a healthier society. Microbiology, cell biology, immunology, and genetic studies offer the physical education curriculum and programs important for disease prevention. For example, using a microscope, Joseph J. Kinyoun—in the Laboratory of Hygiene, which he established as part of the United States Marine Hospital Service (USMHS)—isolated the organism that caused cholera. This laboratory later became the National Institute of Health (Figure 8.2).[17]

Mathematics and statistics are important means of measuring the many components of health and physical education, including food intake, drug dosages, weight measurements, temperature measurement, and blood pressure readings. Sports medicine relies on mathematics and statistics to provide diagnostic and treatments for a wide array of injuries encountered on playgrounds, gyms, and sports arenas.[18]

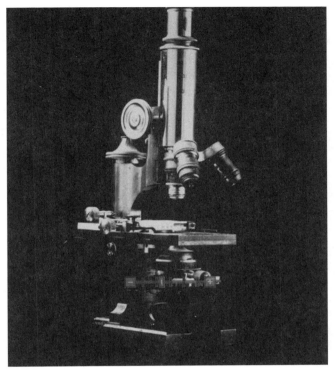

Figure 8.2.
Joseph J. Kinyoun's Zeiss microscope used to discover the organism that causes cholera in his Laboratory of Hygiene, United States Marine Hospital Service. Courtesy of the National Library of Medicine.

BASIC CONCEPT FOR ALL STUDENTS: SCIENTIFIC REASONING, SKILL SETS, AND RELATIONSHIPS

Science and Health

Scientific reasoning reflecting mathematical precision embraces all life and underpins good health and physical activities. All students must be encouraged to consider their health in terms of what good science has to offer them about healthy living. Students—no matter the age or grade—must be taught the values of science, mathematics, and the scientific methods. Good health in modern society is directly associated with good science conducted over the years. Small discoveries, such as washing one's hands, have saved millions of lives.

Scientific Reasoning and Skill Sets

Scientific reasoning is a fundamental skill that all students must acquire. Good health behaviors and attitudes of students can be increased by understanding how to apply scientific methods in everyday life. (See suggested resources in Appendix A.)

Learning Outcomes

Students will:

- Demonstrate reasoning skills by using scientific principles. The basis of the scientific method is asking questions, observing, and then trying to answer questions.
- Pose questions and that can be answered by using scientific principles in observing and recording events in the world that surrounds us.
- Find answers to questions through experimental evidence. Experimental evidence is what makes all of the observations and answers in science valid, which means truthful or confirmed. Biology for 4Kids is one resource: www.biology4kids.com/files/studies_scimethod.html.
- Formulate a research topic.
- Develop hypotheses.
- Conceptualize definitions.
- Define the role of scientific theory and conceptual models.
- Conduct research procedures (how to go about doing research).
- Gather and analyze data.
- Test and revise hypotheses or models.
- Draw conclusions and suggest more study and research.

Most students, no matter what age, can understand many if not most of these concepts. The following are some suggestions that are designed to show the close relationship between health and science and the scientific method.

Questions and/or Activities (Adjust for Age and Abilities)

For Older Students

- Have students research and define scientific theory. Have students discuss what scientists mean when they use the term "theory." Encourage students to observe how theory is used differently by many people who are not scientists.
- Ask students to define and explain the differences between a scientific theory and a scientific law.
- Have students define scientific hypothesis and how it differs from a scientific theory.
- Introduce or review the concept of evolution. Have students research how evolutionary concepts are used in medical research, development of new medicines, and the identification and control of diseases.
- Ask students to define genetics. Have students research how DNA has advanced genetic research.
- Ask students to define microbiology and explain how evolutionary theory is the fundamental base of microbiology.
- Encourage students to consider how microbiology often leads to new medicines.
- Ask students to research food contaminations that often cause serious illnesses and explain how microbiology helps identify and prevents the spread of contaminated foods.
- Ask students to define the differences between viruses and bacteria.
- Have students define the immune system and explain why microorganisms can harm the person with a damaged immune system.

For Younger Students

Introduce the process of scientific inquiry by discussing how scientists learn new things that can help people remain healthy. Make sure that students understand these terms and can define them and how they are used in science: asking questions, observing, finding answers through experiments, and reasoning based on evidence.

- Introduce students to basic science inquiry skills of asking questions and making observations. Introduce the five senses: seeing, hearing, touching, smelling, and tasting. Have them define and discuss the five senses and how those can be used in scientific research. Introduce these instruments: magnifying lens, microscope, ruler, thermometer, scale, balance, or stopwatch. Have students discuss how these are used in scientific research.
- Introduce the concept of taking notes as an important part of scientific research. Introduce how scientists record their observations by taking notes and making charts and graphs.
- Have students select an object, such as an apple, as an experiment. Remind them to use their five senses in this experience. Have them describe it. Remind them to consider color, size, and shape and its different parts. Ask students if it has a smell. Ask them to describe, compare, and discuss how the smell is different from other fruits, such as an orange or a banana. Ask students to describe how an apple differs from a flower. Encourage students to touch it and describe its weight and texture. Ask students if an apple has a sound. Have students take a bite from an apple. Ask them if they hear the apple make a sound? What kind of sounds do they hear? Have your students discuss how an apple tastes and compare that with other students' observations. Ask students to think of other ways to describe an apple. Remind students to be safe and careful with foods and to eat and taste only safe foods.[19]
- Introduce the concept of energy and food and that all living things need food for energy and life. Discuss how the sun produces both food and energy. Introduce the concepts of food chains. Indicate that animals in the food chains rely on each other for food and energy. Introduce the concept of predators and prey. Describe a predator as a living thing that hunts and eats animals and prey as animal eaten by a predator. Have students discuss why it is necessary to have predators and prey. Have students consider what might happen if there were no predators that preyed on rats. Have students discuss what might be in a food chain in their area. Have them discuss and describe the food chain relationships of plants, insects, birds, cats, and foxes or coyotes. Have them make a paper food chain. Introduce the killer whale and have students discuss what it preys on. Ask students to consider why the killer whale is at the top of the oceans' food chains.[20]

MATHEMATICS, STATISTICS AND HEALTH: A BRIEF OVERVIEW

As mentioned, a basic understanding of mathematics and statistics is necessary for good health and the understanding behaviors necessary for healthy living. National standards in most English-speaking countries are consistently uniform in what they consider necessary for mastery of basic mathematical concepts. Rightly so, these standards show a progression of mathematical skills, beginning with the earliest grades. All these play important roles in health care and disease control. In 1977, Davis and Peart noted the following skills as essential mathematical concepts for health care personnel.[21] Likewise, these skills are necessary for all students in maintaining healthy living:

- The expression of numbers as figures and words
- Addition, subtraction, multiplication, and division of whole numbers, fractions, and decimals
- Ratios and proportions
- Percents
- Measurement
- Roman numerals

- Word problems that reinforce student learning and demonstrate the applicability of the mathematical concept to situations encountered in allied health

In 1996, Hayden, Howard, and Davis added these: system of measurements, organizing and reporting statistical data, and using the computer.[22] In 2005, in her listings, Summers included knowledge of "gauges, medications, intravenous solutions, and other emulsions."[23] As we just noted, many if not all of these concepts are fundamental to all students as they seek to maintain a healthy lifestyle.

UNESCO provides the following list of skills for mathematics as related to health across the curriculum. Some of these concepts have been modified to make them broader in social and cultural settings than implied by UNESCO.

Concept: Body Measurements

- Measuring the body (height, arms, weight)
- Charting the body through graphs and models (age, weight, height)

Concept: Water and Liquids Measurements

- Measuring liquids (water containers, distances from supply sources)
- Using statistics and graphs showing water consumption
- Determining the cost of water

Concept: Nutrition

- Reading nutrition labels, charts, and directions and knowing how to make food selections based on good judgments and decision-making skills (Figure 8.3)

Figure 8.3.
"Make Healthy Choices." Observational skills and informed decisions about food choices is fundamental to good health. Line drawing by Richard H. Hendler based on an image from the U.S. Department of Agriculture. Courtesy of the USDA.

Concept: Medicine, Diseases, and Immunization

• Reading and understanding charts showing health and mortality demographics
• Understanding medical dosages (metric notations)
• Conduct surveys and display data concerning health issues
• Comparison of local health data with national data
• Using mathematics to chart the spread of specific diseases (e.g., AIDS)

Concept: Population, Resources, and Health

• Comparison of family data with national data
• Comparison of population growth and local land use and expansion
• Understanding how to find and read national population statistical growth
• Making mathematically based predictions about population growth and resources
• Understanding how to find and use percentages to illustrate growth rates

Learning Outcomes (Adjust for Age and Abilities)

Students will:

• Measure body heights and express those in metric and other forms of measurements.
• Find and use electronic charts that will convert measurements.
• Prepare and discuss measurement charts and graphs.
• Define and describe measurements of central tendencies: mean, medium, and mode.
• Explain and use central tendency statistics to show how natural resources are used (e.g., water use expressed by mean, medium, and mode).
• Calculate the cost of natural resources use per family or individual for a given time period (e.g., how much does it cost for an individual to use water for a week).
• Define and explain directions for mixing prepared food for use.
• Define and explain the directions for taking medicine in terms of dosages and time period for taking dosages.
• Conduct and discuss a survey of recent class illnesses and express those in various mathematic concepts: percentage, ratios, and proportions.
• Compile national data and compare with local surveys or existing data. Discuss those findings using appropriate mathematical concepts.
• Find and discuss statistics that show the spread of AIDS in selected countries.
• Find and explain local data, and show the spread of land use for a given period of time. Compare this with population growth.
• Find and explain national data on populations. Express those population findings in terms of percentages.

Questions and/or Activities (Adjust for Age and Abilities)

For Older Students

• Research these health agencies: the U.S. Centers for Disease Control and Prevention, Health Canada, the Department of Health (Great Britain), and the Federal Ministry of Health Australia. Find their Web sites and critique the kinds of health statistic found there.
• Define health demographics.

- How many people die of heart disease in the United States, Canada, and the United Kingdom? Compile and discuss sources for these statistics.
- Find statistical data and show how many people have died of AIDS in the United Kingdom and Canada for a given period of time. Compare these with U.S. figures.
- Discuss and explain how governments trace the spread of diseases. Discuss where we can find information about new diseases expressed in numbers? What kinds of numerical expressions are generally used? How easily read and understood is this information?

For Younger Students

- Help students understand the concepts of observation and measurements, especially as related to nutrition.
- Explain the concept of estimation to younger children. Explain the concept of circumference. Have students estimate their own upper arm circumference and those of their classmates. Have students compare their findings with each other. Have students then measure their own arms with a tape measure and compare their estimations with their actual measurements. Explain that measurements can be expressed in inches or centimeters.
- Explain a health record to younger children. Have the class discuss what they would want included in a health record. Make sure they include some basic mathematical concepts (e.g., weight and height). Have students record the age, height, and weight of family members and/ or friends and list those in their health records. Discuss with and ask students to explain the health reasons for measuring and recording the height, age, and weight of people.

Figure 8.4.
"How Much Is Too Much Salt?" Good nutrition requires the ability to observe and measure. Line drawing by Richard H. Hendler from an illustration in the History of Medicine Collection, National Library of Medicine. Courtesy of the Library.

TEXTBOOKS IN PHYSICAL EDUCATION AND HEALTH: A RATIONALE

Textbooks play an important role in health instruction in all levels of instruction. Figure 8.5 shows students exploring textbook pages concerning parasitology in a biology class conducted by the Department of Defense (DoD).

Building on our discussion in Chapter 3, textbook selection requires a tremendous amount of time and effort. In the United States, 20 states make their selections on a statewide basis, meaning that once textbooks are selected, all public schools within the state must select from the approved lists. The Ontario province in Canada follows a similar approach,[24] but for the most part, Canadian provinces leave textbook selection to local schools.[25]

Texas, California, and Florida are important states that make statewide selections. Because they purchase huge quantities of textbooks and textbook writers follow the lead of educators in those states, their selections influence school textbook adoptions all over the United States. In recent decades, the state selection of textbooks has become a political process where differing values are often hotly contested.

This is especially true in health where sexuality information has a natural home. The inclusion of family and individual lifestyles, such as same sex families, single parents, and adoption by single persons, have increased as social and political issues have found

Figure 8.5.
Textbook and microscope in use in a military biology class. Courtesy of the National Library of Medicine.

their ways into health textbooks. The teaching of evolution as a scientific theory is another seminal controversial issue in textbook selection.[26,27]

Often, instruction in health and physical education is tied to textbooks. Understanding the role and contents of textbooks is important for school librarians. Limited resources for materials often tie teachers to textbooks, and school librarians need to know the textbooks in use, as textbooks influence the focus that instruction will take. School librarians can use resources suggested in textbooks and the contents of textbooks for collection development and collaborative teaching with classroom teachers. Finally, good, modern textbooks reflect major trends and issues facing youth in health and physical development.

The following overview of adopted textbooks used both in the United States and Canada will help the school library understand the emphasized content of North American health and physical education. Textbooks reflect expected curriculum goals and content, as outlined by states, provinces, and national standards.

Recent examples of textbooks that have been widely adopted for use in North American schools are found in Appendix B of this book. These titles were selected originally from the Texas Instructional Materials Current Adoption Bulletin and the Ontario Ministry of Education's Trillium List. The titles were reviewed against other lists of adopted textbooks to ascertain a commonality of selection. These lists included those from the Baltimore City Schools and the states of Indiana, North Carolina, and Mississippi. Mississippi offers a very user-friendly listing with good search tools.[28] Textbook titles listed in Appendix B, for the most part, come from publisher descriptions because these descriptions highlight the marketing techniques used to promote these products, and they illustrate the close relationship that the texts have to current national, provincial, and state standards. Furthermore, descriptions of content and the instructional approaches offer school librarians new ways of fostering collaborative teaching activities in health and physical education.

One of the fundamental expectations of school librarians is to enhance learning in as many ways as possible. Collaboration is one that can fit nicely into physical and health instruction. A brief review of publishers' descriptions of their textbooks offers many avenues for collaboration and collection development. As we examined these selected textbooks, we developed the following list of contents that seems common in modern physical education and health education textbooks:

- Career planning
- Character education
- Communication skills
- Critical thinking skills
- Cultural diversity (multiculturalism)
- Decision-making and goal-setting
- Drug and substance abuse
- Ethics
- Exercise and exercise management
- Family health and family lifecycles
- Family roles and expectations in modern society
- Information technology
- Leadership
- Legal issues and responsibilities
- Learning life skills within a real-life context
- Mass media and health
- Medical terminology and language structures
- Participation in sports and recreation
- Personal asset recognition and management
- Risk assessment and management
- Safety
- Standards of health care practices
- Tolerance
- Violence and bullying

REVIEW OF HEALTH AND PHYSICAL EDUCATION LESSONS PLANS

Health and physical education instructors have produced a tremendous amount of curriculum guides, lesson plans, and materials over the years. Fortunately, the development of the Internet has made these materials widely accessible. The extent of such materials is so vast that this chapter will only attempt to selectively list and describe some of these in order to provide an overview of curriculum approaches available.

American Dental Association. Smile Smarts Oral Health Curriculum.
This oral health curriculum for grades K–8 grade offers modular lessons plans, support materials, hands-on demonstrations, and student activities to improve awareness of dental health. This curriculum is inclusive offering activities, resources, and background information for the teacher. Available at www.ada.org/public/education/teachers/smilesmarts/index.asp.

Education Development Center Inc. (EDC).
"EDC is a global nonprofit organization that designs, delivers and evaluates innovative programs to address some of the world's most urgent challenges in education, health, and economic opportunity." Its health and human development programs include Teenage Health Teaching Modules (THTM), which offer a "comprehensive health curriculum for grades 6 to 12." Available at www.thtm.org.

Edmund J. Sass. Health, Nutrition, P.E., and Sexuality Education.
Site contains access listings to lesson plans for a variety of health and physical education topics. Includes units such as Germs Everywhere, Examining Ideas About Body Image for grades 6–8, and Surgeon General's Report for grades 9–12, based on national physical education and health standards. Available at www.cloudnet.com/~edrbsass/edpe.htm.

EL Paso Collaborative Health Literacy Curriculum.
Although not specifically developed for youth, these health lessons strive for inclusiveness to help meet health concerns throughout communities. Units include diabetes, breast health, menopause, lead poisoning, household hazards, and nutrition. Teaching resources are provided within each unit. Available at healthliteracy.worlded.org/docs/elpaso.

ERIC. The Educator's Reference Desk. Lessons Plans.
Contains detailed lessons plans in most areas of the curriculum supported by teachers, including health and physical education. Examples of plans in health include body systems, family life, mental health, and safety. Available at www.eduref.org/cgi-bin/lessons.cgi/Health.

Massachusetts University. Massachusetts Worker Education Roundtable.
"The Massachusetts Worker Education Roundtable is a network of worker education programs dedicated to promoting partnerships of employers, unions and educators that provide high quality education as well as training for Massachusetts union members." While focused on adult workers, his curriculum helps teenagers contribute to a healthy work environment. Available at www.umass.edu/roundtable/projects/Health-Safety-ESOL.pdf.

Joe Paslov. Physical Education Lesson Plan Page.
A site "dedicated to providing a space for physical education teachers to share lesson ideas." Units include swim lessons, presidential tests, volleyball, kickball, blind game, and team handball. Available at pazz.tripod.com/lesson.html.

PE Central. The Web Site for Health and Physical Education Teachers.
"PE Central exists to assist teachers, parents, and others who work with youngsters to guide them in the process of becoming physically active and healthy for a lifetime." Detailed lesson plans and resources are offered to teachers. Content includes balancing, body awareness, fitness,

cooperative learning, and dance. Lesson plans are available at www.pecentral.org/lessonideas/
pelessonplans.html.

P.E.links4u. Teaching Unit Plans. Central Washington University.

Offers outline units created by physical educator majors and minors at Central Washington
University. Although varying in quality, the site offers references for further development. Units
include archery, football, golf, rafting, and skiing. Available at www.pelinks4u.org/links/
unitplans.shtml.

teAchnology. The Online Teacher Resource.

"Provides a wide array of teaching support for teachers in all areas of the curriculum. Some 28,500
lesson plans are available including those for physical education." Available at www.teach
-nology.com.

United Nations CyberSchoolBus. Fighting Disease: Health at the End of the Millennium.

Offers information about some of the world's most prevalent diseases and provides a detailed
instructional unit on how to combat infectious diseases. Available at www.un.org/cyberschool
bus/special/health/index.html.

United States. Centers for Disease Control and Prevention. Healthy Youth!

This curriculum is designed to help schools "conduct a clear, complete, and consistent analysis of health education curricula based on the National Health Education Curricula." Curriculum
modules include alcohol and other drugs; healthy eating, mental and emotional health; personal
health and wellness; physical activity; safety; sexual health; tobacco, violence prevention. Each
module offers specific instructional guidance for presenting information. New topics are added
regularly. Available at www.cdc.gov/healthyyouth/HECAT/index.htm.

**United States. Department of Health and Human Services. Administration for Children and
Families. Head Start Dental Health Curriculum.**

Developed by the Charlottesville City Schools Adult Education Program, this curriculum for
young children in Head Start programs covers such items as visiting the dentist, awareness of the
mouth, importance of keeping teen and gums clean, and tooth brushing. Available at
www.bmcc.org/Headstart/Dental.

**United States. Department of Health and Human Services. Health Resources and Services
Administration. Health Education Curriculum.**

This curriculum guide (a part of Adopt-A-Curriculum) is designed to expose students to
careers in health care, with an added focus of helping to prevent dropout, encourage health career
education, and recognize the importance of personal discipline in drug prevention. Content
includes effective communication, observations, journal-keeping, and cultural competence.
Available at bhpr.hrsa.gov/adoptaschool.

United States. National Institute Health. Curriculum Supplement Series.

Provides teacher guides to lessons on the science behind health issues. Includes methods on
how to integrate biomedical discoveries with instructional methods. Sponsored by the Institute's
Office of Scientific Education. Guides are available for elementary, middle, and high schools.
Available at science-education.nih.gov/customers.nsf/WebPages/CSHome.

**University of Texas Health Science Center at San Antonio. The Teacher Enrichment Initia-
tives (TEI).**

The Teacher Enrichment Initiatives (TEI), discussed in Chapter 3, is a partnership between
UTHSCSA researchers and health professionals and San Antonio–area school teachers involving
the development of health science curricula. The initiatives provide "curriculum that enhances
teacher content knowledge through carefully researched background pieces, in depth health science content based upon current biomedical research, [and] inquiry investigations and discrepant
experiences for students." Available at teachhealthk-12.uthscsa.edu.

Utah Education Network. Health Education.

This is a consortium of Utah public education partners, including the Utah State Library. Among its activities is the development of curriculum in a wide variety of areas, including health. Detailed lesson plans are offered, including appropriate links. Available at www.uen.org/core/health/index.shtml.

RESOURCES

Resources for science, mathematics, statistics, and physical education, including health, are listed with annotations in Appendix A. Selected health and physical education textbooks are listed and described in Appendix B.

REFLECTIONS

As we see from this discussion, health instruction comes in many curricula and in many formats. Along with trade books, textbooks and Internet sources offer teachers and school librarians a wealth of ideas and avenues for collaboration. Other disciplines found in the social sciences, such as sociology, history, and community development, further enhance the richness of comprehensive health and physical education. Social psychology has increased our understanding of how physical education and health programs help us in understanding the role of sports in human societies and the role of health throughout life.

NOTES

1. Von Staden, Heinrich. "Health." In *Encyclopedia of Ancient Greece*. Ed. by Nigel Guy Wilson, pp. 337–338. New York: Rutledge, 2006.

2. Von Staden, Heinrich. "Health."

3. "Fitness Focus: A Brief History of Physical Education." www.lakeviewjhs.net/pe/fitness7/q4_1.pdf. Assessed Feb. 23, 2009.

4. Welch, Paula. "Dio Lewis Normal Institute for Physical Education," *The Journal of Physical Education, Recreation & Dance*, 65 (March 1, 1994) 29 (3). http://find.galegroup.com.ezproxy.lib.utexas.edu/gtx/infomark.do?&contentSet=IAC-Documents&type=retrieve&tabID=T002&prodId=AONE&docId=A15414913&source=gale&srcprod=AONE&userGroupName=txshracd2598&version=1.0. Accessed March 9, 2010.

5. "Physical Education" psychology.wikia.com/wiki/Physical education. Accessed Feb. 24, 2009.

6. CDC. "Current Trends: The Effectiveness of School Health Education." September 26, 1986. www.cdc.gov/mmwr/preview/mmwrhtml/00000796.htm. Accessed Feb. 25, 2009.

7. CDC. "Healthy Youth! Coordinated School Health Program." www.cdc.gov/healthyyouth/CSHP. Accessed March 8, 2009.

8. New Jersey State Department of Education. Comprehensive Health Education and Physical Education Curriculum Framework, Summer 1999. www.state.nj.us/education/frameworks/chpe. Accessed Nov. 26, 2009.

9. New Jersey State Department of Education. Quoting Marx, E., Wooley, S., and Northrup, D. *Health Is Academic: A Guide to Coordinated School Health*. Columbia

University, Teachers College Press, 1998. University of Texas Health Science Center at San Antonio www.state.nj.us/education/frameworks/chpe. Accessed Nov. 26, 2009.

10. *New Jersey Core Curriculum Content Standards for Comprehensive Health and Physical Education Grade 8. Teen Health Course 3*. 2005. www.glencoe.com/correlations/PDFs/0565NJ.pdf. Accessed Nov. 27, 2008.

11. New Jersey State Department of Education. *Curriculum Framework*.

12. "History of Physical Education: Now and Then." people.dbq.edu/students/jveach/images/PEPP%20pack/History%20of%20Physical%20Education.ppt. Assessed Feb. 25, 2009.

13. "History of Physical Education: Now and Then."

14. "Sport in History: Promises and Problems." http://intelevents.athollsweb.co.uk/index.php; http://www.sports.stir.ac.uk/research/conferences/index.php. Accessed March 8, 2010.

15. *Abstinence Education: Assessing the Accuracy and Effectiveness of Federally Funded Programs. Testimony Before the Committee on Oversight and Government Reform, House of Representatives*. Washington, D.C. U.S. Government Accountability Office, 2008.

16. Public Health Agency of Canada. *Canadian Guidelines for Sexual Health Education*. Rev. ed. Ottawa, Ontario: Ministry of Health, 2008. Note: A 2009 revision is projected by the publisher.

17. Roberts, William Clifford. "Facts and Ideas from Anywhere." www.ncbi.nlm.nih.gov/pmc/articles/PMC1200677. Accessed Oct. 25, 2009.

18. RMIT University. "Program Guide, Bachelor of Applied Science (Physical Education)." rmit.net.au/browse;ID=BP041. Accessed March 21, 2010.

19. "Making Observations." www.brainpopjr.com/science/scienceskills/makingobservations/grownups.weml. Accessed March 9, 2010.

20. "Food Chain: Background Information and Activities." www.brainpopjr.com/science/animals/foodchain/grownups.weml. Accessed Feb. 25, 2009.

21. Davis, Kathryn, and Pamela Peart. "Personal Achievement Mathematics: Health Occupations." Unpublished paper. Cedar Rapids, IA: Kirkwood Community College, 1977. ED 194 167.

22. Hayden, Jerome D. and T. Howard, and H. T. Davis. *Fundamental Mathematics for Health Careers*. 3rd. ed. Albany, N.Y.: Delmar Publishers, 1996.

23. Simmers, Louise. *Practical Problems in Mathematics for Health Occupations*, 2nd ed. Clifton Park, N.Y.: Thomson Delmar Learning, 2005.

24. Ontario Ministry of Education. "Guidelines for Approval of Textbooks," 2006. www.edu.gov.on.ca/trilliumlist/guide.pdf. Accessed Feb. 24, 2006.

25. Thomas, Doug. "Textbook Selection: Censorship or Citizenship?" HumanistNetworkNews.org. May 14, 2008. americanhumanist.org/hnn/archives/index.php?id=348&article=3. Accessed Feb. 26, 2009.

26. Barna, Joel. *The Texas Textbook Controversy*. Austin, Tex.: House Study Group, 1984.

27. Cline, Austin. "Norma Gabler, Textbook Censor: 1923–2007." Friday August 3, 2007. atheism.about.com/b/2007/08/03/norma-gabler-textbook-censor-1923-2007.htm. Accessed Feb. 24, 2009.

28. "Texas Instructional Materials Current Adoption Bulletin." ritter.tea.state.tx.us/textbooks/materials/bulletin/programs.pdf; the Ontario Ministry of Education Trillium List (www.curriculum.org/occ/trillium/index.shtml); Baltimore City Schools (www.boarddocs.com/mabe/bcpss/Board.nsf/. . ./$FILE); Indiana (www.doe.in.gov/olr/textbook/welcome.html); North Carolina www .ncpublicschools.org/textbook/adopted; Mississippi (www.schoolbook-ms.com/ catalogs/data/MS-Cat4.pdf). Accessed March 3, 2009.

9

Globalization, Instruction, and Youth Health

WHAT IS GLOBALIZATION?

Globalization offers many ways to integrate health education throughout the curriculum. The word itself encompasses economic, environmental, political, and cultural aspects of life.[1] This definition reflects much of the modern school curriculum and instruction. For example, globalization has natural homes in cultural studies such as literature and foreign languages as well as in science and mathematics, social sciences (including history, geography, and civics), psychology, sociology, business, economics, human ecology (home economics), and technology education (formerly industrial arts).

Some authorities see globalization as a continuing process rather than a finished product. Overall, it involves and engages the world through a variety of concepts, including:[2]

- Economic and commercial links and processes
- Technological changes, such as communications and computerizations
- Global infrastructure developments, such as international organizations and justice systems
- Cultural developments, including the sharing of cultural values as well as conflicts in cultural values
- Development of a global citizenship where the care of the world is viewed as everyone and every country's responsibility
- Awareness of inequality and inclusion in income and resources and how to include more people and countries in the world's resources
- Leadership and globalization both at local, national, and international levels, including businesses, consumers of goods, competitions, investments, labor, and ethics

In terms of health, globalization involves:

- Nutrition, causing both hunger and obesity
- Climate changes affecting health
- Transportation policies
- Poverty and inequality
- Working conditions, labor relations, and health
- Population movements and health
- Women's health
- Children's health
- Entrepreneurship

YOUTH IN A GLOBALIZED WORLD

Today's youth, no matter where they might live, exist in a complex world different from previous generations. This world requires increased levels of skills and development, including physical and cognitive skills, the acquisition of knowledge, and the acquiring of positive values, attitudes, and beliefs. Experts generally contend that youth are at optional ages for this learning and development.[3]

Certainly, variations in schooling exist throughout the world. This is especially true for secondary education, where attendance and enrollment levels fall and where we see a widening gap in education attainment between males and females and among different countries. School is important to and is positively associated with young people's health. As we have noted in earlier chapters, skill-based school health programs endorsed by UNESCO promote healthy youth. Together with supporting school-based health education, globalization requires:

- Attention to school quality
- Addressing the needs of the poor
- Increasing school enrollments and lowering dropout rates sing the needs of the poor
- Ensuring gender equality in education and in the individual classroom
- Reaching more students with health intervention strategies and health information

Additionally and in concert with these, youth at all ages need to be given opportunities to learn decision-making skills and be allowed to take part in decisions and events that will affect their lives, education, and health.

TEACHING GLOBALIZATION AND HEALTH: A FUNDAMENTAL RELATIONSHIP

Globalization in terms of health is a cultural process. Often, this involves conflicting values and expectations about health information, health management and care, and social and political responsibilities. Systematic health instruction and information provided within their school environment is one of the important means of helping youth of all ages better understand these cultural dynamics and how they as individuals and as citizens can live better within the context of change. Figure 9.1 visually illustrates the concept of health being a worldwide concern in our changing and dynamic world.

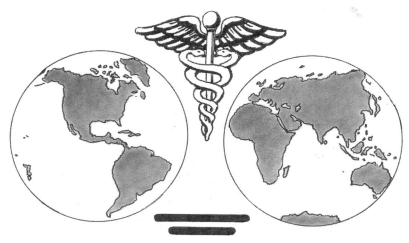

Figure 9.1.
Health is a worldwide concern in times of change. Line drawing by Richard H. Hendler.

GLOBALIZATION THEMES

The following 12 themes suggest the wide impact of globalization on health instruction and information.[4] From this list, we have prepared a number of instructional units to help teach the impact of globalization on health. These themes and units cross most curriculum areas and can be used in a variety of instructional settings already discussed in other chapters.

Theme 1: Food and Water

- Food trade
- Food systems
- Consumption of animal fats
- Sweets and sugars
- Animals as food sources
- Water purity and supply
- Food security
- Role of women in food security

Theme 2. Climate and Weather Changes

- Diseases influenced by climate and weather
- Environmental changes because of climate and weather

Theme 3. Ecological Changes

- Land clearance
- Deforestation

Theme 4. Populations and Migrations

- Population displacements
- Refuges and displacements
- Urbanization and health
- Rural-to-urban immigration
- Migration and developed countries
- Women, health, and migration

Theme 5. Diseases

- Infectious diseases
- New emergent infections

Theme 6. Medical Care, Interventions, and Public Health

- Pharmacological interventions
- Tobacco regulations and advertisements
- Transnational tobacco industry and its global impact
- World Health Organization (WHO) and tobacco
- Tobacco and politics
- Caregivers
- Measurements and assessment for health care and improvements
- Intellectual property rights, medical care, and globalization.

Theme 7. Information and Communication Technology

- Communication and the Internet
- Delivery of medical services and information
- Geographic technology and linking information about individuals and infections
- Communicating health information

Theme 8. Travel and Transportation

- Automobile culture and health (pollution, climate change, accidents, rural-urban displacements)
- Transporting of goods and diseases

Theme 9. Justice and Litigation Systems

- Access to courts and legal advocates
- Human rights

Theme 10. Labor and Work

- Labor, work, and the influences of globalization (migrant workers)
- Occupational diseases
- Health and unemployment

- Labor standards and laws
- Commerce and health

Theme 11. Governments and Health Policies

- Local, state, and national governments and health policies
- How governments promote good health behaviors (see Figures 9.2 and 9.3)
- The role of international organizations in promoting health
- Costs, profits, and investments in markets
- Business responsibilities and ethics

Figure 9.2.
Public health information campaign on preventing diseases, United States Agency for International Development, South Pacific Commission, New Caledonia, 1987. Courtesy of the U.S. Agency for International Development.

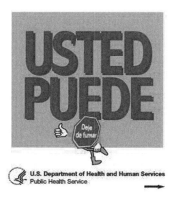

Figure 9.3.
Government warnings in Spanish about the dangers of smoking. Courtesy of the U.S. Department of Health and Human Services, Public Health Service.

Theme 12. Market Demands

- Market identification and cultivation
- Profit motivation
- Investment strategies
- Social and culture values and marketing approaches
- Developing of products for emerging markets
- Product development and protection of products rights
- Advertising strategies
- Social values and development of marketing
- Impact of local environments resulting from marketing and product distribution

GLOBALIZATION, HEALTH INFORMATION, AND INSTRUCTION: SOME EXAMPLES

Technology Education

Technology education (formerly industrial arts) is necessary in understanding globalization because it helps to integrate science, technology, engineering, mathematics, and health education. It is based on "problem solving learning activities,especially for middle and high school students."[5] The Standards for Technology Literacy for technology education are closely connected to globalization through the study of environmental issues, agriculture, energy, fuel consumption and use, power, and transportation and motor vehicles.[6,7] Many other aspects of globalization allow students to consider health in relationship to core elements of technology. See Chapter 8 for suggestions on how it can be taught in relationship to health, science, and mathematics. Useful lesson plans are also available at:

Discovery Education: school.discoveryeducation.com/lessonplans/tech.html
Thirteen Ed Online: www.thirteen.org/edonline/lessons/index_tech.html

Agriculture Education

Agriculture education is broad-based and can be well-integrated into health education and globalization studies. Agricultural studies augments mathematics and science, rural sociology and psychology, medicine and health care delivery in rural and remote areas, rural community development and outreach, labor management and use, immigration policies, governances, economics, and other aspects of globalization.[8] Lesson plans are available at:

The U.S. Department of Agriculture: www.usda.gov/wps/portal/!ut/p/_s.7_0_A/7_0_1OB?navtype
    =SU&navid=EDUCATION_OUTREACH
Oregon Agriculture in the Classroom Foundation: aitc.oregonstate.edu/resources/lesson.htm (for
    related lesson suggestions on health and economics)

See also Chapters 7, 8, and 10.

Economics Education

Economics education study is another broad area that affects health education and globalization. The Economics Department at the University of Texas at Austin says:

"Economics trains students to think objectively and independently about a wide range of economic issues and problems, giving them insights that will serve them as individuals and citizens."[9] The Council on Economic Education's national standards[10] for K–12 students include the following areas of study:

- Scarcity
- Marginal cost/benefit
- Allocation of goods and services
- Role of incentives
- Gain from trade
- Specialization and trade
- Markets: price and quantity determination
- Role of price in market systems
- Role of competition
- Role of economic institutions
- Role of money
- Role of interest rates
- Role of resources in determining income
- Profit and the entrepreneur
- Growth investment in factories, machinery, new technology, and in the health, education, and training of people can raise future standards of living
- Role of government
- Using cost/benefit analysis to evaluate government programs
- Macroeconomy income/employment, unemployment, and inflation
- Monetary and fiscal policy

Lesson plans for each of these standards are available at the Council on Economic Education at www.councilforeconed.org/ea/standards.

Many if not all of these standards involve globalization and can be easily modified to discuss health issues. Other concepts relating to economics and health are found in Chapters 7, 8, and 10.

Human Ecology (Home Economics)

Human ecology has many attributes and goals, ranging from home management to health, which can be directly applied to globalization and health instruction. This content involves personal development, family relationship and life skills, healthy and safe foods, nutrition, healthy living, healthy food choices, child development, financial literacy, consumerism, and resource management.[11] Such skills address problems associated with globalization and individual responsibilities for improving personal and world health. Human ecology lessons plans are available at: Communities and Schools Promoting Health: www.safehealthyschools.org/family_studies/family_studies_gateway _table.htm; LessonPlanet: www.lessonplanet.com. See Chapters 7, 8, and 10 for additional ways that human ecology supports health instruction.

Selected Instructional Thematic Procedures

The following selective instructional procedures are based on some of the themes listed previously as well as appropriate content areas just discussed. These units first present general learning outcomes, followed by specific instructional goals and procedures for both older and younger students. Because both older and younger students can study globalization concepts jointly, selected units combine instructional suggestions. Other units, based on concepts, are separated into younger and older student categories. This arrangement will allow instructors to make selections based on the characteristics of their classes.

Themes and Procedures

1. Food and Water

Learning Outcomes

Students will:

- Demonstrate knowledge of basic terms, concepts, and data related to food and water and global health issues.
- Demonstrate knowledge of the world's food trade.
- Identify major food systems that serve people around the world.
- Identify problems with impure water systems around the world and make suggestions as how water can be made safe for cooking and drinking.
- Identify problems associated with the consumption of too much animal fat, sweets, and sugars.
- Consider animals as food sources around the world.
- Define food security and water security.
- Explain the role of men and women in food security.

Questions and/or Activities (Adjust According to Age and Abilities)

For Older Students

- Begin this unit by having students identify these terms: marketing strategies and promotion techniques, food security and water security, food systems, government policies, and gender and gender roles.
- Have students investigate how governmental policies made in developed countries, such as the United States, Canada, and European countries, affect the food trade and water standards.
- Ask students to consider the mechanics that both help and hinder the marketing of food to and from developing countries.
- Encourage students to consider the impact of western marketing strategies and techniques that both discourage and promote good attitudes and behaviors about food and water (e.g., the marketing of baby milk formula to African mothers, the influence of fast food in both developed and developing countries.) Have students research and explain major waterborne diseases and discuss standard promotional and educational strategies designed to eliminate or lessen the affects of the diseases.
- Ask students to explain how climate changes in the next 20 years are likely to affect food and water supplies around the world.
- Have students select two countries to research and explain how they are or can be fostering cross-border communication related to food and water availability.
- Have students consider alternatives to animals as food sources. Ask students to explain why animals and fish have become such as important sources of food for people around the world.
- Students need to be aware of diet as a health behavior. Have students research and explain medically why consuming too much animal fat, sugar, and sweets is not a good health behavior.

- Have students research traditional roles that men and women have historically played in food and water security. Ask students to consider whether these roles are changing or need to change.

For Younger Students

- Help students define and understand the concept of food trade and food systems. Encourage students to identify people who are involved in the food trade in communities. Make a chart of food providers in their community and have them consider how these food providers help bring food to their families. Introduce the idea of a farmer's market or flea market and explain the role that farmers play in a local farmer's market. Introduce the concept of small shopkeepers in such various countries. Have students discuss how similar these providers are to those in their own communities and how they all are a part of the world food trade and food systems.
- Introduce the role that both men and women play in helping provide food in countries around the world. Be sure to help students consider how women in poorer countries help provide food for their families.
- Introduce the concept of clean water and how clean water is necessary for good health. Explain how boiling water makes water safe for drinking and cooking. Introduce the concept that in some areas of some countries, water is not always safe to use for cooking or drinking. Introduce some programs that are helping to bring clean water to these countries. These programs can include:
  - Cooperative Housing Foundation (CHF) www.chfinternational.org/water)
  - Deep Springs International (deepspringsinternational.org); and the International Medical Corps (www.imcworldwide.org/Page.aspx?pid=183)
- Locate countries that are especially suffering from poor water security and ask students to compare these countries with water security in their own cities, towns, states, and provinces. Lesson plans centering on water security are available at World Wise Schools: Water in Africa (www.peacecorp.gov/wws/educators/enrichment/africa/lessons/byarea.html).
- Help students consider how their local communities keep water safe for use. Some discussion points that cause bad water in their local communities can include:
  - Leaves and grass clippings
  - Swimming pool chemicals
  - Hazardous chemicals
  - Soaps and detergents
  - Trash and litter
  - Animal and human waste
  - Dirt
  - Oil and other chemicals from cars
  - Air pollution from cars
  - Pesticides and fertilizers

2. Climate and Weather Changes

Learning Outcomes

Students will:

- Demonstrate knowledge of basic terms, concepts, and data related to climate and weather changes.
- Demonstrate knowledge of climate changes throughout the world.

- Identify major examples of climate changes.
- Identify health problems affected by climate changes.
- Explain the roles of governments and industry in affecting climate changes.
- Identify ways that climate and weather changes affect populations and population migration.
- Demonstrate how ecological systems are affected by climate changes.
- Identify diseases that are directly caused by climate changes or are exuberated by climate changes.

Questions and/or Activities (Adjust According to Age and Abilities)

For Older Students

- Have students define public health security and how this is related to climate change.
- Have students research and describe some of the key concepts listed below that are associated with climate change:
  o **Aerosols:** Solid or liquid particles suspended within the atmosphere
  o **Carbon dioxide (CO_2):** CO_2 is a colorless, odorless, nonpoisonous gas that is a normal part of the ambient air. Of the six greenhouse gases normally targeted, CO_2 contributes the most to human-induced global warming. Human activities such as fossil fuel combustion and deforestation have increased atmospheric concentrations of CO_2 by approximately 30 percent since the industrial revolution. CO_2 is the standard used to determine the "global warming potentials" (GWPs) of other gases. CO_2 has been assigned a 100-year GWP of 1 (i.e., the warming effects over a 100-year timeframe relative to other gases).
  o **Climate:** The long-term average weather of a region, including typical weather patterns, the frequency and intensity of storms, cold spells, and heat waves. Climate is not the same as weather.
  o **Ecosystem:** A community of organisms and its physical environment
  o **Emissions:** The release of substances (e.g., greenhouse gases) into the atmosphere
  o **Energy resources:** The available supply and price of fossil and alternative resources will play a huge role in estimating how much a greenhouse gas constraint will cost. In the U.S. context, natural gas supply (and thus price) is particularly important, as it is expected to be a transition fuel to a lower carbon economy.
  o **Enhanced greenhouse effect:** The increase in the natural greenhouse effect resulting from increases in atmospheric concentrations of GHGs because of emissions from human activities.
  o **Fossil fuel:** A hydrocarbon deposit, such as petroleum, coal, or natural gas, derived from the accumulated remains of ancient plants and animals and used as fuel. Carbon dioxide and other greenhouse gases generated by burning fossil fuels are considered to be one of the principal causes of climate change.
  o **Greenhouse effect:** The insulating effect of atmospheric greenhouse gases (e.g., water vapor, carbon dioxide, methane, etc.) that keeps the Earth's temperature about 60°F warmer than it would be otherwise.
  o **Kyoto Protocol:** An international agreement adopted in December 1997 in Kyoto, Japan. The protocol sets binding emission targets for developed countries that would reduce their emissions on average 5.2 percent below 1990 levels.
  o **Renewable energy:** Energy obtained from sources, such as geothermal, wind, photovoltaic, solar, and biomass
  o **Stratosphere:** The region of Earth's atmosphere 10–50 km above the surface of the planet
  o **Sulfate aerosols:** Sulfur-based particles derived from emissions of sulfur dioxide (SO_2) from the burning of fossil fuels (particularly coal). Sulfate aerosols reflect incoming light

from the sun, shading and cooling Earth's surface (see "radiative forcing"), and thus offset some of the warming historically caused by greenhouse gases.
- ○ **Water vapor (H_2O):** Water vapor is the primary gas responsible for the greenhouse effect. It is believed that increases in temperature caused by anthropogenic emissions of greenhouse gases will increase the amount of water vapor in the atmosphere, resulting in additional warming
- ○ **Weather:** Describes the short-term (i.e., hourly and daily) state of the atmosphere. Weather is not the same as climate (PEW Center on Global Climate Change, "Glossary of Key Terms," www.pewclimate.org/global-warming-basics/full_glossary/glossary.php and The Free Dictionary by FARLEX at www.thefreedictionary.com/fossil+fuel.
- Ask students to identify and provide specific examples of climate changes and report on specific areas of the world where climate change is well-documented.
- Ask students to research and identify major health problems caused by climate change.
- Have students identify, explain, and offer specific examples of how the U.S. and other governments are attempting to lessen the affects of climate change on health and the environment.
- Have students research the Kyoto treaty and discuss why the United States refused to sign this treaty. Identify other countries also refused to sign treaty, and provide their reasons.
- Ask students to collect examples from the popular media that give evidence of how industry is addressing in positive and negative ways the effects of climate change.
- Have student research political-based discussions on climate change, noting the arguments in support of recognizing climate change and arguments that do not support climate change.

For Young Students

- Introduce and define the Arctic and Antarctic regions of the world.
- Introduce the concepts of global warming and climate change, carbon-based fuels, and carbon dioxide, that affect the Arctic and Antarctic regions.
- Explain that many scientists believe that carbon dioxide causes climate changes because it traps heat from the sun and heats Earth.
- Have students identify major effects of climate change on animals of the Arctic and Antarctic regions (e.g., effects of climate change on polar bears, arctic wolves, penguins, whales).
- Discuss with students how global warming is affecting the health of these animals (e.g., finding food, finding places to nest and raise their young, changes in food supplies).
- Have students list and discuss ways that they can help prevent harmful climate change by saving energy. Some discussion points:
- ○ Turn off lights and computers when not in use.
- ○ Encourage students to use energy-efficient light bulbs.
- ○ Plant trees because trees take carbon dioxide from the air.
- ○ Recycle and use materials that are made of recycled materials.
- ○ Reduce or eliminate using paper or plastic shopping bags by carrying a canvas tote bag when shopping.

3. Ecological Changes

Learning Outcomes
Students will:

- Define ecology and provide examples of ecological systems.
- Identify and give examples of deforestation and land clearance, and explain where and why this is occurring.

- Define desertification and explain human activities that have caused it.
- Explain how desertification and poor land management can affect health.
- Explain how land clearance and deforestation affect human health.
- Document and explain how deforestation and land clearance affects food security and medical treatments and research.
- Identify ways that deforestation and land clearance affect climate change and human health.
- Explain how forests help purify air and improve air quality.
- Identify ways that reforestation and forest management can help combat the adverse effects of deforestation and land clearance.
- Explain how reforestation and land clearance affect population movements, population displacements, and health care.

Questions and/or Activities (Adjust According to Age and Abilities)

For Older Students

- Introduce the concepts of land clearance and deforestations, and explain the economic and political factors that help promote this use of land resources.
- Have students consider the benefits of forests to medical and pharmaceutical resources.
- Identify and discuss ways that deforestation affects human health in terms of spreading infectious diseases (e.g., malaria).
- Because deforestation affects the ecological systems, identify cases where infectious diseases have been reduced and/or eliminated because of land clearance.
- Have students identify ways that deforestation affects food security and nutrition of native populations that have depended on the forest for food.
- Introduce the need for land management. Explain the history of the Dust Bowl that occurred in the United States in the 1930s. Compare modern desertification with Dust Bowl conditions. What characteristics do they have in common?

For Younger Students

Many of the suggestions given previously can be used with younger students. These include:

- Land management
- Climate change and how it affect human life
- Deforestation and land clearance
- Food security
- Benefits of natural resources for health
- Management of ecosystems

4. Populations and Migrations

Learning Outcomes

Students will:

- Define population displacements, and provide current examples of population displacements.
- Explain the causes of refugee displacements.
- Define and provide example of urbanization and how this affects health and health care.
- Explain the causes of rural-to-urban immigration.
- Define and explain migration in developed countries.

- Explain the effects of migration on the health of women and children.
- Explain how governments respond to population displacements.
- Discuss the effects of population displacement on food and water security.

Questions and/or Activities (Adjust According to Age and Abilities)

For Older Students

- Introduce the terms "immigration," "migration," "refugee," and "political asylum" and have students relate these terms to population displacement.
- Have students identify population displacements, as discussed in the popular media (e.g., countries such as Afghanistan, Rwanda, Iraq, Somalia, Sudan).
- Have student construct maps showing where populations that are displaced come from and where they go.
- Ask students to name reasons that cause population displacements.
- Ask students to explain how population displacements cause health problems, especially among children and women.
- Have students research and report on the diseases encountered by people who are displaced. Ask them to consider these health problems:
  - Waterborne diseases
  - Contaminated foods
  - Lack of nutritious foods
  - Supply and transportation of populations
  - Terrorism
  - Political instability
- Have students define and provide examples of urban-rural immigration. Ask students to consider health problems that can occur with this type of population displacement.
- Have students consider how governments generally provide help with this type of immigration through public health services.
- Population displacement occurs in developed countries. What causes this type of displacement? Ask students to consider the concept of public health services provided by governments. Have students consider how public health services address issues of both urban-rural immigration and population displacement in developed countries.

For Younger Students

Use some of the activities and questions given previously with younger students. These include:

- Introduce the terms "immigration," "migration," "refugee," and "political asylum."
- Discussion the terms "populations" and "population displacements."
- Discuss reasons for population displacement.
- Have students research and map population displacement because of various causes.
- Discuss why population displacements especially affect women and children.
- Identify some of the health problems caused by population displacement.
- How do governments and other aid organizations care for displaced persons?
- Define urban-rural immigration. Have students discuss why this occurs in the United States and other developed countries.
- Explain how public health services help with population displacement.
- What kinds of diseases generally occur with displaced populations?

5. Diseases

Learning Outcomes
Students will:

- Assess the historical spread of infectious diseases.
- Demonstrate knowledge of terms related to the study of global health.
- Identify the political, social, economic, and environmental effects of the rising incidences of infectious diseases.
- Define and explain the most important ways that global health has been affected by globalization (e.g., increased travel; increased trade; foodborne illnesses; urbanization, climate change, and assorted environmental issues; microbial drug resistance; breakdowns in public health systems).

Questions and/or Activities (Adjust According to Age and Abilities)

For Older Students

- Have students research and explain these terms as related to globalization and health: economic consequences; political consequences societal impacts; governmental responsibilities.
- Ask students to discuss this question: If infectious diseases have been around for centuries, why do we often consider them new phenomena?
- Ask students to consider how climate changes around the world can affect health.

For Younger Students

- Help students define and understand these concepts:
  - Infectious diseases
  - Transmission of infectious diseases
  - Preventions of infectious disease
  - Quarantine
  - Vaccination
  - Food safety
  - Water purity
- Malaria is the world's most common infectious disease. Help students understand how it is spread so widely. Note: " . . . Malaria is a mosquito-borne disease that affects more than 500 million people annually, causing between 1 and 3 million deaths. It is most common in tropical and subtropical climates and is found in 90 countries, but 90% of all cases are found in Sub-Saharan Africa. Most of its victims are children. . . . Malaria was almost eradicated 30 years ago; now it is on the rise again."[12]
- Have students find examples of how communities help prevent infectious disease. Have students especially consider how their school, city government, and state government help prevent infectious diseases.
- Children are especially susceptible to infectious diseases. Have students consider how the availability of health facilities, such as health clinics and hospitals, can help children who contact infectious diseases.
- Discuss the concepts both pro and con that medical care is a human right and should be enforced through legislation and government policy.[13]

6. Medical Care, Interventions, and Public Health

Learning Outcomes

Students will:

- Define pharmacological interventions in disease control.
- Explain tobacco regulations in selected countries and areas of the world.
- Analyze tobacco advertisements and how they are designed to appeal to selected audiences.
- Discuss the transnational tobacco industry and its global impact on health by using marketing techniques designed to appeal to people.
- Describe the World Health Organization (WHO) and its campaigns against tobacco use.
- Analyze tobacco in terms of political issues that both support and discourage its use.
- Define the roles of health caregivers within social and cultural contexts.
- Explain how society measures and assesses health care and improvements.
- Define intellectual property rights and how property rights affect medical care within a global context.
- Discuss and explain public health services.
- Critique women and children health issues.
- Discuss and explain government health polices and the role of local, state, provincial, national, and international governmental actions in providing health care.
- Have students research for examples of how various countries provide public health care. Have students make comparisons between countries that approach public health care differently.

Questions and/or Activities (Adjust According to Age and Abilities)

For Older Students

- Define marketing for students. Have then research general marketing strategies used by pharmaceutical companies. How can students demonstrate if these strategies benefit society? Some elements of global marketing of pharmaceutical products include:
  - Message design and impact
  - Cultural influences (national, regional, local)
  - Prevailing values, norms, traditions, beliefs, religion, rituals, and artifacts
  - Means for reaching the global consumer market (e-commerce, business-to-business, and strategic supply chain management)
  - Conducting market research
  - Importing and exporting practices
  - Influence of Internet technology on marketing
  - Develops and promotes new products and services through marketing strategies
  - Techniques used in advertising, public relations, and publicity within a global context
- Ask students to research laws that regulate the use of tobacco where they live and then select another region of the world to compare tobacco regulations and laws with their own.
- Introduce WHO and give some examples of its activities. Inform students that WHO conducts Tobacco Free Initiative (TFI) programs. As part of this initiative, on May 31, 2009, it sponsored World No Tobacco Day. Ask students to research how WHO works to lessen the use of tobacco among youth. For information on WHO and its activities, visit its Web site at www.who.int/about/en.
- Have students select and research a specific group of health caregivers, workers, or organizations that support health caregivers and workers and their clients. For a list of organizations,

visit Caregivers at www.beyondtheveil.net/cglinks.html#caregivers. Have older students consider specific fields of health care workers in terms of career requirements, education, and opportunities. Broadly speaking, these include:
   o Nursing
   o Rehabilitation
   o Pharmacy
   o Radiology
   o Physician/medical doctor
   o Dentistry
   o Dietitian
   o Emergency medical technician (EMT)/paramedics
   o Physician assistant
   o Psychological, behavioral, and mental health
   o Medical researcher
   o Therapist (e.g., recreational therapist)
   o Social work/social worker
   o Specialty fields, surgical services (surgical technician/surgical technologist), and various other types of technicians/technologists.
   o Administration/management (including but not limited to hospital and nursing home administrators)
   o Information systems/technology/computers/IT (including but not limited to computer programmer and systems analyst)
   o Medical records
• Have students investigate volunteer services within medical services. Ask students to provide examples of how volunteers work in developing countries.
• Have students consider how necessary it is to measure medical successes. Refer them to the U.S. Department of Health and Human Services Agency for Health Care and Quality and the services of the U.S. Department of Agriculture and have them investigate some of the attributes recommended by the agency that make for good health care. Visit the Agency for Health Care Research and Quality at www.ahrq.gov. After students review these suggestions, have them explain how they are or are not workable when placed within a global context.
• Introduce the concept of intellectual property rights as related to drug development and marketing. Have students research this concept based on these assumptions and then prepare to debate:
   o Intellectual property rights allow the pharmaceutical industry to receive justifiable revenues based on the high expenses involved in drug research, development, and marketing. This is a marketing right that companies must have to survive or the opposite.
   o Intellectual property rights causes drug prices to be unaffordable in many countries, and this prevents poor people living in developing and poor countries from receiving drugs that will improve their health or even save their lives.
• Discuss the role that intellectual property rights have on the availability of drugs in developing countries. Discuss how pharmaceutical companies and governments work together to supply needed drugs to those who need them based on agreements.
• Introduce students to the concepts of public health (e.g., prevention of disease and dealing with large population groups). Have students research some of the major activities of public health services. Ask students to explain how public health operates in developing countries and to discuss how different and/or similar public health services are in developing countries compared to their own country. Have students research and explain how laws and regulations influence public health actions. Have students give examples in their own communities.

- Introduce the concept of the health needs of women and children within a global context. Have students research and compare women and children's health in major North American and European countries with those in selected developing countries. Have students (based on age and ability) discuss how social and cultural issues affect the health care provided to women and children. Have students consider some of these specific issues:
  - Organizations that support improvement in women and children's health
  - Labor and workplace conditions caused by globalization
  - Women's health, poverty, and rights to health care
  - Persistence of discrimination against women and children and their health needs
  - Adolescent women and their cultural and social vulnerability
  - Childbirth and maternity death
  - Terrorism and its effects on women and children's health
  - Women and children as displaced populations (refugee situations)
  - Aging women and their need for health care
  - Local community support for women and children's health
  - The relationship (positive and negative) of global pharmaceutical industry and women and children's health
  - Violence against children and women
  - Sexual exploration of women and children
  - Reproductive rights of women
  - The universalism (global) movement for the improvement of women and children's health
  - The HIV situation on the continent of Africa

For Younger Students

Young students can benefit from some of the questions and activities listed previously. Consider these as especially useful for younger students:

- Define marketing.
- Discuss examples of marketing and how marketing can influence health attitudes and behaviors.
- Provide examples of health laws and how they affect health behaviors and attitudes.
- Introduce WHO and provide examples of its work throughout the world.
- Introduce the term "health care worker" and then ask students to name health care workers where they live.
- Explain volunteer health care workers. Ask students how they can become volunteer health care workers as they grow older.
- Introduce students to some specific government agencies that are involved in health care services (e.g., the U.S. Department of Health and Human Services; the U.S. Department of Agriculture; and state, provincial, and local health authors).
- Ask students to consider the special needs women and children have for health care.

7. Information and Communication Technology

Learning Outcomes

Students will:

- Describe and discuss:
  - The delivery of health care services and information via communication technologies
  - Communication and the Internet

  ○ Delivery of medical services and information
  ○ Geographic technology and linking information about individuals and infections

Questions and/or Activities (Adjust According to Age and Abilities)

For Older Students

- Introduce students to the concept of information technology. Explain that information technology is widespread and that it includes information about medicine and health care.
- Explain the concept of digital divide as applied to developed and developing countries.
- Have students research how medical and other types of health care services and information can be carried through information technologies.
- Have students research and then debate the values of information technology within a global context (e.g., security and privacy involved with personal information).
- Have students select a country that is generally considered a developing country to see how much basic information they can find about the health care needs of the country and how citizens of that country get information about health care needs. Have students debate, discuss, and develop the outline of a program for bringing information technology to that country with the help of governmental (both local and international) and nongovernmental agencies.
- Have students discuss how governmental agencies, such as the WHO and the CDC, can use information technology to track the spread of infectious diseases.
- Ask students to research and discuss the various types of medical and health care information available on the Internet. What are some criteria that must be used to evaluate and accept this information? What types of health information would students want to see available on the Internet? What kinds of information might governments want to exclude from the Internet?

For Younger Students

Younger students can especially profit from the following activities and questions:

- Introduce and explain information technology. Provide examples. Have students discuss how it can be used in health care.
- Ask students to discuss why privacy and security of medical information about a person is important.
- Ask students how a person's information located on medical information technology can be used inappropriately.
- Ask students to discuss what kinds of medical information for kids are available on the Internet.
- Provide some examples of how to judge health information on the Internet for kids (e.g., accuracy, reliability, who provides the information, does it have a commercial base).

8. Travel and Transportation

Learning Outcomes

Students will:

- Describe how the automobile culture affects health (e.g., pollution, climate change, accidents, rural-urban displacements).
- Research and explain how transporting goods across national boundaries spreads infectious diseases.

- Discuss how road safety is a health concern.
- Identify and explain how transportation safety can be improved.
- Explain the role of government policies in transportation issues affecting health.

Questions and Activities (Adjust According to Age and Abilities)

For Older Students

- Begin by explaining road safety and how it relates to health in a globalized context (e.g., world-wide deaths, demands on health care facilities, death of persons ages 15–44 who are generally primary family supporters, financial costs).
- Have students research and provide examples of how the following conditions associated with transportation and cars affect human health:
  - Speed rates on roads and streets
  - Alcohol consumption
  - Use of helmets and seatbelts and other restraining devices
  - Awareness of pedestrian cyclists and their rights
  - Better design of roads
  - Better design for safety of cars and other forms of transportation
  - Government policies and traffic law enforcement
  - Have students define car culture. After conducting background reading and research, have students discuss how car culture affects these conditions:
    Physical inactivity
    Road traffic injuries
    Air pollution
    Traffic noise
    Community disruption and dislocation
    Environmental impacts
    Climate change
    Occupational hazards in the workforce
- Have students consider how governments can construct social, economic, and transportation policies that takes both economic needs and health needs into account.
- Have students debate this statement: "Reducing car reliance is a global problem."

For Younger Students

Motor and transportation issues are important for younger students to understand. Based on some of the previous strategies:

- Ask students to discuss road safety and to provide examples on how to be safe on the road.
- Introduce the term "pedestrian," and have students explain ways to be safe as a pedestrian.
- Have students consider how these factors affect health and safety
  - Speed
  - Alcohol
  - Cell phones and text messaging
  - Not using a seatbelt when riding in a car or on public transportation
  - Not wearing helmets when riding a bicycle or motor bike
- Ask students to discuss how governments can help in providing safe conditions for drivers and pedestrians.

9. Justice and Litigation Systems

Learning Outcomes

Students will:

- Define and demonstrate the relationship between health and human rights.
- Identify and discuss major issues regarding health and human rights contained in selected international agreements and declarations.
- Identify and describe governmental agencies and private organizations that work to ensure that health is a human right.
- Describe the issues involved in recognizing health as a human right.
- Prepare to debate if access to courts of law and legal advocates (e.g., lawyers) are necessary in the promoting of health and health-related rights.

Questions and Activities (Adjust According to Age and Abilities)

For Older Students

- Ask students to define and discuss rights as understood in society. Review or ask students to define "human rights." Help students arrive at a consensus definition of "human rights. Based on this discussion, ask students to consider the idea that health care is a basic human right. Make sure that both the pros and cons of this issue are brought into the discussion. Helpful sources for this discuss include these sites:
  - **Pro:** www.nhchc.org/humanright.html
  - **Con:** www.pubmedcentral.nih.gov/articlerender.fcgi?artid=112691
- Introduce the Universal Declaration of Human Rights and then ask students to consider how this document might improve the health care for people throughout the world. Ask students to research this idea and provide evidence that it has or has not helped improve the health care of people throughout the world. The Universal Declaration of Human Rights is available at www.un.org/en/documents/udhr.
- Ask students to debate how courts can influence health care (e.g., rulings granting rights to health care vs. rulings that limit rights to health care, work-related accidents and diseases, insurance benefits, class action suits, rights to sue for health cost recoveries, etc.).
- Have students find and examples of recent court rulings affecting health care.
- Have students define a legal advocate and give reasons that legal advocates are generally necessary in court proceedings.

For Younger Students

- Have them brainstorm the word "law." List the word "law" on a board or clip chart. Ask students to supply words that can be added to "law" (e.g., driving laws). Next, have students name a word they think of when seeing or hearing "law." Give a few examples to promote thinking (e.g., laws keep us safe). As suggestions are given, place them on the chalkboard around the term "law."
- Introduce the idea of health laws. Ask students to name ways that health laws keep us save. To encourage discussion, suggest concepts (e.g., food laws make our food safe to eat).
- Make sure that various heath laws are listed and then have students discuss how different health laws help in daily life (e.g., laws regarding food, drugs, driving and traffic, smoking, hunting and fishing, child safety, chemicals, solid waste, sound and noise controls).
- Introduce students to the concept of rule of law based on such things as constitutions, court rulings, "common law," and regulations. Define these in ways that students can relate to them.

Define the word "constitution." A dictionary definition of constitution that can be used with modification is "the basic principles and laws of a nation, state, or social group that determine the powers and duties of the government and guarantee certain rights to the people in it" (*Merriam-Webster*). Make sure that students understand how democracies operate under a constitutional form of government and systems of laws.

- Help students understand how health laws and regulations are made in their towns, states, provinces, and countries.
- Introduce the concept that health around the world needs to be protected by international oversight. Introduce the WHO, and discuss how this organization helps influence global health through directives and suggestions for laws. For information, visit its site at www.who.int/about/en.

10. Labor and Work

Learning Outcomes

Students will:

- Describe health care and diseases in the contexts of work and workplaces.
- Identify major occupational diseases.
- Explain the reasons that most countries have labor standards and laws.
- Describe how labor has been influenced by globalization (e.g., migrant workers, child labor, and displacement of populations).
- Explain the major relationships between health and unemployment.
- Identify and explain the work that government agencies do to protect the health and safety of workers engaged in various types of work (e.g., national, state, provincial, local, and international governments).

Questions and Activities (Adjust According to Age and Abilities)

For Older Students

- Introduce the concept of work environments to students.
- Have students define what constitutes a hazardous working environment and ask students to identify and explain some major conditions that can contribute to work-related diseases and health problems. Help with discussion by suggesting some specific conditions (e.g., lack of good quality air, poor lighting, use of heavy equipment, noise, lack of emergency escape routes, lack of safety regulations and worker training).
- Ask students to define and give examples of household chores that most students are asked and/or expected to do at home. Ask students to explain how those chores are safe and contribute to healthy living.
- Introduce the concept of child labor and then ask students to describe the difference between family chores and child labor.
- Review or introduce child labor and then ask students to give examples of unhealthy child labor practices.
- Introduce the Convention of the Rights of the Child (http://www.unicef.org/crc) and then ask students to explain how this document can protect the health of children.
- Ask students to explain why most countries have labor standards and laws. Have students identify the major labor agencies in their countries, states, provinces, cities, regions, and areas that are charged with enforcing labor laws and standards. Have students provide examples of how

laws and regulations protect workers from work-related injuries, diseases, and other health conditions.

- Ask students to debate the effects that labor unions have had on working and health conditions in work environments.
- Have students identify how immigrant workers, population displacement, and child laborers affect health and disease in work environments.
- Pose this question to students: "What are the major cause and effect relationships between health, diseases, and unemployment?"
- Have student assess the long-term effects of poor health-related working conditions on a country's economy and societal well-being.
- Ask students to identify reasons that some industries do not look after the health conditions of their workers.
- Have students debate this question: "How does the global society suffer when workers are forced to work in hazardous working conditions?"
- Have students discuss why it is in the interest of businesses to develop policies and procedures that ensure a healthier workforce.
- Ask students to consider and explain how students' consumer decisions might add to the cycle of unhealthy working conditions.
- Have students consider common student jobs and then ask them to list and explain how those jobs can cause health problems. Have them list some rules and regulations that help prevent the development of unhealthy conditions among students who work.
- Provide this definition of child labor: "Child labor, as defined by International Labour Organization (ILO) is work done by children under the age of 12; work by children under the age of 15 that prevents school attendance; and work by children under the age of 18 that is hazardous to their physical or mental health. Child labor is an economic activity or work that interferes with the completion of a child's education or that is harmful to children in any way." ("Lesson Plan on Child Labour," www.un.org/works/goingon/labor/lessonplan_labor.html). Ask students to give examples of health conditions that are implied in this definition.
- The UN Convention on the Rights of the Child states that children under age 18 often need special care that adults do not. The convention is the first legally binding international instrument to incorporate a full range of human rights for children, such as civil, cultural, economic, political, and social. The United States and Somalia did not ratify it. Have students research and explain reasons why the United States failed to ratify this treaty. Make sure that students understand what it means to ratify a treaty in terms of U.S. law.
- What are some special health and disease conditions that farm workers throughout the world face? How can governments protect farm workers who face these conditions?

For Younger Students

Emphasize these questions and activities:

- Introduce the concept of work environments and then ask students to provide examples.
- Introduce the concept of a hazardous working environment and then ask for examples.
- Ask students to name household chores that they perform and then ask students to explain how they contribute to a healthy environment for their families.
- Introduce the concept of child labor and then ask students to conduct research so they can provide examples of child labor.
- Introduce the concept of labor laws and then discuss why labor laws are required in countries.
- Ask students to consider how household purchase can both help and hurt the environment and health.

11. Governments and Health Policies

Learning Outcomes

Students will:

- Explain why it is necessary to have local, state, and national governmental health policies and directives.
- Explain how international organizations promote heath policies.
- Explain and describe the influence of governmental policies on selected issues of importance, such as:
  - Trade policies and health
  - Health care systems development
  - Policies regarding resources and financial allocations
  - Market-orientated concept of health delivery
  - Health cost containment and cost recovery
  - Decentralization vs. centralized of heath care systems
  - Ethics and policy
  - Health and global security and economic development
  - Equality of health care provision
  - Collaboration on policy development and health care delivery
  - Policy and social movements and social activitism (e.g., women's, labor, and environmental movements)

Questions and/or Activities (Adjust for Age and Abilities)

For Older Students

- Have student consider the concept of a government's responsibility to its citizens and the citizens' responsibility to their government regarding health (e.g., participate in policy formation, be informed, finding information, critically examining information, taking care of one's health).
- Ask students to research and explain concepts influencing how health policies are formed at local, state, provincial, and international levels (e.g., expressed needs of new groups arriving on the scene, failures of existing policies to meet needs, needs not foreseen by existing policies,

Figure 9.4.
Emblem of the U.S. Environmental Protection Agency. Courtesy of the U.S. government.

- new research findings, changes in political philosophies, changes in demographics, social, cultural, and economic changes).
- Ask students to explain how conflicts can develop between groups who have different needs and agendas regarding health when policies are being formed.
- Introduce the concepts of negotiation and compromise in developing health policies. Ask students to provide some examples of health policy development drawn from local, state, provincial, and international health policies.
- Have students identify public health policy advocacy groups and then explain their agendas and influences on health policies.
- Often, people who are in the public eye devote time to advocating for health policy and reform. Have students research and report on selected personalities as advocates for health care reform. These might include:
  - Lance Armstrong
  - Paul David "Bono Hewson (professionally known as "Bono")
  - Bill Clinton
  - Elton John
  - Al Gore
  - Magic Johnson
  - Larry Kramer
  - Michael Moore
  - Ralph Nader
  - Maureen Reagan

For Younger Students

Based on the previous, the following questions and activities can be used with younger students:

- Introduce the concept of government health policy. Ask students to consider how citizen can help governments develop good health care policies (e.g., participate in government activities, be informed, find information, look critically at government policies).
- Introduce the concepts of negotiation and compromise when governments develop heath policies.
- Identify people who have been active in promoting how governments develop health care policies.

12. Market Demands

Learning Outcomes

Students will:

- Identify and explain the costs of marketing goods internationally.
- Define profits and explain why profit requirements often interfere with the implement of health care operations in developing countries.
- Demonstrate how markets are identified and cultivated.
- Explain investments in markets.
- Identify and demonstrate the effects of social and cultural values within diversified markets.
- Explain the basic attributes of advertising and explain how advertising is used to market health products and services internationally.

- Identify the concept of social marketing and explain how it is used to promote better health globally (e.g., social marketing attempts with positive messaging to change attitudes and behaviors and reinforce existing positive behaviors and attitudes for public and social good).

Questions and/or Activities (Adjust According to Age and Abilities)

For Older Students

- Have students research and define patients and why most countries have patient laws. Ask students to identify the patient office in their own countries. Have students explain how patients affect the marketing of medical drugs and devices in developing countries.
- One of the major disputes in offering medical drugs at affordable prices internationally is the insistence from pharmaceutical companies that their patient rights and prices must be protected. Have students identify and discuss the major reasons why pharmaceutical companies defend this viewpoint. Make sure that students identify these points:
  - Costs involved in research and development of new drugs that can benefit society
  - Cost of testing new drugs
  - Cost of distribution and marketing of new drugs

International organizations and treaties have addressed problems associated with marketing affordable drugs internationally.

- Have students identify these treaties discuss, stating why they are important in making affordable drugs available.
  - **TRIPS: Agreement on Trade-Related Aspects of Intellectual Property Rights.** Available at www.wto.org/english/tratop_e/trips_e/t_agm2_e.htm; "TRIPS and Pharmaceutical Patents: Fact Sheet. Available at www.wto.org/english/tratop_e/trips_e/factsheet_pharm00_e.htm.
  - **"Globalization and Access to Drugs." A summary of the General Agreement on Tariffs and Trade (GATT)** available at apps.who.int/medicinedocs/en/d/Jwhozip35e/3.1.html.
- Marketing involves many processes. Often, this is referred to as a marketing mix—called the 7 Ps: price, product, physical environment, process, promotion, people, place. In terms of marketing drugs and health services globally, ask students to explain these relationships:
  - Price of drugs in developing countries
  - Price and high-risk diseases
  - Price and price controls through patients and generic drugs
  - Drugs' product designs and usability in relationship to value and high-risk disease
  - Generic drugs and their quality in relation to high-risk disease
  - Methods of moving important drugs to places of use in relation to high-risk diseases
  - Methods of integrating drugs into the culture and society of areas where high-risk diseases occur
- Have students debate these issues as related to the globalized investments in the pharmacological industry:
  - Investments in medical drugs and services are useful because they help transfer knowledge, technology, and management techniques that often initiate changes other than simply the trading of medical drugs and services.
  - Investments in medical drugs and health services can bring about positive social and cultural changes as well as foster economic growth and economic integration of world economies.
- Introduce the terms "culture" and "society," and make sure students have a common understanding of what these terms mean. Next, introduce the term "values," and explain how values

are an important part of society and culture. Students should also be given a definition for socialization.

- Explain that values are acquired through a complex process involving one's culture, social class, friends and associates (reference group norms), family (values, attitudes) and individual preferences. Ask students to consider and explain how marketing of health drugs and services are affected by these issues:
  - Protecting the environment
  - Rural life
  - Religion
  - Human rights
  - Family
  - Women's issues
  - Ethnic heritage
- Have student consider these elements of advertising medical drugs and services to be sold in a global market:
  - Target audience
  - Culture and society of the target audience
  - Persuasion techniques (crating needs and wants)
  - Cost and affordability
  - Creating action to acquire the product
  - Visual images
  - Logo and slogan
  - Text (readability and information)
  - Color, selection of fonts, and spacing
  - Accuracy of information scientific information
  - Symbols of authority
- Ask students to locate a printed medical drug advertisement (or supply one) and have them redesign it for use in a developing country. In doing this, have them identify an audience and the educational level of potential viewers. Have them also consider what visuals and symbols of authority might be useful in making the advertisement more effective. Encourage students to consider this advertisement a social marketing message as well as an advertisement to sell and encourage the use of the drug.
- Introduce students to the concept of social marketing, which includes techniques aimed at promoting better attitudes, behaviors, and reinforcing existing positive behaviors and attitudes for public and social good.
- Introduce the term "public service announcements" as heard on radio and seen in television and ask them to select an example and to analyze it according to its audience, information, visuals, and its sponsorship (en.wikipedia.org/wiki/Public_service_announcement).
- Introduce students to the American Ad Council and have them investigate the activities of this organization in terms of how it helps in developing public service announcements (www.adcouncil.org).

For Young Students

Some of the concepts noted previously can be modified for younger students:

- Define marketing and provide examples from local situations that involve marketing.
- Define patients and patient laws that countries have and then have students discuss how these are important.

- Discuss why patients are important in drug marketing.
- Introduce the concept of market advertisement and market branding.
- Help students locate and identify some pharmaceutical marketing logos and slogans. Discuss that caution must be used when observing logos and slogans and marketing messages.
- Introduce the concept of social values and then have students consider these values in terms of health and the marketing of health products:
  - Protecting the environment
  - Rural life
  - Human rights
  - Family
  - Women and children
  - Men
  - Heritage
- Introduce the concept of public service announcements. Have students identify such announcements and describe them either orally or in writing.
- Introduce students to the American Ad Council and explain how they have helped promote better health care. Its site is www.adcouncil.org.

RESOURCES

Resources that support many of the subjects encompassed in globalization are included in the annotated list found in Appendix A.

REFLECTIONS

Globalization offers many avenues to introduce health information and instruction throughout the curriculum. In addition to important content regarding health for students as well as society, globalization—by its very nature—provides a wealth of opportunities for teachers and school librarians to develop critical thinking skills among students. Similarly, information literacy strategies can be taught by using globalization topics because information about globalization is found in a variety of subjects and formats. Globalization is an important aspect of social development that ensures important roles in the lives of teachers and school librarians.

NOTES

1. "Globalization: Definition." www.mindtools.net/GlobCourse/gdef.shtml. Accessed Dec. 17, 2009.
2. Hicks, Douglas A. "Globalization." In *Encyclopedia of Leadership*. Edited by George R. Goethals, Georgia J. Sorenson, and James Macgregor Burns, vol. 2, pp. 570–577. Thousand Oaks, Calif.: Sage Reference, 2004.
3. "Youth and Education: Trends and Challenges. Growing Up Global." Full report available at National Academic Press, Washington, www.nap.edu. Accessed Sept. 21, 2009.
4. Kawachi, Ichiro and Sarah Warmala, eds. *Globalization and Health*. New York: Oxford, 2007.
5. Globalization 101.org. www.globalization101.org. Accessed Sept. 21, 2009.

6. Busby, Joe and Pam Page Carpenter. "Teaching Students About Clean Fuels and Transportation Technology," *Technology Teacher* 68 (April 2009): 16–21.

7. Moye, Johnny T. "Technology Teacher Supply and Demand: A Critical Situation," *Technology Teacher* 69 (Oct. 2009): 30–36.

8. Wisconsin's Model Academic Standards for Agricultural Education. dpi.state.wi.us/standards/pdf/agried.pdf. Accessed Dec. 8, 2009.

9. University of Texas at Austin. Department of Economics. www.utexas.edu/cola/depts/economics. Accessed Dec. 8, 2009.

10. Council for Economic Education. "National Standards." www.councilforeconed.org/ea/standards. Accessed Dec. 8, 2009.

11. "Texas Essential Knowledge and Skills for Home Economics Education." ritter.tea.state.tx.us/rules/tac/chapter122/index.html. Accessed Dec. 8, 2009.

12. "Common Infectious Diseases Worldwide." www.infoplease.com/ipa/A0903696.html. Accessed Sept. 24, 2009.

13. National Health Care for Homeless Council. "Human Rights, Homelessness and Health Care." www.nhchc.org/humanright.html. Accessed March 21, 2010.

10

Outreach, Health, and the
School Community

DEFINING THE SCHOOL HEALTH COMMUNITY

Defining community is both straightforward and difficult. Community can have both geographical as well as emotional boundaries. Where one lives and goes to school within designated boundaries is the most common way of thinking of a school community. In the broadest sense, community can also have an emotional context in that community can extend to a city, a country, or even a fondly remembered place.[1,2] For this discussion, we will define community as the various areas in which a school has direct geographical ties. This will include the local school and its service area, the area of the city or town where the school is located, the city, and the school district.

At the higher level, in the United States, the states are the primary influential communities for schools because individual states are responsible for education within their borders. Education was not assigned to the federal government in the Constitution, meaning that in theory the U.S. Congress has limited authority over the states in how they choose to educate their children. This has been a much debated point when federal funds are provided for schools. Monetary support for schools, as well as for other programs, from the federal government has often been accomplished through systems called "cooperative federalism." In this way Congress can exercise its powers by offering, mandating, or encouraging the States to implement national programs consistent with national minimum standards, especially when the states accept federal funds. [3] "Cooperative federalism" can influence the way health is taught in schools.

The school community also has an international-community aspect related to the ever-increasing globalization of health issues. The ease of communication between school students in the United States and other countries in the world also adds to this community aspect.

The most obvious connection to the school and school district within the school community is its students, faculty, staff, administrators, and parents. School districts are a part of the school community, as they provide health information literacy programs through curriculum, instruction, health services, staffing, and information provision. The behaviors and modeling of good health practices of school personnel and students play key roles in establishing school community standards.

School districts as well as state and provincial health curriculum guides, mandates, and instruction about how to provide health literacy instruction further define the school's community. When a state mandates a certain number of hours to teaching health in schools and at what levels, school districts must find ways to incorporate this instruction into existing classes or into entirely separate classes with a certified teacher.

National governments in other countries and professional groups play significant roles in defining the local school health community. Organizations for physical education teachers create standards for their area of the curriculum, and districts will add these to their units of instruction.

The premise of this book is that health should be integrated into all classes. The complexity of modern life necessitate that health not be taught simply as a separate topic. Health permeates the lives of students before, during, and certainly after they leave school.

COMMUNITY DEVELOPMENT: CONCEPTS AND SCHOOL HEALTH INFORMATION LITERACY

In providing health information, the local school is a partner and player in community development. Because the best definition of this concept is provided by the Federation for Community Development Learning in Great Britain we are using it here:

The process of developing active and sustainable communities based on social justice and mutual respect. It is about influencing power structures to remove the barriers that prevent people from participating in the issues that affect their lives. . . .

Community workers facilitate the participation of people in this process. They enable connections to be made between communities and with the development of wider policies and programmes. . . .

    . . .

Community Development expresses values of fairness, equality, accountability, opportunity, choice, participation, mutuality, reciprocity and continuous learning. Educating, enabling and empowering are at the core of Community Development.[4]

Within a health information literacy context, community development places emphasis on how "to organize, use, and increase the capacity and resources within the community as opposed to depending on outside resources."[5] Ideally, this should come from the community, but it often comes from external sources.[6] School libraries as an integral part of the school community, and its service areas become important in community development. At a fundamental level, school librarians join with teachers and staff in providing resources and instruction, and they are involved with curriculum development and refinement. At the next level, librarians can work to bring health information and the necessary skills to access health information to the school service environment through both school-based services as well as outreach programs.

SCHOOL PROGRAMS

School health information programs can be mounted in many ways to serve the school population. Based on good planning, the school librarian can become involved by offering:

Help to Parents

- Develop resources that will be of use to parents. These can be delivered in several ways, including special collections listed on the school library Web site, where useful links and other types of external as well as internal sources are displayed.
- Provide bibliographies of health materials available for them to use in the school library and refer them to the public library for further resources. If the public library does not offer assistance in online searching, offer this to parents on teacher conference days. Well-taught students can help with this training.
- Be available together with other staff members to offer basic consultations about health information resources.
- Develop lists of referral sources and contacts to community resources for parents and older students. Seek to educate and involve the faculty and staff members in this process.

Help to Staff

- Create a series of information meetings with staff where health issues and resources are discussed. Such meetings can provide opportunities to introduce health resources in the library, including databases, and to present health authorities from the community to discuss their concerns, resources, and health information agendas.

Help for Students

- Encourage teachers to discuss health issues in conjunction with their lessons plans. These discussions can offer information that can be combined with instructional units. School librarians can encourage teachers to make sure that students understand the importance of personal hygiene in the control of diseases.
- Develop age-appropriate health information resources in easily accessible collections and formats.
- Plan all-school health fairs, workshops, and conferences where external health information sources are displayed. These displays can include not only materials about services and good health practices, but they can also include demonstrations by experts from the community about various health issues. Include here poster sessions that involve students' work regarding health issues.
- Be involved in direct instruction with students either as individuals or as a teaching team.

OUTREACH TO THE COMMUNITY

In basic terms, library outreach is taking school library services out into the larger community where services are needed and often where an underserved population resides or where the population does not view the school library as a viable place to provide community resources. Library outreach has been a mainstay of library services since the latter part of the nineteenth century. In those early days, services were

Figure 10.1.
Library service, Kelly Field Library, ca. 1920 (l). WPA Bookmobile services. Courtesy of the U.S. federal government and the Library of Congress.

extended by public and school libraries, including state and provincial libraries, to both urban and rural areas.

Health outreach services have also been a part of public health initiatives since the mid- to late nineteenth century. Borrowing from these two traditions, school librarians can play an important role in furthering health information services and in promoting better health information literacy. Many of the services outlined previously are useful at the school level and can be extended into the community.

REACHING THE WIDER SCHOOL COMMUNITY WITH HEALTH INFORMATION

In addition to the school health fair, there are a number of ways to involve the larger school community. These include conference programs and workshops where members of the school community are invited and encouraged to participate. The first example, the Community Health Fair, has many possibilities for the school librarian:

- **Resources in and from the school library.** Biblioteca Américus, a library in the South Texas Independent School District serving Mercedes, San Benito, and Edinburg, offers a good example of community outreach services sponsored by a school library.[7]
- **The Community Health Fair.** The community health fair is similar in design to the school level health fair, except that it more inclusive of the community. Participants come both from the school and the larger health community, including hospitals, clinics, public health agencies, health organizations, health practitioners, and libraries of various types, including public libraries and special medical collections. The school librarian, with help from students, designs brochures showing the community the resources available through the school library. Copies of bibliographies distributed to teachers and students could be on display. With the school librarian on the planning committee, attention can be paid to locating agencies that provide consumer health information services and information that is free and easily distributed. If they are unable to participate in the fair, the school librarian could offer to display their resources.

Figure 10.2.
Conference attendees at the GetHIP health conference, San Antonio, Texas. Courtesy of
the University of Texas Health Science Center in San Antonio. Published with permission.

With the proper technology in the booth or on the table at the fair, students could display their
abilities to search available databases and share their findings with their audience.

- **Workshops and conferences.** Workshops and conferences are similar to health fairs, except
they are focused more directly on specific issues and topics and generally include a highly
selected group of presenters that have expertise in health issues identified as the conference
theme. Like health fairs, these will involve the coordinated work of a planning committee.

- An example of such a large event is the GetHIP: Health Information Plus conference held on
Saturday, June 7, 2008, in San Antonio, Texas. The conference involved an almost year-long
series of planning sessions of library and health experts from the San Antonio–Austin area.
Some 121 school librarians, school nurses, teachers, school administrators, health educators,
health sciences librarians, and others attended the conference. The overall objective of the
conference was to "promote a coordinated approach to school health." The highlights of the
conference were keynote and panel presentations, an experience fair that "allowed attendees
to exchange ideas with colleagues from a variety of schools, libraries and other organizations
engaged in schools and public health." Small group sessions held in the afternoon produced
"specific ideas for collaborating across professional lines to promote a team approach to school
health," following the CDC's Coordinated School Health Program model. Much of the materials from the workshop are available at www.library.uthscsa.edu/events/gethip.cfm.

BASIC GUIDES TO PLANNING AND MANAGING HEALTH FAIRS AND CONFERENCES

Basic planning strategies for health fairs, conferences, and workshops are similar in almost all health information literacy programs. At one time, the American Academy of Pediatrics (www.aap.org) offered an inclusive guide in their planning kit for health fairs. Unfortunately this Web-based guide appears to be no longer available; but its suggestons are summarized below:

- **Allow enough time for planning.** Ten months is required for good planning and organizing of events and details. Schedule the fair or event at times other than important and competing events in the community.
- **Determine your message and your audience.** The message can be specific to a theme or it can be general health information. Likewise, the audience can be general or more specific as to communities and situations.
- **Form a planning committee.** Use informed and professional volunteers to help with planning that includes program development and strategies as well as arrangements (registration, publicity, logistics, exhibitors, sponsors, and evaluation).
- **Select a location.** Select a convenient place for the fair, workshop, or conference. Be sure to consider parking, housing, dining facilities, public transportation, and safety.
- **Staffing needs.** Use both informed professionals as well as dedicated volunteers. Student groups, schools, community service organizations, church groups, senior citizen centers, and advocacy groups are good places to start looking for volunteers. Depending on the situation, volunteers can include students, parents, professionals from the community, and school staff and faculty.
- **Displays and exhibitors.** Secure exhibitors, which can be both profit and not-for profit organizations. Be sure to develop an exhibitor policy that outlines exhibitors' responsibilities and what you will or will not supply as the event sponsor. Selection of exhibitors can be by invitation only or based on application, with or without a fee for exhibiting. Whatever the case, make sure that the exhibitors represent the overall theme of the fair or conference. Exhibitors can be recruited from many sources. These include various types of health professionals, local and state health departments, community groups, public, school, and medical libraries, police and fire departments, school PTAs, YMCAs, health clubs, and national and regional health organizations.
- **Funders and sponsors.** Sponsors will generally be needed to offer financial support. Sponsors can include community groups, community foundations, businesses and labor groups, individuals within the community, business leaders, and government funding sources. Often, businesses will be glad to help advertise the fair or conference in various ways. Public recognition can be provided for their contributions.
- **Publicity.** Publicity will be necessary. Publicize your fair, workshop, or conference in a variety of ways. Use the local newspapers, television, and radio outlets, prepare news releases, and post on available Web sites and community calendars. Develop your publicity to reflect professional design standards. Create a logo that will reflect the overall theme of the fair or conference. Make sure that advertisements are placed in high traffic areas American Academy of Pediatrics, such as libraries, childcare facilities, hospitals, health care facilities, and churches. Appropriate materials can also be sent home with students at various schools in the area. Press conferences and appearances on local television and radio can also be used effectively.
- **Evaluation.** Evaluation is necessary and is an ongoing process. From the beginning, decisions and ideas must be continually evaluated in terms of how they meet the identified and agreed-to goals,

objectives, and audience needs of the event. Formal evaluation forms can be created for participants, planning committees, exhibitors, and funders and sponsors, and others.

- **Outcome measures should be developed to ascertain how well the objectives were met.** Outcome measures are the: "Determination and evaluation of the results of an activity, plan, process, or program and their comparison with the intended or projected results."[8] An outcome measure is generally stated in quantitative terms that can be measured through calculation or recording tabulation or based on an activity, effort, or process that is expressed in numbers. Quantitative measures include counting, recording, tabulating, and displaying the results of your activity or effort that can be expressed in numbers. Stating outcomes in behavioral terms connected to an objective is an important means of measuring outcomes.[9] In developing outcome measures, consider the participants as actors and design activities that can be measured and that can be seen and/or observed. Evidence for this can be derived from a broad range of activities that are embedded in the program plan. Plan the outcome measurements so they can be displayed in narrative or numerical form, allowing for summations and conclusions.[10]
- **Trained observer ratings.** These are based on an observation instrument, specific procedures, and a standardized rating scale.
- **Types of evaluations.** Output evaluation for a community event can include:
  Questionnaires. Data can include needs, expectations, knowledge, attitudes, self-perception, skills, behaviors, life situations, status, experience in program, results from programs, demographics.
  Mail surveys. Content and development are much like a questionnaire.
  Phone surveys. Content development is based on questionnaire development, but a special protocol must be used.
  Trained observer ratings. These are based on an observation instrument, specific procedures, and a standardized rating scale.
  Informal self-reports. These are from staff, participants, administrators, etc.
- **Follow-ups (financial and otherwise).** After the event, thank-you letters must be sent to all persons on the planning committee, volunteers, funders, sponsors, and any others who have contributed in any way to the event's successes and operations. Settling accounts and paying bills in a timely fashion and meeting financial obligations are mandatory. Throughout the process, good bookkeeping and accounting procedures must be followed in accordance with laws and institutional requirements.

DEVELOPING OBJECTIVES AND ACTIVITIES

In planning, the National Library of Medicine suggests these starting points:

- Who is the target audience?
- What are the major health information needs?
- What access problems exist?
- What are the highest priorities to address?

NLM suggests positive behavior changes in health information and care can be obtained through the following objectives:[11]

- Increase awareness of health information sources.
- Increase specific knowledge about health information sources.
- Influence positive attitudes about health information sources.
- Influence beliefs about health information sources.

- Facilitate technology access and willingness to use information technology.
- Develop skills necessary for the better use of health information resources.
- Reinforce already-existing positive behaviors and attitudes.
- Build community and/or institutional support for programs and services.

Objectives that are especially needed for schools:

- Increase teacher and staff awareness of the importance of health information in curriculum and other areas of student life.
- Increase positive parental attitudes and behaviors about health information.
- Make health information easily accessible.
- Increase the participation of health providers in the community in contributing to the school's health information program.
- Increase students' health information literacy performance.

As just stated, good outcome measurements depend on good, behavior-focused objectives.

COORDINATED SCHOOL HEALTH PROGRAM CONFERENCE: GETHIP

The GetHIP conference held at the University of Texas Health Science Center in San Antonio, Texas, in June 2008 provides an example of a well-developed and well-received health conference. The planners of the conference developed these conference goals stated in behavioral terms:

- Discuss best practices relevant to school health and identify specific information resources.
- Explore strategies for disseminating current information about school health issues and health careers.
- Identify specific opportunities for collaboration among school librarians, school nurses, teachers, school administrators, health educators, and health sciences librarians, resulting in a team approach to school heath issues.

This CDC model is useful in planning because it recognizes eight interaction components: families, health care workers, the media, religious organizations, community organizations, and youth. The CSHP envisioned the school as an important agent in bringing all the elements together to promote better health of the nation's youth (CDC). These components are:

1. **Health education:** A planned, sequential K–12 curriculum that addresses the physical, mental, emotional, and social dimensions of health. The curriculum is designed to motivate and assist students to maintain and improve their health, prevent disease, and reduce health-related risk behaviors. It allows students to develop and demonstrate increasingly sophisticated health-related knowledge, attitudes, skills, and practices. The comprehensive health education curriculum includes a variety of topics, such as personal health, family health, community health, consumer health, environmental health, sexuality education, mental and emotional health, injury prevention and safety, nutrition, prevention and control of disease, and substance use and abuse. Qualified, trained teachers provide health education.

2. **Physical education:** A planned, sequential K–12 curriculum that provides cognitive content and learning experiences in a variety of activity areas, such as basic movement skills; physical fitness; rhythms and dance; games; team, dual, and individual sports; tumbling and gymnastics; and aquatics. Quality physical education should promote—through a variety of planned physical activities—each student's optimum physical, mental, emotional, and social development and should promote activities and sports that all students enjoy and can pursue throughout their lives. Qualified, trained teachers teach physical activity.

3. **Health services:** Services provided for students to appraise, protect, and promote health. These services are designed to ensure access or referral to primary health care services or both, foster appropriate use of primary health care services, prevent and control communicable diseases and other health problems, provide emergency care for illness or injury, promote and provide optimum sanitary conditions for a safe school facility and school environment, and provide educational and counseling opportunities for promoting and maintaining individual, family, and community health. Qualified professionals, such as physicians, nurses, dentists, health educators, and other allied health personnel, provide these services.

4. **Nutrition services:** Access to a variety of nutritious and appealing meals that accommodate the health and nutrition needs of all students. School nutrition programs reflect the U.S. Dietary Guidelines for Americans and other criteria to achieve nutrition integrity. The school nutrition services offer students a learning laboratory for classroom nutrition and health education and serve as a resource for linkages with nutrition-related community services. Qualified child nutrition professionals provide these services.

5. **Counseling and psychological services:** Services provided to improve students' mental, emotional, and social health. These services include individual and group assessments, interventions, and referrals. Organizational assessment and consultation skills of counselors and psychologists contribute not only to the health of students but also to the health of the school environment. Professionals such as certified school counselors, psychologists, and social workers provide these services.

6. **Healthy school environment**: The physical and aesthetic surroundings and the psychosocial climate and culture of the school. Factors that influence the physical environment include the school building and the area surrounding it, any biological or chemical agents that are detrimental to health, and physical conditions such as temperature, noise, and lighting. The psychological environment includes the physical, emotional, and social conditions that affect the well-being of students and staff.

7. **Health promotion for staff:** Opportunities for school staff to improve their health status through activities such as health assessments, health education and health-related fitness activities. These opportunities encourage school staff to pursue a healthy lifestyle that contributes to their improved health status, improved morale, and a greater personal commitment to the school's overall coordinated health program. This personal commitment often transfers into greater commitment to the health of students and creates positive role modeling. Health promotion activities have improved productivity, decreased absenteeism, and reduced health insurance costs.

8. **Family/community involvement:** An integrated school, parent, and community approach for enhancing the health and well-being of students. School health advisory councils, coalitions, and broadly based constituencies for school health can build support for school health program efforts. Schools actively solicit parent involvement and engage community resources and services to respond more effectively to the health-related needs of students.[12]

Figure 10.3.
Logo designed for the conference on health information for librarians and school health professionals serving K–12 students. Courtesy of the University of Texas Health Science Center in San Antonio. Published with permission.

ACTIVITIES FOR HEALTH FAIRS, WORKSHOPS, AND CONFERENCES

Family and Consumer Science, a part of the Texas A&M system, suggests the following activities suitable for a health event. These activities can be tailored to fit appropriate audiences and are designed to meet the needs of several groups, such as children, teen parents, adolescents (youth), adult parents, teenagers, grandparents, adults, all audiences, and older adults:

- Disability Awareness (children, youth, teens)
- Occupant Protection (all)
  - Child Safety Seat (parents, grandparents)
  - Pick-Ups 'N Kids (parents, grandparents)
  - It's Your Choice (adults)
  - Beat the Odds (teens)
  - Safe & Sober (teens, adults)
  - You Booze, You Cruise, You Lose (teens, adults)
  - Speed Interactive Board (teens, adults)
- Poisonous Snakes (all)
- Poison Prevention (all)
- Skin Cancer Prevention (all)
- Tobacco Use Prevention (all)
- Traffic Safety (all)
- Safety Belts and Child Safety Seats (all)
  - Child Safety Seats (parents, grandparents)
  - Pick-Ups 'N Kids (parents, grandparents)
  - Booster Seat Exhibit (parents, grandparents)
  - Pickup Truck Exhibit (teens, adults)
  - Safety Belt Exhibit (teens, adults)
  - Vince & Larry Costumes (children, teens, adults)
  - Rollover Convincers (children, teens, adults)
  - Traffic Safety Program (all)
- Drinking and Driving (teens, adults)
- Bicycle/Pedestrian Safety (children, youth, teens)

- Zoonosis Control (youth, teens)
- Bicycle Rodeo (children, youth, teens)
- Child Health (teen parents, adult parents, grandparents)
  - How to care for a child with fever
  - Preventing and treating colds and flu
  - Dealing with bed-wetting
  - Preventing ear infections and swimmer's ear
- Fire Prevention and Safety (children, youth, teen parents, adult parents)
- Health Care/Self-Care (adults, older adults)
  - How to select a doctor or clinic
  - How to participate in making decisions with your health care professional
  - Choosing the right kind of health care coverage (e.g., HMO, Preferred Provider, etc.)
  - Cutting health care costs and being a wise consumer of medical care
- Heart Disease and Stroke Prevention and Early Detection of Heart Attack and Stroke (children, youth, teens)
- Occupant Protection (children, youth, teens)
- Physical Activity (all)
- Prenatal Care (teen parents, adult parents)
- Women's Health (adults, older adults)
- Stress Management (adults, youth, teens, older adults)
- Tobacco Use Prevention (all)

Other topics can include:

- Sexuality (youth, teens, older adults)
- Violence and Youth Safety (children, youth, teens, teen Parents, adults)
- Grooming and Health (children, youth, teens, teen parents)
- Food and Diet (all)
- Growth and Development (all)
- Social and Cultural Issues (all)
- Disease Identification and Prevention (all)
- How to use the Internet for Health Information (all)[13]

TAKING CARE OF DETAILS

No matter how well we plan for an event, everyday operational details can often determine its overall success. Here are some basic suggestions for tracking important details, developed with some modification by the Public Libraries of Columbus and Franklin County, Ohio. We have made slight modifications to this fine inclusive checklist.

Implementation

- Confirm program participants and dates.
- Plan for setup (booths, speaker platforms, etc.).
- Make sure all equipment and materials are on hand.
- Consider furniture needs, lighting and electrical needs, audio projections, and assistance with equipment.

- Make sure you have all program participants contact information (address, phones, and e-mails).
- Make sure these details are confirmed: dates, times, place, transportation for program participants, directions and parking considerations for all participants, staff and volunteer responsibilities, and catering for refreshment and food and/or directions to nearby restaurants.
- Printing and delivery of programs
- Registration and continuing education credit
- Determine how continuing education credit is obtained. Check with official offices for regulations. Make sure that participants are notified about the availability of this and cost in announcements. In registering for the fair or conference, make the application for continuing education credit easy and transparent.
- Establish registration procedures. Will preregistration be required or will it be open to walkins? Will there be a cost for registration? If so, how will the cost be determined?
- Decide what materials and equipment will be needed at the registration desk. Will credit or debit cards be accepted? If photographs are to be taken, have a release form available at time of registration.

Housekeeping and Hospitality

- Make sure arrangements have been secured with the housekeeping staff so everything will be set up and taken down in a timely fashion.
- Plan for appropriate decorations in keeping with the theme of the conference.
- Appoint greeters and staffers that can greet both program participants as well as attendees, and make sure they have direction information regarding the overall program arrangements and physical facilities.

REFLECTIONS

Outreach to the community has been one of the lasting hallmarks of public libraries and public health services. As schools take on more and more community responsibilities, outreach in various forms is expected to be offered by the school and its faculty including the school librarian. Health care and health information are an excellent means of serving the school community and the larger community. All members of the school's community can be served by well-planned outreach programs, such as school health fairs, conferences, and workshops. Not only will outreach meet a vital informational need in the community, but it will also further the information literacy mission of the school library, extending it far beyond the walls of the library. Indeed, outreach allows the school library media center to become a library without walls.

Although outreach is important service to the school and community, do not neglect those within the school. Health information can be provided to teachers, staff, and parents through programming, collections, and resource development. Collaboration with teachers in teaching health information and resources is fundamental. The school librarian can also be available for consultations and to make referrals to resources and services to students, teachers, and staff. School librarians—working together with parents, teachers, and staff—can be a powerful force in providing health information to their communities and improving the health literacy of the entire community.

NOTES

1. Rabinowitz, D. "Community Studies: Anthropological," in *International Encyclopedia of Social and Behavioral Sciences*, ed. Neil J. Smelser and Paul V. Baltes, vol. 4 Amsterdam: Elsevier, 2001, p. 2387.

2. Jacobs, B. D. "Community Sociology," in *International Encyclopedia of Social and Behavioral Sciences*, ed. Neil J. Smelser and Paul V. Baltes, vol. 4. Amsterdam: Elsevier, 2001, p. 2383.

3. Constitution. Available at en Wikipedia.org/wiki/Tenth_Amendment_to_the United States_Constitution#Federal_funding. Accessed March 7, 2010.

4. Federation for Community Development Learning. www.fcdl.org.uk/about/definition.htm. Accessed Nov. 4, 2008.

5. Bracht, Nel, ed. "Health Promotion at the Community Level." *New Advances*. 2nd ed. Thousand Oaks, Calif.: Sage Publications, 1999, pp. 5–6.

6. Bracht.

7. Biblioteca Américas. ¡VIVA! bla.stisd.net/viva.html. Accessed Nov. 7, 2008.

8. "Outcome measure." BusinessDictionary.com. www.businessdictionary.com/definition/outcome-measure.html. Accessed Nov. 2, 2008.

9. "Outcome measure." BusinessDictionary.com.

10. University of Texas, Division of Instructional Innovation and Assessment (DIIA). "Academic Unit Assessment Plan Evaluation, 2006–2008. Assessment for All Departments: Information Studies, M.S." Unpublished document.

11. Burroughs, Catherine. *Guide to Planning, Evaluation and Improving Health Information Outreach*. Draft, Dec. 17, 1999, 12. n.p.: National Library of Medicine, Pacific Northwest Region, 1999. See also the *Planning and Evaluating Health Information Outreach Projects* series at nnlm.gov/evaluation/booklets/index.html#A2. Accessed Oct. 14, 2008.

12. University of Texas Health Science Center at San Antonio. "GetHIP." www.library.uthscsa.edu/events/gethip.cfm. Accessed Nov. 2, 2008.

13. Family and Consumer Sciences. fcs.tamu.edu/health/health_fair_planning_guide/evaluating_the_health_fair.php. Accessed Nov. 2, 2008.

11

Into the Future: Health, Curriculum, and Librarians

THE SCIENCE OF PREDICTING THE FUTURE

Predicting the future is difficult, but it seems to be a part of human nature to want to know what lies ahead with some degree of confidence. Strategic planning that most institutions conduct is just one example of forecasting. Such plans are attempts to anticipate future needs and to lay plans as to how to place those plans into operation within a designated future timeframe. Figure 11.1 indicates that planning begins with:

1. A review of the current situation
2. Selecting what is valuable from the present to carry into the future
3. Design for the future based on past experiences and anticipated needs

Over the years, prediction of the future has become an academic and/or popular practice based on logic. Nicholas Rescher, professor of philosophy at the University of Pittsburgh, in his 1998 book, *Predicting the Future: An Introduction to the Theory of Forecasting* lists three important characteristics associated with solid forecasting:[1]

- Past and present information should be obtained in a timely manner that is both accurate in facts, reliable and dependable overtime.
- The data obtained must demonstrate "discernible patterns."
- The patterns must be stable, consistent, and likely to continue into the future.

Rescher advises that the data must be evaluated in terms of "temporal patterns." After that, one can set about projecting such patterns into the future in the most efficient way possible.[2]

Predictions for medicine in the future are based on data from present-day medical advances and research as well as from social and cultural patterns. Most of these

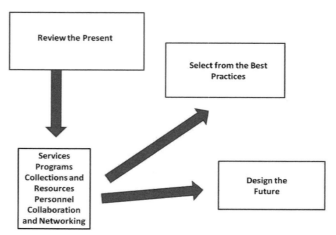

Figure 11.1.
A simple planning diagram for the future. Based on a concept by Vijay Govindarajan.[3]

predictions will affect how medical information is taught and provided to youth as consumers. The following discussion is based on articles by Donald A. B. Lindberg, Betsy L. Humphreys, and Leroy Hood. Although Lindberg and Humphreys write about medical libraries, much of what they say can be adjusted and applied to health information programs in school.[4,5]

PARTICIPATORY MEDICAL APPROACHES

Participatory medicine is based on the assumption that patients will have to assume more control of their health care. To do this, they must have the knowledge to make health care decisions. This means they must be educated to assume a participatory role. Participatory medicine involves such elements as knowing their own health characteristics, such as personal genetic data, and also having an understanding of the effects of environments on health and personal health behaviors. For example, patients must have knowledge and accept the facts that cancer is closely associated with the use of tobacco and exposure to the sun.[6]

The implications of participatory medicine for the school librarian and the school library media center are obvious: These implications involve:

- Promotion of critical thinking skills as related to personal health care
- Evaluation of health information
- Encouraging the informed used of information technology that provides access to health information
- Providing comfortable and inviting facilities for personal health study and research

INFORMATION TECHNOLOGY AND COMMUNICATION

Very much aligned with participatory medicine is the use of information technology. This involves:

- Providing easy access to electronic information and telecommunications in a variety of locations

- Expanding the use of a wide variety of information communication devices
- Offering facilities that have instant communication capabilities
- Training users and developing guidelines for use of databases and communication devices

NETWORKING AND COLLABORATION

As curriculum becomes more inclusive, we will see teachers, school librarians, and students networking and collaborating with parents, colleagues, and community agencies involved in a wide variety of service learning and participatory activities. These activities may occur off campus as well as within the school environments and in virtual settings. This means that communication technology must meet a high level of efficiency.

FACILITIES: THE SCHOOL LIBRARY AS PLACE

In order to meet demands for health information in the future, the school library must be a place that is:

- Centrally located and easy to reach
- Physically attractive
- Technically equipped
- Accommodating for individual study and research, large group instruction, and small group work
- Able to offer facilities for the production of multimedia and virtual collections
- Provide data and information in a variety of languages that are required by the users

SCHOOL LIBRARIAN AS MENTOR

The school librarian will see an increase in role expectations, such as:

- Facilitator of instruction and programming
- Mentor to teachers, students, and community
- Guide to information resources
- Customizer of information for presentations and individual information requests

COLLECTION DEVELOPMENT

As the availability of electronic resources increases, the paper-based collection will decrease, allowing more space for the accommodations mentioned previously. Nevertheless, school librarians will be required to keep abreast of present and emerging health information formats and health needs. A brief list could well include these topics:

- Customized drug development
- Genetics and diseases
- Evaluation of health information
- Infectious diseases and their eradication
- Climate change and health

- Screening for health defects
- Complementary medicine
- Globalization and health issues
- Antibodies and health issues
- Demographics and health issues
- Health disparities
- High-risk environments and behaviors
- Government policies and health issues
- Integration of public health services and programs into schools environments
- Health networking and communication
- Youth health issues, including teen pregnancies
- Nutrition and food in cultures
- Dietary behaviors
- Sports medicine and training

REFLECTIONS

Health instruction and health literacy are important aspects of future development. Their vigorous integration into curriculum areas by using appealing teaching themes, media, and databases are paramount of the future health of youth. Trade books, textbooks, Internet sources, commercial databases, and present-day and future communication technologies offer teachers and school librarians a wealth of ideas and avenues to bring better health information to youth today and in the future. Concentrated health instruction that promotes health literacy will help change for the better attitudes and behaviors of youth about their health and the health of their friends and families now and in the coming decades.

NOTES

1. Rescher, Nicholas. *Predicting the Future: An Introduction to the Theory of Forecasting.* State University of New York Press, 1998, p. 86.

2. Rescher.

3. "Vijay Govindarajan's Blog. Strategy & Innovation, Oct. 30, 2009." www.vijay govindarajan.com. Accessed Oct 30, 2009.

4. Lindberg, Donald A. B. and Betsy L. Humphreys. "2015—The Future of Medical Libraries." *The New England Journal of Medicine* 352 (March 27, 2005): 1067–1070.

5. Hood, Leroy. "A Doctor's Vision of the Future of Medicine," *Newsweek*, July 13, 2009. www.newsweek.com/id/204227. Accessed Oct. 16, 2009.

6. Hood.

Appendix A

Resources

CHAPTER 4. SEARCHING FOR HEALTH INFORMATION AND DEVELOPING LIBRARY USE SKILLS

For Older Students

Goodstein, Anastasia. *Totally Wired: What Teens and Tweens Are Really Doing Online*. 1st ed. Saint Martin's Griffin, 2007.

Hock, Randolph. *The Extreme Searcher's Internet Handbook: A Guide for the Serious Searcher*. CyberAge Books, 2004.

Keen, Andrew. *The Cult of the Amateur: How Today's Internet is Killing Our Culture*. 1st ed. Doubleday/Currency, 2007.

Maran, Ruth and others. *Computers*. Thomson/Course Technology, 2005.

Mintz, Anne P. *Misinformation on the Internet*. CyberAge Books, 2002.

Networking and How the Internet Works. 3rd ed. Prentice Hall, 2000.

Oppel, Andrew J. *Databases Demystified*. McGraw-Hill/Osborne, 2004.

Schell, Bernadette H. *The Internet and Society: A Reference Handbook*. Contemporary World Issues series. ABC-CLIO, 2007.

Stein, Richard Joseph. *Internet Safety*. Reference Shelf series, v. 81, no. 2. H. W. Wilson Co., 2009.

Taniar, David and others. *Web-Powered Databases*. Idea Group Pub, 2003.

Zittrain, Johathan. *The Future of the Internet and How to Stop It*. Yale University Press, 2008.

For Younger Students

Gaines, Ann. *Ace Your Internet Research*. Ace It! Information Literacy series. Enslow Publishers, 2009.

Goranson, Christopher. *Everything You Need to Know about Misinformation on the Internet.* I Need to Know Library series. Rosen Publishing Group, 2002.

Gordon, Sherri Mabry. *Downloading Copyrighted Stuff from the Internet: Stealing or Fair Use?* Issues in Focus Today series. Enslow Publishers, 2005.

Herumin, Wendy. *Censorship on the Internet: From Filters to Freedom of Speech.* Issues in Focus Today series. Enslow, 2004.

McLeese, Don. *The Internet and E-mail.* Let's Explore Technology Communications series. Rourke, 2009.

Oxlade, Chris. *My First Internet Guide.* Heinemann Library, 2007.

Rosner, Marc Alan. *Science Fair Success Using the Internet.* Science Fair Success series. Revised and updated ed. Enslow Publishers, 2006.

For Librarians and Teachers

Bell, Suzanne S. *Librarian's Guide to Online Searching.* Libraries Unlimited, 2006.

Crane, Beverley E. *Using Web 2.0 Tools in the K–12 Classroom.* Neal-Schuman, 2009.

Daccord, Thomas. *The Best of History Sites.* Neal-Schuman, 2007.

De Abreu, Belinha S. *Teaching Media Literacy.* How-to-Do-It Manuals for Libraries series, no. 156. Neal-Schuman, 2007.

Hunt, Finna and Birks, Jane. *More Hands-On Information Literacy Activities.* Neal-Schuman, 2008.

Schlessinger Media. *Library Skills for Children.* Schlessinger Media, 2004.

Thomas, Nancy Pickering. *Information Literacy and Information Skills Instruction: Applying Research to Practice in the School Library Media Center.* Libraries Unlimited, 2004.

Descriptions of databases are available in Chapter 4.

CHAPTER 5. MATERIALS FOR HEALTH INSTRUCTION AND INFORMATION

An extensive listing and descriptions of health-related Internet databases and selection aids are found in the discussion in Chapter 5.

CHAPTER 6. LITERATURE, THE ARTS, PERFORMANCE ACTIVITIES, AND LANGUAGES

Suggested Resources: Drama and Fiction

For Older Students

Anderson, Maxwell and March, William. *Bad Seed: A Play in Two Acts: A Dramatization of William March's Novel The Bad Seed.* Dramatists Play Service, 1985.

Auburn, David. *Proof: A Play.* Faber and Faber, 2001.

Brancato, Robin. *Winning.* Bantam, 1978.

Brooks, Geraldine. *Year of Wonders: A Novel of the Plague.* Viking, 2001.

Carden, William, Berline, Pamela and the HB Playwrights Foundation & Theatre. *HB Playwrights Short Play Festival 2001: The Hospital Plays.* Contemporary Playwrights series. Smith and Kraus, 2003.

Camus, Albert. *The Plague.* Vintage, 1991.

Craven, Margaret. *I Heard the Own Call My Name*. Doubleday, 1973.

Cronin, A. J. *The Citadel*. Back Bay Books, 1983.

Crutcher, Chris. *Staying Fat for Sarah Byrnes: An American Indian Odyssey*. Paw Prints, 2008.

Gibson, William. *The Miracle Worker: A Play for Television*. Knopf, 1957.

Guest, Judith. *Ordinary People*. Viking Press, 1976.

Gunter, Jon. *Death Be Not Proud: A Memoir*. HarperCollins, 2007.

Lewis, Sinclair. *Arrowsmith*. Signet Classics, 1998. Originally published in 1925.

March, William. *The Bad Seed: A Novel*. 1st Ecco ed. Ecco Press. Distributed by W. W. Norton, 1997.

Mersand, Joseph E., Ibsen, Henrik, Kingsley, Sidney and Howard, Sidney Coe. *Three Plays about Doctors*. The ANTA Series of Distinguished Plays. Washington Square Press, 1961.

Morgan, Nicola. *Fleshmarket*. Delacorte Press, 2004.

Sinclair, Upton. *The Jungle*. Various editions. Originally published in 1905.

Todd, Lee Savitt. *Medical Readers' Theater: A Guide and Scripts*. University of Iowa Press, 2002.

Wilder, Thornton. *Our Town: A Play in Three Acts*. Harper, 1960.

For Younger Students

Atkin, Flora B. *Hold That Tiger: How a Family Copes with a Medical Crisis: A Play for Young People and Families*. New Plays, 1986.

Brooks, Jerome. *The Big Dipper Marathon*. Pocket Books, 1982.

Coerr, Eleanor. *Sadako and the Thousand Paper Cranes*. Puffin Books, 1999.

Giblin, James and Dooling, Michael. *The Boy Who Saved Cleveland: Based on a True Story*. Henry Holt, 2006.

Havill, Steven. *Race for the Dying*. Thomas Dunne Books, 2009.

Hennigan, Katherine. *Ida B: . . . and Her Plans to Maximize Fun, Avoid Disaster, and (Possibly) Save the World*. Greenwillow Books, 2004.

Koertge, Ron. *Shakespeare Bats Cleanup*. Candlewick Press, 2003.

McDaniel, Lurlene. *A Rose for Melinda*. Bantam Books, 2002.

Rus, Jeff. *Paralyzed*. Orca Sports series. Orca Sports series. Orca Book Publishers, 2008.

Voigt, Cynthia. *Izzy, Willy-Nilly*. Paw Prints, 2008.

Weaver, Lydia. *Close to Home: A Story of the Polio Epidemic*. Sagebrush Education, 1999.

For Preschool and Primary Grades

Agee, Jon. *Terrific*. Michael di Capua Books/Hyperion, 2005.

Appelt, Kathi. *The Underneath*. Atheneum Books for Young Readers, 2008.

Beaty, Andrea and Lemaitre, Pascal. *Dr. Ted*. Atheneum Books for Young Readers, 2008.

Beinstein, Phoebe and A&J Studios. *Say Ahhh!: Dora Goes to the Doctor*. Dora the Explorer series, no. 26. Simon Spotlight, 2008.

Collins, Nile and Coombe, Marten. *The Insulin Discovery: The Story of Dr. Frederick Banting and Charles Best*. Active Lives: Biographies on Stage series. Clean Slate Press [Auckland, New Zealand], 2007.

Cousins. Lucy. *Maisy Goes to the Hospital*. Candlewick Press, 2007.

Guest, Elissa Haden and Davenior, Christine. *Iris and Walter: The School Play*. Harcourt, 2003.

Jon Scieszka and Design Garage. *Uh-Oh, Max*. Ready-to-Read series. Aladdin Paperbacks, 2009.

Klein, Adria F. and Gallagher-Cole, Mernie. *Max Goes to the Doctor*. Read-It! Readers series, Purple level. Picture Window Books, 2008.

McDonald, Megan and Reynolds, Peter. *Judy Moody, M.D.: The Doctor Is In!* Candlewick Press, 2004.

Millman, Isaac. *Moses Sees a Play*. Farrar, Straus and Giroux, 2004.

Wells, Rosemary. *Felix Feels Better*. Candlewick Press, 2001.

Wells, Rosemary and Wheeler, Jody. *The School Play*. Hyperion Books for Children, 2001.

Wilson, Karma and Chapman, Jane. *Bear Feels Sick*. M. K. McElderry Books, 2007.

York, Vanessa and Mounsey-Smith, Karen. *Nightingale Power: The Story of Florence Nightingale and Sidney Herbert*. Active Lives: Biographies on Stage series. Clean Slate Press [Auckland, New Zealand], 2007.

BIOGRAPHICAL MATERIALS

Extraordinary People and Experiences

Gonzales, Doreen. *AIDS: Ten Stories of Courage*. Enslow Publishers, 1996.

Irwin, Cait, Evans, Dwight L. and Andrews, Linda Wasmer. *Monochrome Days: A Firsthand Account of One Teenager's Experience with Depression*. Annenberg Foundation Trust at Sunnylands' Adolescent Mental Health Initiative series. Oxford University Press, 2007.

Keller, Helen. *The Story of My Life*. Penguin, 2002. Reprint.

Kent, Deborah and Quinlan, Kathryn A. *Extraordinary People with Disabilities*. Children's Press, 1996.

Kisor, Henry and Percy, Walker. *What's That Pig Outdoors? A Memoir of Deafness*. Farrar, Straus and Giroux, 1990.

Krementz, Jill. *How It Feels to Fight for Your Life*. Little, Brown, 1989.

———. *How It Feels When a Parent Dies*. Knopf, 1988.

Lance Armstrong Foundation. *Live Strong: Inspirational Stories from Cancer Survivors—from Diagnosis to Treatment and Beyond*. Broadway Books, 2005.

Lavender, Kee. *Lesson in Taxidermy*. Akaskie Books, 2005.

Reeve, Christopher. *Still Me*. Arrow, 1999.

Winick, Judd. *Pedro and Me: Friendship, Loss, and What I Learned*. Henry Holt, 2002.

Biographies of Artists

Andersen, Wayne V. *Cézanne and the Eternal Feminine*. Contemporary Artists and their Critics series. Cambridge University Press, 2004.

Boris, Janet. *Frida Kahlo*. ArtEd series. Harry N. Abrams, 2001.

———. *Roy Lichtenstein*. ArtEd Series. Harry N. Abrams, 2001.

Cezanne in Provence. Created by Jackson Frost; Norman Allen; Jacqueline Bisset; Paul Cézanne; and WETA-TV (Washington, D.C.); PBS Home Video, 2006. Available on DVD.

Deitch, Jeffrey, Haring, Keith, Geiss, Suzanne and Gruen, Julia. *Keith Haring*. Rizzoli, 2008.

Koestenbaum, Wayne. *Andy Warhol*. Penguin Lives series. Viking, 2001.

Kudlinski, Kathleen V. and Henderson, Meryl. *Dr. Seuss: Young Author and Artist*. 1st Aladdin Paperbacks ed. Childhood of Famous Americans series. Aladdin Paperbacks, 2005.

Landau, Ellen G. *Jackson Pollock.*, Harry N. Abrams, 2000.

Mason, Miriam E. and Morrison, Cathy. *John Audubon, Young Naturalist*. New ed. Young Patriots series, 12. Patria Press, 2006.

McFeely, William S. *Portrait: The Life of Thomas Eakins*. W. W. Norton, 2007.

McNeese, Tim. *Salvador Dalí*. Great Hispanic Heritage series. Chelsea House Publishers, 2006.

Mis, Melody S. *Paul Cezanne*. 1st. ed. PowerKids Press, 2008.

Porcu, Costantino. *Dalí*. Skira, 2009.

Souder, William. *Under a Wild Sky: John James Audubon and the Making of the Birds of America*. 1st ed. North Point Press, 2004.

Weston, Nancy. *Daniel Maclise: Irish Artist in Victorian London*. Four Courts Press, 2001.

Biographies of Athletes

Armstrong, Lance and Jenkins, Sally. *Every Second Counts*. Broadway Books, 2003.

———. *It's Not about the Bike: My Journey Back to Life*. Putnam, 2000.

Connor, Jim. *Comeback!: Four True Stories*. Step into Reading series, Book 4. Random House, 1992.

Coyle, Daniel. *Lance Armstrong's War. One Man's Battle against Fate, Fame, Love, Death, Scandal, and a Few Other Rivals on the Road to the Tour de France*. HarperCollins, 2005.

Duplacey, James. *Muhammed Ali: Athlete, Activist, Ambassador*. Warwick Publishing, 2001.

Great Achievers. Lives of the Physically Challenged Series. Chelsea House, 1997.

Hall, Jonathan. *Mark McGwire: A Biography*. Pocket Books, 1998.

———. *Mark McGwire: A Biography*. American Printing House for the Blind, 2000. Cassette tape, one sound cassette: mono., NAB standard.

Harrington, Geri and Callahan, John. *Jackie Joyner-Kersee: Champion Athlete*. Facts on File, 1995.

Hatch, Robert and Hatch, William. *The Hero Project: 2 Teens, 1 Notebook, 13 Extraordinary Interviews*. McGraw-Hill, 2006.

Macht, Norman and Callhan, John. *Roy Campanella: Baseball Star*. Facts on File, 1995.

Macht, Norman and Lewis, Jerry. *Jim Abbott: Major League Pitcher*. Facts on File, 1994.

Rappoport, Ken. *Profiles in Sports Courage*. Peachtree, 2006.

Rennebohm, Peter. *Be Not Afraid: Ben Peyton's Story: A Seventeen-Year-Old Hockey Player's Fight to Overcome a Devastating Injury*. North Star Press of St. Cloud, 2004.

Robinson, Tom. *Donovan McNabb: Leader On and Off the Field*. Sports Stars with Heart series. Enslow Publishers, 2008.

Scranton, Pierce E. *Playing Hurt: Treating and Evaluating the Warriors of the NFL*. Brassey's, 2001.

Stewart, Mark, *Sweet Victory: Lance Armstrong's Incredible Journey: The Amazing Story of the Greatest Comeback in Sports*. Millbrook Press, 2000.

Biographies of Dancers

Barasch, Lynn. *Knockin' on Wood: Starring Peg Leg Bates*. Lee & Row, 2004.

Daneman, Meredith. *Margot Fonteyn*. Viking, 2004.

Glover, Savion and Weber, Bruce. *Savion!: My Life in Tap*. New York: W. Morrow and Co., 2000.

Gottlie, Robert. *George Balanchine: The Ballet Maker*. HarperCollins/Atlas Books, 2004.

Haselhurst, Maureen. *Born to Dance: The Story of Rudolf Nureyev*. Oxford University Press, 2003.

Kavanagh, Julie. *Nureyev: The Life*. 1st American ed. Pantheon Books, 2007.

Kozodoy, Ruth. *Isadora Duncan*. American Women of Achievement series. Facts on File, 1987.
Pinkney, David. *Alvin Ailey*. 1st ed. Hyperion Books for Children.
Plisetskaia, Maiia Mikhailovna, with others. *I, Maya Plisetskaya*. Yale University Press, 2001.
Stuart, Otis. *Perpetual Motion: The Public and Private Lives of Rudolf Nureyev*. Simon & Schuster, 1995.
Thompson, Lauren and Estrin, James. *Ballerina Dreams: A True Story*. Feiwel and Friends, 2007.

Biographies of Musicians

Geck, Martin. *Johann Sebastian Bach: Life and Work*: Harcourt, 2006.
Halperin, Ian. *Unmasked: The Final Years of Michael Jackson*. 1st Simon Spotlight Entertainment hardcover ed., Simon Spotlight Entertainment, 2009.
Kallen, Stuart A. *Great Composers*. Lucent Books, 2000.
Krohn, Katherine. *Michael Jackson: Ultimate Music Legend*. Gateway Biographies series. Lerner, 2010.
Pratt, Mary K. *Michael Jackson: King of Pop*. Lives Cut Short series. ABDO Pub. Co., 2010.
Ritz, David. *Ray Charles: Voice of Soul* by Facts on File, 1994.
Taraborrelli, J. Randy. *Michael Jackson: The Magic, the Madness, the Whole Story, 1958–2009*. 1st Grand Central Publishing ed. Grand Central Publishing, 2009.
Williams, Peter F. *J.S. Bach*. Cambridge: Cambridge University Press, 2007.

Hearing and Health

Chasin, Marshall. *Hearing Loss in Musicians: Prevention & Management*. Plural Publishing, 2008.
Heelan, James Riggio. *Can You Hear a Rainbow?: The Story of a Deaf Boy Named Chris*. 1st ed. Peachtree Publishers, 2002.
Hyman, Jane. *Deafness*. F. Watts, 1980.
Jennings, Terry J. *Sound*. Smart Apple Media, 2009.
Pringle, Laurence P. *Hearing*. Benchmark Books, 2000.
Showers, Paul and Keller, Holly. *Ears Are for Hearing*. Crowell, 1990.

Dance and Athletic Health

Arnheim, Daniel D. *Dance Injuries: Their Prevention and Care*. Princeton Book Company, 3rd ed. 1991.
Balcavae, Dynise. *Steroids*. Junior Drug Awareness series. Chelsea House Publishers, 2000.
Ballard, Carol and Pickett, Robert. *Exercise*. Blackbirch Press and Thomson/Gale, 2004.
Barringer, Janice and Schlesinger, Sarah. *The Pointe Book: Shoes, Training & Technique*. 2nd. ed. Princeton Book Company, 2004.
Bellenir, Karen. *Fitness Information for Teens: Health Tips about Exercise, Physical Well-Being, and Health Maintenance Including Facts about Aerobic and Anaerobic Conditioning, Stretching, Body Shape and Body Image, Sports Training, Nutrition, and Activities for Non-Athletes*. Teen Health series. Omnigraphics, 2004.
Clippinger, Karen S. *Dance Anatomy and Kinesiology*. Human Kinetics Publishers, 2007.

Dimon, Theodore. *Anatomy of the Moving Body: A Basic Course in Bones, Muscles, and Joints.* 2nd. ed. Random House, 2008.

Dosil, Joaquin. *Eating Disorders in Athletes.* John Wiley & Sons, 2008.

Edelson, Edward. *Sports Medicine.* 21st Century Health and Wellness series. Chelsea House Publishers, 2000.

Ferguson Publishing. *Careers in Focus: Coaches and Fitness Professionals.* Ferguson, 2008.

Gardner, Robert and Conklin, Gardner Barbara. *Health Science Projects about Sports Performance.* Enslow Publishers, 2002.

Hyde, Natalie. *Live It—Fairness.* Crabtree Character Sketches series. Crabtree Publishing, 2010.

Janda, David. *The Awakening of a Surgeon: A Family Guide to Preventing Sports Injuries and Death.* Michigan Orthopaedic Center, 2004.

Janowski, Connie. *The Human Body.* Mission Science series. Compass Point Books, 2009.

Koutedakis, Yiannis, Sharp, N. C. Craig, Boreham, Colin and others. *The Fit and Healthy Dancer.* John Wiley & Sons, 1999.

Magill, Lenny, Durkin, Todd, Eveland, Brian and Time Zone Multimedia. *Flexibility for Performance: For Professionals.* Time Zone Multimedia, 2006. DVD. Lawton, Sandra Augustyn. *Eating Disorders Information for Teens: Health Tips about Anorexia, Bulimia, Binge Eating, and Other Eating Disorders.* Teen Health and Exercise series. Omnigraphics, 2005.

Marcovitz, Hal. *Caffeine.* Drug Education Library series. Lucent Books, 2006.

Mason, Paul. *Biking.* Recreational Sports series. Smart Apple Media, 2008.

McCloskey, John and Bailes, Julian E. *When Winning Costs Too Much: Steroids, Supplements, and Scandal in Today's Sport.* Taylor Trade Pub, 2005. Distributed by the National Book Network.

McMahon, Patricia. *Dancing Wheels.* Houghton Mifflin, 2000.

Minigh, Jennifer L. *Sports Medicine. Health and Medical Issues.* Today series. Greenwood Press, 2007.

Morris, Neil. *Food for Sports.* Energy Foods series. Heinemann Library, 2006.

Nagler, Michelle H. *Get Fit! Eat Right! Be Active!: Girls' Guide to Health & Fitness.* Scholastic, 2001.

Omalu, Bennet. *Play Hard, Die Young: Football Dementia, Depression and Death.* Neo-Forenxis Books, 2008.

Pasternak, Harley and Boldt, Ethan. *5-Factor Fitness: The Diet and Fitness Secret of Hollywood's A-List.* Berkley, 2005.

Ruskin, Ron. *Personal Development, Health and Physical Education.* HSC Study Cards series. Jacaranda [Milton, Queensland], 2002.

Schaefer, A. R. *Steroids.* 21st Century Library: Health at Risk series. Cherry Lake Publishing, 2009.

Spilken, Terry. *Dancer's Foot Book.* Princeton Book Company, 1990.

Spilsbury, Louise. *Why Should I Get Off the Couch?: And Other Questions about Health and Exercise.* Heinemann Infosearch series. Heinemann Library, 2003.

Trevor Romain and PorchLight Home Entertainment. *If You Don't Take Care of Your Body, Where Else Are You Going to Live?* Trevor Romain collection. Porchlight Entertainment, 2008. DVD.

Turner, Chérie. *Marathon Cycling.* Ultra Sports series. Rosen Publishing Group, 2002.

Watkins, Andrea and Clarkson, Priscilla M. *Dancing Longer Dancing Stronger: A Dancer's Guide to Improving Technique and Preventing Injury.* Princeton Book Company, 1990.

Woolf-May, Kate and Bird, Stephen R. *Exercise Prescription: Physiological Foundations: A Guide for Health, Sport and Exercise Professionals*. Churchill Livingstone, 2006.

Art and Health

For Older Students

Barcsay, Jenō. *Jenō Barcsay's Anatomy for the Artist: Drawings and Text*. MetroBooks, 2002.
Bender, George A. and Thom, Robert A. *Parke-Davis's Pictorial Annals of Medicine and Pharmacy*. Warner-Lambert Co., 1999.
Currie-McGhee, L. K. *Tattoos and Body Piercing*. Lucent Books, 2006.
Hayes, Bill. *The Anatomist: A True Story of Gray's Anatomy*. Ballantine Books, 2008.
Kyle, Robert A. and Shampo, M. A. *Medicine and Stamps*. R. E. Krieger Publishing, 1980. Originally published by the American Medical Association, 2nd, 1970.
McCann, Michael. *Artist Beware*. Watson-Guptill Publications, 1979.
McCann, Michael and Babin, Angela. *Health Hazards Manual for Artists*. 6th ed. Lyons Press, 2008.
McNiff, Shaun. *Art as Medicine: Creating a Therapy of the Imagination*. Piatkus, 1994, 1992.
Rifkin, Benjamin A. and Ackerman, Michael J. *Anatomy: From the Renaissance to the Digital Age*. Abrams, 2006.
Rossol, Monona. *The Artist's Complete Health & Safety Guide*. 2nd. Allworth Press, 1994.
Wilkinson, Beth. *Coping with the Dangers of Tattooing, Body Piercing, and Branding*. Rosen Publishing Group, 1998.

For Younger Students

Bull, Peter. *Flowers & Plants*. Kingfisher (London), 2008.
Court, Rob. *How to Draw People*. Child's World, 2007.
Esterer, Arnulf K. and Esterer, Louise A. *Signs and Symbols*. Messner, 1980.
Temple, Kathryn. *Drawing: The Only Drawing Book You'll Ever Need to Be the Artist You've Always Wanted to Be*. Lark Books, 2005.

Foreign Languages

Folklore and Mythology

For Novice Readers

Aesop. *The Sick Lion* at www.elook.org/literature/aesop/fables/423.html.
———. *The Sick Lion: And the Hare and the Tortoise*. Award Publications Ltd., 2001.
Aesop Fables. An extensive list of Aesop Fables is available at eLook.org: www.elook.org/literature/aesop/fables.
Arnold, Katya and Suteev V. *That Apple is Mine*. Holiday House, 2000.
Brodsky, Beverly. *The Crystal Apple: A Russian Tale*. Viking Press, 1974.
Cleveland, Rob and Baird Hoffmire. *The Magic Apple: A Middle Eastern Folktale*. Paw Prints, 2006.
Desclot, Miquel and Ignasi Blanch. *Blancanieves* (*Snow White*). Bilingual. Chronicle Books, 2008. A more authentic version of the tale is found at en.wikipedia.org/wiki/Snow_White.

Grimm Brothers. Full-text versions of most of the Grimm Brothers' folktales are available at www.pitt.edu/~dash/grimmtales.html.

Hunia, Fran. *Blanche-Neige et les Sept Nains*. Scholastic-TAB, 1984.

Hürlimann, Bettina and Nussbaumer, Paul. *William Tell and His Son*. Brace & World, 1965.

Nuttall, Gina. *Is Lion Sick?* QEB, 2005.

Rylant, Cynthia and Corace, Jen. *Hansel and Gretel*. Hyperion Books for Children, 2008.

Shah, Indries and Santiago, Rose Mary. *The Farmer's Wife*. Hoopoe Books, 1998.

Sibley, Raymond, Grimm, Jacob and Aitchison, Martin. *Snow White and the Seven Dwarfs*. Ladybird Favorite Tales series. Ladybird Books USA, 1996.

Yeoman, John and Swiderska, Barbara. *The Apple of Youth, and Other Russian Folk Stories*. Franklin Watts, 1967.

Fiction and Drama

For Intermediate Students

French

Bondoux, Anne-Laure. *The Killer's Tears*. Translated from the French by Y. Maudet. Delacorte, 2006.

Mourlevat, Jean-Claude. *The Pull of the Ocean*. Translated from the French by Y. Maudet. Delacorte, 2006.

German

Bach, Tamara. *Girl from Mars*. Translated from the German by Shelley Tanaka. Groundwood, 2008.

Holub, Josef. *An Innocent Soldier*. Translated by Michael Hofmann. New York: Alfred A. Levine Books, 2005.

Russian

Anisimov, Andreĭ. *Bomba dlia Al'-Kaidy* (Бомба дИя АИь-Каиды) (*Bomb for Al-Qaeda*). AST/Astrel (Moscow), 2007.

Poliakova, Tat'iana. *Vse Tochki Nad I* (Все точки над i) (*Dot All of Your "I"s*). EKSMO (Moscow), 2007.

Twain, Mark. *Prikliucheniia Gekl'berri Finna: Roman* English translations: *Adventures of Huckleberry Finn: A Novel*. Detskaia Literatura (Moscow), 2007.

Spanish

Harris, Dorothy Joan. Melany: *Historia de una Anorexica*. English translation: *Even If It Kills Me*. Grupo Editorial Norma, 2002.

Sánchez, Carlos. *Cuanhtémos Sangre de Campeón sin Cadenas: La Primera Novela de Asertividad para Adolescentes y Adultos*. English translation: *Campion Blood without Chains*. Serie Juvenil. Selectas Diamante, 2002.

Taylor, Barbara. *Supervivencia: Vida en los Hábitos mas Inhóspitos*. Translation of *Survival*. Planeta Junior, 2002.

VanCleave, Janice Pratt. *Alimentos y Nutrición para Niños y Jovenes: Actividades Superdivertidas para el Aprendizaje de la Ciencia*. English translation: *Food and Nnutrition for Every Kid*. Limusa-Wiley, 2002.

For Advanced-Level Students

French

Camus, Albert. *La Peste*. English translation: *The Plague*. Translated by Stuart Gilbert. Modern Library College series. McGraw-Hill, 1965.

Flaubert, Gustave. *Madame Bovary*. Pocket [Paris], 2006. Translated by Elcanor Marx Aveling. Barnes & Noble Classics, 2005.

Hugo, Victor. *Les Misérables*. Borders Group, 2009.

———. *Notre-Dame de Paris*. English translation: *The Hunchback of Notre-Dame*. Ann Arbor Media, 2006.

Rostand, Edmond. *Cyano de Bergerac*. Translated by Gertrude Hall. Barnes & Noble Classics series. Barnes & Noble, 2004.

German

Hesse, Hermann. *Demian: Die Geschichte von Emil Sinclair's Jugend*. English translation: *Demian: The Story of Emil Sinclair's Youth*. Harper Perennial Modern Classics, 1999.

———. *Der Zauberberg*. English translation: *The Magic Mountain*. Translated by Luann Walther and John E. Woods. Paw Prints, 2008.

Remarque, Erich Maria. *Im Westen nichts Neues*. English translation: *All Quiet on the Western Front*. Paw Prints, 2008.

Russian

Solzhenitsyn, Aleksandr Isaevich. Раковый Корпус. Flegon Press, 1968. English translation: *Cancer Ward*. Random House, 1983, 1969.

Spanish

Picoult, Jodi. *Por la Vida de Mi Hermana*. English translation: *My Sister's Keeper*. Simon & Schuster, 2008.

Sabato, Ernesto. *El Tunel*. English translation: *The Tunnel* 28th ed. Catedra, 2006.

Umbral, Francisco. *Mortal y Rosa*. English translation: *Mortal and Rose*. Letras Hispánicas Series, 393. Ediciones Cátedra: Ediciones Destino, 2008.

CHAPTER 7. CONNECTIONS TO GOOD HEALTH: SOCIAL AND BEHAVIORAL SCIENCES, AND LANGUAGES

Sociology of Health (Living Together and Social Responsibilities)

Ancona, George. *Barrio: José's Neighborhood*. San Diego: Harcourt Brace, 1998.

Berenstain, Stan and Berenstain, Jan. *The Berenstain Bears and Too Much Junk Food*. Random House, 1985.

Birch, Robin. *Health*. Macmillan Education, 2002.

Bird, Chloe E., Conrad, Allen and Fremont, M. *Handbook of Medical Sociology*. 5th ed. Prentice Hall, 2000.

Bohland, Mark A. *Problem Based Learning: Mystery Disease*. Edited by Dianne Draze and Sonsie Conroy. Dandy Lion Publications, 2003.

Bradby, Hannah. *Medical Sociology: An Introduction*. Sage Publications, 2009.

Caeeley, Judity. *On the Town: A Community Adventure*. Greenwillow Books, 2002.

Cockerham, William C. *Medical Sociology*. Prentice Hall, 2008.

Exploring Health Care Careers. 3rd ed. Ferguson, 2006.

Finkelstein, Eric and Zuckerman, Laurie. *The Fattening of America: How the Economy Makes Us Fat, If It Matters, and What to Do about It*. John Wiley & Sons, 2008.

Freedman, Jeri. *Steroids: High Risk Performance Drugs*. Drug Abuse and Society series. Rosen Publishing. Group, 2009.

Gabe, Jonathan, Bury, Michael and Elston, Mary Ann. *Key Concepts in Medical Sociology*. Sage Publications, 2004.

Geisert, Bonnie and Geisert, Arthur. *Desert Town*. Houghton Mifflin, 2001.

———. *Prairie Town*. Houghton Mifflin, 1998.

———. *River Town*. Houghton Mifflin, 1999.

Hodge, Robyn. *People and Population*. Australia Focus series. Echidna Books, 2006.

Kalman, Bobbie. *Hospital Workers in the Emergency Room*. Crabtree Publishing, 2005.

———. *What Is a Community from A to Z?* Crabtree Publishing, 2000.

McPherson, Stephanie Sammartino. *The Workers' Detective: A Story about Dr. Alice Hamilton*. A Carolrhoda Creative Minds Book series. Carolrhoda Books, 1992.

McClafferty, Carla Killough. *The Head Bone's Connected to the Neck Bone: The Weird, Wacky, and Wonderful X-ray*. Farrar, Straus and Giroux, 2001.

Médecins sans Frontières (Association). *Doctors Without Borders: Helping Those in Need. Faces: People, Places, and Cultures*, v. 21, no. 7. Cobblestone Publishing, 2005.

Miller, Debra A. *Biodiversity. Current Controversies* series. Greenhaven Press, 2008.

Parker, Steve. *The History of Medicine*. Gareth Stevens Information Library series. Gareth Stevens Children's Books, 1992.

Provensen, Alice and Provensen, Martin. *Town & Country*. Crown Publishers, 1985.

Riegelman, Richard. *Public Health 101: Healthy People-Healthy Populations*. Jones and Barlett Publishers, 2010.

Walker, Ida. *Steroids: Pumped Up and Dangerous*. Illicit and Misused Drugs series. Mason Crest Publishers, 2008.

History and Geography of Health and Medical Discoveries

Aberth, John. *The First Horseman: Disease in Human History*. Connections: Key Themes in World History series. Prentice Hall, 2007.

Allen, Peter L. *The Wages of Sin: Sex and Disease, Past and Present*. University of Chicago Press, 2000.

Barnard, Bryn. *Outbreak: Plagues That Changed History*. Crown Publishers, 2005.

Barnes, David S. *The Great Stink of Paris and the Nineteenth-Century Struggle against Filth and Germs*. Johns Hopkins University Press, 2006.

Boehm, Kate. *Fighting Disease*. National Geographic Reading Expeditions: Human Body series. National Geographic Society, 2003.

Bookworm. Earth Matters series. Marshall Cavendish Benchmark. Various dates.

Crawford, Dorothy H. *Deadly Companions: How Microbes Shaped Our History*. Oxford University Press, 2007.

Dobson, Mary J. *Disease: The Extraordinary Stories Behind History's Deadliest Killers*. Quercus, 2007.

Elgin, Kathy. *Health and Disease*. Changing Times series. Compass Point Books, 2005.

Farrell, Jeanette. *Visitors from Afar—A Journey to the Long-Ago Time—The Speckled Monster Helps Conquer the New World—Fighting Back with Inoculation—The Jenners of Berkeley Invisible Enemies: Stories of Infectious Disease.* Farrar, Straus and Giroux, 1998.

Getz, David. *Purple Death: The Mysterious Flu of 1918.* Henry Holt, 2000.

Giblin, James and Frampton, David. *When Plague Strikes: The Black Death, Smallpox, AIDS.* HarperCollins, 1995.

Harrison, Mark. *Disease and the Modern World: 1500 to the Present Day.* Themes in History series. Polity, 2004.

Haydon, Julie. *Making a Map.* Early Fluency series. Rigby, 2002.

Henderson, D. A. *Smallpox: The Death of a Disease: The Inside Story of Eradicating a Worldwide Killer.* Prometheus Books, 2009.

Hunter, Susan S. *Black Death: AIDS in Africa.* Palgrave Macmillan, 2003.

Link, Kurt. *Understanding New, Resurgent, and Resistant Diseases: How Man and Globalization Create and Spread Illness.* Praeger Publishers, 2007.

Making Your Own Map. Lollipop Dragon's World of Maps and Globes series. Clearvue & SVE, 2005. Video.

MapPoint 2009 Academic. Microsoft for Windows. DVD. Distributed by Academic Superstore.

Map Skills for Children. Schlessinger Media; Summer Productions, 2004. DVD set.

Marrin, Albert. *Dr. Jenner and the Speckled Monster: The Search for the Smallpox Vaccine.* Dutton Children's Books, 2002.

Mason, Paul. *Population.* Planet Under Pressure series. Heinemann Library, 2006.

Morton, Satin. *Death in the Pot: The Impact of Food Poisoning on History.* Prometheus Books, 2007.

Parker, Steve. *Population.* QEB Changes n series. QEB, 2010.

Peters, Stephanie True. *Smallpox in the New World.* Epidemic! series. Benchmark Books, 2005.

Power, Michael L and Schulkin, Jay. *The Evolution of Obesity.* Johns Hopkins University Press, 2009.

Ridgway, Tom. *Smallpox.* Epidemics series. Rosen Publishing Group, 2001.

Robinson, Arthur H. and others. *Elements of Cartography.* 6th ed. John Wiley & Sons, 1995.

Russell, Cheryl and New Strategist Publications Inc. *Best Customers: Demographics of Consumer Demand.* 5th ed. New Strategist Publications, 2008.

Senior, Kathryn, Antram, David and Salariya, David. *You Wouldn't Want to Be Sick in the 16th Century: Diseases You'd Rather Not Catch.* Franklin Watts, 2002.

Sherman, Irwin W. *Twelve Diseases That Changed Our World.* ASM Press, 2007.

Snyder, Tom. *Neighborhood MapMachine Deluxe.* CD set. Distributed by Academic Superstore.

Spangenburg, Ray and Moser, Diane. *Modern Science, 1896–1945.* History of Science series. Facts on File, 2004.

Stewart, Gail B. *Population. Ripped from the Headlines.* The Environment series. Erickson Press, 2008.

Townsend, John. *Pox, Pus & Plague: A History of Disease and Infection.* A Painful History of Medicine series. Raintree, 2006.

U.S. Central Intelligence Agency. *CIA World Fact Book.* https://www.cia.gov/library/publications/the_world_factbook.

Uschan, Michael V. and the Tuskegee Institute. *The Tuskegee Experiments: Forty Years of Medical Racism.* Lucent Library of Black History. Lucent Books, 2006.

Wellner, Alison Stein. *Best of Health: Demographics of Health Care Consumers.* New Strategist Publications, 2000.

Youngerman, Barry. *Pandemics and Global Health.* Global issues set, 15 vols. Facts on File, 2008.

Psychological and Developmental Health

American Medical Association, Pfeifer, Kate Gruenwald and Middleman, Amy B. *Boy's Guide to Becoming a Teen*. Jossey-Bass, 2006.

As Real as Your Life. DVD. All Game Productions. www.asrealasyourlife.com.

Blume, Judy and Kids Fund Foundation. *Letters to Judy: What Your Kids Wish They Could Tell You*. Putnam, 1986.

Bode, Janet. *For Better, for Worse: A Guide to Surviving Divorce for Preteens and Their* Families. Simon & Schuster Books for Young Readers, 2001.

———. *Kids Still Having Kids*. Rev. ed. Franklin Watts: Chivers, 2000.

Bowman, Robin. *It's Complicated: The American Teenager*. Umbrage Editions, 2007.

Building Self-Esteem: You've Got the Power. Linx Educational Publishing, 2009. DVD.

Clayton, Lawrence. *Amphetamines and Other Stimulants*. The Drug Abuse Prevention Library series. Rosen Publishing Group, 2001.

———. *Barbiturates and Other Depressants*. The Drug Abuse Prevention Library series. Rosen Publishing Group, 2001.

DeGezelle, Terri. *Illness*. The Real Deal series. Heinemann Library, 2009.

———. *Moving*. The Real Deal series. Heinemann Library, 2009.

Esherick, Joan. *Diet and Your Emotions: The Comfort Food Falsehood*. Obesity: Modern Day Epidemic series. Mason Crest Publishers, 2006.

Favor, Leli J. and Freed, Kira. *Food as Foe: Nutrition and Eating Disorders*. Food and You series. Marshall Cavendish Benchmark, 2009.

Fisanick, Christina. *Addiction*. Opposing Viewpoints series. Greenhaven Press, 2009.

Harper, Hill. *Letters to a Young Brother: MANifest Your Destiny*. Paw Prints, 2008.

Heathcliff Unleashed. LBS Communications, Inc.; NCircle Entertainment. Distributed by NCircle Entertainment, 2009. DVD.

Hewitt, Sally. *My Stepfamily. How Can I Deal with ___?* Smart Apple Media, 2009.

Hubner, John. *Last Chance in Texas: The Redemption of Criminal Youth*. Random House, 2005.

Hyde, Margaret O. *Safe Sex 101: An Overview for Teens*. Teen Overview series. Twenty-First Century Books, 2006.

Hyde, Margaret O. and Forsyth, Elizabeth Held. *Depression: What You Need to Know*. Franklin Watts, 2002.

Keel, Pamela K. *Eating Disorders*. Psychological Disorders series. Chelsea House Publishers, 2006.

Koegel, Lynn Kern, LeZebnik, Claire Scovell and LaZebnik, Andrew. *Growing Up on the Spectrum: A Guide to Life, Love, and Learning for Teens and Young Adults with Autism and Asperger's*. Viking, 2009.

Krementz, Jill. *How It Feels When a Parent Dies*. Peter Smith, 2000.

———. *How It Feels When Parents Divorce*. Paw Prints, 2008.

Lawton, Sandra Augustyn. *Eating Disorders Information for Teens: Health Tips about Anorexia, Bulimia, Binge Eating, and Other Eating Disorders Including Information about Risk Factors, Prevention, Diagnosis, Treatment, Health Consequences, and Other Related Issues*. Teen Health series. 2nd. Omnigraphics, 2009.

Love, Ann and Drake, Jane. *Talking Tails: The Incredible Connection Between People* and Their Pets. Tundra Books, 2010.

Mattern, Joanne. *Bullying*. The Real Deal series. Heinemann Library, 2009.

———. *Death*. The Real Deal series. Heinemann Library, 2009.

McPherson Stephanie, Sammartino. *Stressed Out in School?: Learning to Deal with Academic Pressure*. Issues in Focus Today series. Enslow Publishers, 2010.

Medina, Sarah. *Abuse and Neglect*. Emotional Health Issues series. Gareth Stevens, 2009.

————. *Know the Facts about Relationships*. Know the Facts series. Rosen Central, 2010.

Orr, Tamra. *Home and Family Relationships Teens*. Being Gay, Lesbian, Bisexual, or Transgender series. Rosen Publishing Group, 2010.

————. *When the Mirror Lies: Anorexia, Bulimia, and Other Eating Disorders*. Franklin Watts, 2007.

Parker, Victoria. *Good Relationships*. Exploring Citizenship series: Heinemann Library, 2009.

Powell, Jillian. *Self-Harm and Suicide*. Emotional Health Issues series. North American ed. Gareth Stevens, 2009.

Sayer, Melissa. *Too Fat? Too Thin?: The Healthy Eating Handbook*. Really Useful Handbooks series. Crabtree Publishing, 2009.

Sis, Peter. *The Wall: Growing Up Behind the Iron Curtain*. Farrar, Straus & Giroux/Frances Foster, 2007.

Shapiro, Ouisie. *Autism and Me: Sibling Stories*. Albert Whitman, 2009.

Tammet, Daniel. *Born on a Blue Day: A Memoir: Inside the Extraordinary Mind of an Autistic Savant*. Simon & Schuster/Free Press, 2007.

Teen Health series. Omnigraphics, 2009.

Warbrick, Caroline. *Taking Action against Eating Disorders*. Taking Action series. Rosen Central, 2010.

Warburton, Lianne and Callfas, Diana. *Amphetamines and Other Stimulants*. Junior Drug Awareness series. Chelsea House, 2008.

Willett, Edward. *Frequently Asked Questions about Exercise Addiction*. FAQ: Teen Life series. Rosen Publishing Group, 2009.

Wood, Douglas. *Chickadee's Message*. Adventure Publications, 2009.

Wyborny, Sheila. *Anxiety Disorders*. Diseases and Disorders series. Lucent Books, 2009.

Zeckhausen, Dina. *Full Mouse, Empty Mouse: A Tale of Food and Feelings*. Magination Press, 2008.

Governments and Health

Anderson, Judith and Christian Aid. *Fighting Disease*. Working for Our Future series. Sea-to-Sea Publications, 2010.

Anderson, Judith, Christian Aid and UN Millennium Project. *Ending Poverty and Hunger*. Working for Our Future series. Franklin Watts, 2007.

Bedesky, Baron. *What Is a Government?* Your Guide to Government series. Crabtree Publishing, 2009.

Cheney, Glenn Alan. *They Never Knew: The Victims of Nuclear Testing*. An Impact Book series. Franklin Watts, 1996.

Edwards, George C., Wattenberg, Martin P., and Lineberry, Robert L. *Government in America: People, Politics, and Policy*. 9th ed. Pearson Longman, 2008. Recording for the Blind & Dyslexic, 2009. Audiobook on CD.

Europa World Yearbook. Europa Publications. Annual.

Gale Virtual Reference Library. www.gale.cengage.com.

Haerens, Margaret. *Malnutrition*. Opposing Viewpoints series. Greenhaven Press, 2009.

Mintzer, Richard. *The National Institutes of Health*. Your Government—How It Works. Chelsea House, 2002.

Niethammer, Carolyn J. *Keeping the Rope Straight: Annie Dodge Wauneka's Life of Service to the Navajo*. Salina Bookshelf, 2006.

Ptacek, Greg. *Champion for Children's Health: A Story about Dr. S. Josephine Baker.* A Carolrhoda Creative Minds Book series. Carolrhoda Books, 1994.

Ruffin, David C. *The Duties and Responsibilities of the Secretary of Health and Human Services.* Your Government in Action series. PowerKids Press, 2005.

The Statesman's Yearbook: The Politics, Cultures and Economies of the World. Barry Turner, ed. Macmillan. Annual.

Thomson Gale. *Junior Worldmark Encyclopedia of the Canadian Provinces.* Gale Virtual Reference Library series. 5th ed. UXL, 2007.

Time for Kids Almanac. Time Inc. Annual.

Torr, James D. *Genetic Engineering.* Current Controversies series. Greenhaven Press, 2006. Recording for the Blind & Dyslexic, 2007. Audiobook on CD.

Victory Gardens of WWII: The American Farmers Pitch-In. OnDeck Home Entertainment. 1998. VHS.

Watson Jr., Thomas J., Institute for International Studies (Brown University), and Choices for the 21st Century Education Program. *The U.S. Role in a Changing World.* Choices for the 21st Century series. The Choices Program, Watson Institute for International Studies, Brown University, 2008.

Whitaker's Almanack. A&C Black. Annual.

Young, Mitchell. *Government Spending.* Opposing Viewpoints series. Greenhaven Press, 2009.

CHAPTER 8. CONNECTIONS: HEALTH, PHYSICAL EDUCATION, SCIENCE, AND MATHEMATICS

Mathematics and Health

Benjamin-Lesmeister, Michele. *Math Principles and Practice: Preparing for Health Career Success.* 2nd ed. Pearson Education, 2004.

Consortium for Foundation Mathematics. *Mathematics in Action: An Introduction to Algebraic, Graphical, and Numerical Problem Solving.* 3rd ed. Addison Wesley, 2007.

Health Care Skills Math and Medication Dosage Skills. DVD video. The School Co., 2008.

Medina, Sarah. *Graphing Water.* Real World Data series. Heinemann, 2009.

Minden, Cecilia. *Breakfast by the Numbers. Real World Math: Health and Wellness.* 21st Century Skills Library series. Cherry Lake Publishing, 2008.

———. *Lunch by the Numbers. Real World Math: Health and Wellness.* 21st Century Skills Library series. Cherry Lake Publishing, 2008.

———. *Restaurants by the Numbers: Real World Math: Health and Wellness.* 21st Century Skills Library series. Cherry Lake Publishing, 2008.

Quadling, Douglas and Neill, Hugh. *Mathematics for the IB Diploma Standard Level.* 1st ed. Cambridge University Press, 2007.

Roche, Susan, ed. *Statistics.* Figure It Out series. Published for the [New Zealand] Ministry of Education by Learning Media, 2008.

Speedstudy Basic Statistics. Selectsoft, 2007. CD for computer.

Thomas, Isabel. *Graphing Food and Nutrition.* Real World Data series. Heinemann Library, 2009.

———. *Graphing Population.* Real World Data series. Heinemann Library, 2009.

Timmons, Daniel L. and Johnson, Catherine W. *Math Skills for Allied Health Careers.* Pearson Prentice Hall, 2008.

Trivieri, Lawrence. *Basic Mathematics*. 2nd ed. fully rev. and updated. Collins College Outlines series. Collins, 2006.

Science and Health

Gardner, Robert. *Health Science Projects about Anatomy and Physiology*. Science Project series. Enslow Publishers, 2001.

———. *Health Science Projects about Heredity*. Science Projects series. Enslow Publishers, 2001.

———. *Science Projects about Kitchen Chemistry*. Science Projects series. Enslow Publishers, 2001.

———. *Science Projects about Methods of Measuring*. Science Projects series. Enslow Publishers, 2000.

———. *Health Science Projects about Nutrition*. Science Projects series. Enslow Publishers, 2002.

———. *Science Projects about the Environment and Ecology*. Science Projects series. Enslow Publishers, 1999.

———. *Science Projects about the Physics of Sports*. Science Projects series. Enslow Publishers, 2000.

———. *Health Science Projects about Your Senses*. Science Projects series. Enslow Publishers, 2001.

CHAPTER 9. GLOBALIZATION, INSTRUCTION, AND YOUTH HEALTH

For School Librarians and Teachers

Bennett, Belinda, Carney, Terry and Karpin, Isabel. *Brave New World of Health*. Federation Press, 2008.

Biographical information. Consult World Cat at www.worldcat.org and Health Activists at en.wikipedia.org/wiki/Category:Health_activists.

Center for Governmental Studies. Policy Archives. www.cgs.org.

Edmundson, Andrea. *Globalized e-Learning Cultural Challenges*. IGI, 2006.

Farese, Lois, Kimbrell, Grady and Woloszky, Carl A. *Marketing Essentials: Student Activity Workbook*. Glencoe/McGraw-Hill, 2002.

Francis, Greg, Inoue, Keiko, Orrick, Stefanie and the Stanford Program on International and Cross-Cultural Education. *Examining Human Rights in Global Context*. The Program, 2001.

"Global Awareness" is a teaching unit developed by Sarah White. www.galeschools.com/lesson_plans/secondary/social_science/global.htm.

Johnson, Barry L. *Environmental Policy and Public Health*. CRC Press, 2007.

United Nations. "Economic Commission for Africa: Commission on HIV/AIDS and Governance in Africa. Securing Our Future: Report of the Commission on HIV/AIDS and Governance in Africa." Commission on HIV/AIDS and Governance in Africa, 2008.

"What's Going On: Lessons Plan on Child Labor." A lesson plan developed by the United Nations on child labor. www.un.org/works/goingon/labor/lessonplan_labor.html.

Work Safe Alberta. *Workplace Health and Safety Teachers' Toolkit*. Work Safe Alberta, 2006. Visual material kit. employment.alberta.ca/SFW/3133.html

Resources for Students

Bowden, Rob. *Globalization: The Impact on Our Lives. 21st Century Debates* series. Raintree, 2004.

Hibbert, Adam. *Face the Facts: Globalization*. Raintree, 2005.

Teichmann, Iris. *Globalization*. Smart Apple Media, 2002, 2004.

Food and Water

China Food for a Billion Plus. DVD. A Voyageur Experience in Global Geography series. Agency for Instructional Technology. Visual Education Centre. Distributed by Visual Education Centre Limited, 2005. DVD.

Climate and Weather Changes

An Inconvenient Truth. Gore, Al, and others. Paramount, 2006. DVD.

David, Laurie and Gordon, Cambria. *The Down-to-Earth Guide to Global Warming*. Orchard Books, 2007.

Global Warming. Green Matters: What in the World Is Going On? series. Film Ideas, 2008. DVD and VHS.

Gore, Al. *An Inconvenient Truth: The Crisis of Global Warming*. Viking, 2007.

Jewitt, Kathryn and Legg, Gerald. *Ice World*. Paragon, 2008.

What Does Science Say about Climate Change? Classroom Encounters with Global Change Scientists series. Rita Chang & Alan Fine, 2005. DVD.

Ecological Changes

Global Environmental Issues. Global Issues for Students series. Schlessinger Media, 2004. DVD.

Kidd, J. S. and Kidd, Renee A. *Potent Natural Medicines: Mother Nature's Pharmacy*. Science & Society series. Chelsea House, 2006.

Kovach, Robert and McGuide, Bill. *Firefly Guide to Global Hazards*. Firefly Books, 2004.

Piwkedge, Fred. *Pharmacy in the Forest: How Medicines Are Found in the Natural World*. Atheneum Books for Young Readers, 1998.

Populations and Migrations

Ellis, Deborah. *Children of War: Voices of Iraqi Refugees*. Groundwood Books/House of Anansi Press, 2009.

Gifford, Clive. *Refugees*. World Issues series. Chrysalis Children's Books, 2004.

Hill, Ken and Maman, Joseph L. *War, Humanitarian Crises, Population Displacement, and Fertility: A Review of Evidence*. National Academies Press, 2004.

Medical Care and Interventions (Public Health)

Global Health Council. "The Importance of Child Health." Available at www.globalhealth.org/childhealth.

————. "The Importance of Women's Health." Available at www.globalhealth.org/womens _health.

Grahame, Deborah A. *World Health Organization*. International Organizations series. World Almanac, 2004.

Jacobsen, Kathryn H. *Introduction to Global Health*. Jones and Bartlett Publishing, 2008.

Médecins sans Frontieères (Association). *Doctors Without Borders: Helping Those in Need. Faces:* People, Places, and Cultures series, v. 21, no. 7. Cobblestone Publishing, 2005.

Murray, Anne Firth. *From Outrage to Courage: Women Taking Action for Health and Justice*. Common Courage Press, 2008.

Quan, Kathy. *The Everything Guide to Careers in Health Care: Find the Job That's Right for You*. Everything series. Adams Media, 2007.

Rx for Survival: A Global Health Challenge. WGBH Boston Video, 2005. DVD, CD for computer, NTSC color broadcast system, widescreen format.

Suen, Anastasia. *Doctors Without Borders*. Reading Power: Helping Organizations series. PowerKids Press, 2002.

Turshen, Meredeth. *Women's Health Movements: A Global Force for Change*. Palgrave Macmillan, 2007.

U.S. Department of Health and Human Services. "Women'sHealth.gov." www.womenshealth.gov.

Information and Communication Technology

Dawn Hillier. *Communicating Health Risks to the Public: A Global Perspective*. I'm Safe series. Gower, 2007.

Kaiser Family Foundation. "How Changes in Medical Technology Affect Health Care Cost." www.kff.org/insurance/snapshot/chcm030807oth.cfm.

Pierce, Alan J. *Introduction to Technology*. Glencoe/McGraw-Hill, 2005.

Routh, Kristina. *Medicine*. Technology All Around Us series. Smart Apple Media, 2006.

U.S. Central Intelligence Agency. "World Factbook." https://www.cia.gov/library/publications/ the-world-factbook.

U.S. National Library of Medicine. "Medline." www.nlm.nih.gov/databases/databases _medline.html.

————. "MedlinePlus." medlineplus.gov.

Travel and Transportation

Bragdon, Clifford R. *Transportation Security*. The Butterworth-Heinemann Homeland Security series. BH/Elsevier, 2008.

Gerdes, Louise I. *Transportation*. Opposing Viewpoints series. Greenhaven, 2008.

Gordon, Wendy and Gordon, Paul. *I'm Safe! in the Car*. Child Safety Solutions/BackYard Books, 2003.

Llewellyn, Claire and Gordon, Mike. *On the Road*. Watch Out! series. Barron's Educational Series, 2006.

Katz, Bruce and Puentes, Robert. *Taking the High Road: A Metropolitan Agenda for Transportation Reform*. James A. Johnson Metro series. Brookings Institution Press, 2005.

Kemp. Roger L. *Cities and Cars: A Handbook of Best Practices*. McFarland & Co., 2007.

Macmillan Reference USA. *Encyclopedia of Transportation*. Macmillan Reference USA, 2000.

Mattern, Joanne. *Staying Safe in the Car*. Safety First series. Weekly Reader Early Learning Library, 2007.

Shiftan, Yoram, Button, Kenneth John and Nijkamp, Peter. *Transportation Planning (Classics in Planning)*. An Elgar Reference Collection series. Edward Elgar, 2007.

Winters, Adam. *Everything You Need to Know about Being a Teen Driver*. The Need to Know Library series. Rosen Publishing Group, 2000.

Justice and Litigation Systems

Amnesty International. *We Are All Born Free: The Universal Declaration of Human Rights in Pictures*. Frances Lincoln Children's, 2008.

Banks, Deena. *Amnesty International*. International Organizations series. World Almanac Library, 2004.

Bell, Daniel and Coicaud, Jean-Marc. *Ethics in Action: The Ethical Challenges of International Human Rights Nongovernmental Organizations*. Cambridge University Press, 2007.

Brysk, Alison. *Globalization and Human Rights*. University of California Press, 2002.

Cook, Rebecca J. and Ngwena, C. G. *Health and Human Rights*. The International Library of Medicine, Ethics, and Law series. Ashgate, 2007.

Herumin, Wendy. *Child Labor Today: A Human Rights Issue*. Issues in Focus Today series. Enslow Publishers, 2008.

Human Rights. Global Issues for Students series. Russ Mitchell; Jeffrey W Litzke; Schlessinger Media; and CBS News. Schlessinger Media: CBS News Productions, 2004. DVD.

Hunnicutt, Susan. *Corporate Social Responsibility*. Opposing Viewpoints series. Greenhaven Press, 2009.

Hunt, Lynn Avery. *Inventing Human Rights: A History*. 1st ed. W. W. Norton, 2007.

Ishay, Micheline. *The History of Human Rights: From Ancient Times to the Globalization Era*. University of California Press, 2004.

Kramer, Ann. *Human Rights: Who Decides?* Behind the News series. Heinemann Library, 2007.

MacDonald, Theodore H. *The Global Human Right to Health: Dream or Possibility?* Radcliffe Publishing, 2007.

Marks, Stephen P. and the François-Xavier Bagnoud Center for Health and Human Rights. *Health and Human Rights: Basic International Documents*. Harvard Series on Health and Human Rights series. Harvard University, Francois-Xavier Bagnoud Center for Health and Human Rights, 2004.

McGowan, Keith. *Human Rights*. Lucent Overview series. Lucent Books, 2003.

O'Neil, Edward. *Awakening Hippocrates: A Primer on Health, Poverty, and Global Service*. American Medical Association, 2006.

Phillips, Douglas A. and Gritzner, Charles F. *Human Rights*. Global Connections series. Chelsea House Publishers, 2009.

Puybaret, Eric and the United Nations General Assembly. *Universal Declaration of Human Rights*. United Nations and Gautier-Languereau, 2008.

Robinson, Mary, EPals, and the United Nations General Assembly. *Every Human Has Rights: A Photographic Declaration for Kids*. National Geographic, 2009.

Rothman, David J. and Rothman, Sheila M. *Trust Is Not Enough: Bringing Human Rights to Medicine*. New York Review Books, 2006.

Stevenson, Bruce and Stevenson, Maeve. *Freedom. Towards Human Rights and Social Justice*. Pearson Education, 2000.

Watson, Susan. *Understanding Human Rights.* 1st ed. Global Citizenship series. Smart Apple
    Media, 2004.

World Health Organization. *The Right to Health.* OHCHR, 2008.

Young, Mitchell. *Free Trade.* Opposing Viewpoints series. Greenhaven Press, 2009.

Labor and Work

Canadian Centre for Occupational Health and Safety. *Workplace Health and Wellness Guide.* 2nd ed.
    CCOHS, 2008.

Forastieri, Valentina and the International Labour Office. *Children at Work: Health and Safety
    Risk.* ILO Child Labour Collection series. ILO, 2002.

Gourley, Catherine. *Society's Sisters: Stories of Women Who Fought for Social Justice in
    America.* Twenty-First Century Books, 2003.

Hanson, Anders. *Workplace Health Promotion: A Salutogenic Approach.* AuthorHouse, 2007.

Hlavac, Christine E., Mosher, Kevin M., and Sherman, James B. *Practical and Legal Issues of
    Employee Wellness Programs.* Lorman Education Services, 2007.

Lee, Albert S. and Southworth, James W. *Practical and Legal Issues of Employee Wellness
    Programs.* Lorman Education Services, 2008.

Levine, Marvin J. *Children for Hire: The Perils of Child Labor in the United States.* Praeger,
    2003.

Lewis, Joan and Thornbory, Greta. *Employment Law and Occupational Health: A
Practical Handbook.* Blackwell Publishing, 2006.

Polopolus, Leo and others. *Occupational Safety and Health Act.* University of Florida
    Cooperative Extension Service, Institute of Food and Agricultural Sciences, EDIS, 2003.
    eBook.

Work and the Workplace. Pro/Con series. Grolier, 2005.

Governments and Health Policies

Bennett, Belinda, Carney, Terry, and Karpin, Isable *Brave New World of Health.* Federation
    Press, 2008.

Center for Governmental Studies (Los Angeles, Calif.); IUPUI (campus). University Library.
    Center for Governmental Studies, Policy Archives, 2008.

Close Up Foundation. *Current Issues: Critical Policy Choices Facing the U.S. and the World.*
    Recording for the Blind & Dyslexic, 2007. Audiobook on CD.

Harmon, Daniel E. *The Food and Drug Administration.* Chelsea House Publishers, 2002.

Johnson, Berry L. *Environmental Policy and Public Health.* CRC Press, 2007.

Schroeder, Christopher H., and Steinzor, Rena. *A New Progressive Agenda for Public Health and the
    Environment: A Project of the Center for Progressive Regulation; Center for Progressive
    Regulation (U.S.).* Carolina Academic Press, 2005.

Syrett, Keith. *Law, Legitimacy, and the Rationing of Healthcare: A Contextual and Comparative
    Perspective.* Cambridge Law, Medicine, and Ethics series. Cambridge University Press,
    2007.

United Nations. Economic Commission for Africa. Commission on HIV/AIDS and Governance
    in Africa." Securing Our Future: Report of the Commission on HIV/AIDS and Governance
    in Africa." Commission on HIV/AIDS and Governance in Africa, 2008.

Market Demands

Burstein, John. *Big Fat Lies: Advertising Tricks*. Slim Goodbody's Lighten Up! series. Crabtree Publishing, 2008.

Earle, Richard. *Art of Cause Marketing: How to Use Advertising to Change Personal Behavior and Public Policy*. 1st ed. McGraw-Hill Companies, 2002.

Gifford, Clive. *Advertising & Marketing*. Developing the Marketplace. Influence and Persuasion series. Heinemann Library, 2005.

Grewal, Dhruv and Levy, Michael. *Marketing*. McGraw-Hill, 2008.

Heller, Steven and Talarico, Lita. *Design Entrepreneur: Turning Graphic Design into Goods That Sell*. Design Field Guide series. Rockport Publishers, 2008.

Lüsted, Amidon Marcia and McIlrath, Mary. *Advertising to Children*. Essential Viewpoints series. ABDO Publishing, 2009.

Milton, Bess. *Advertising*. Paw Prints, 2008.

Snell, Clete. *Peddling Poison: The Tobacco Industry and Kids*. Criminal Justice, Delinquency, and Corrections series. Greenwood Publishing Group, 2005.

Appendix B

A Selected List of Health and Physical Education Textbooks Used in North American Schools

AMERICAN TEXTBOOKS

HEALTH AND FITNESS

Decisions for Health. Holt, Rinehart, and Winston. Grades 7–8.

Introduces and reinforces students' life skills and understanding of age-appropriate health content through hands-on and cross-curricular activities, guided and independent practice, and application in real-life contexts. All activities are labeled as Basic, General, or Advanced to address varied levels of student learning. Includes editions modified for Texas and California adoption.

Family Health Needs. Curriculum Caddy. CEV Multimedia, Ltd. Grades 7–9.

Families come in all shapes, sizes, and forms, and there is a universal link between an individual and his or her family's health. The Microsoft PowerPoint presentation explores the diverse aspects of a family and a family's health.

Great Big Body Shop. Children's Health Market. Grades K–6.

Provides a fully articulated cross-curricular approach for school districts that require additional concentration in one or more of the following specific areas: substance abuse prevention; social and emotional health; character education; violence prevention (including bullying); critical thinking; asset building; reading, communication, technology, and other learning skills.

Harcourt Health and Fitness series. Harcourt Brace School Publishers. Grades 1–6.

Features printable student Activity Book pages and select teaching resources pages, such as school-home connection letters, patterns/organizers, a health and safety handbook, Webliography, teacher and parent links to health resources, teaching transparencies, and full-color diagrams of the human body and selected health concepts.

The Human in Health and Disease. Mosby & W. B. Sanders. Grades 9–12.
> Presents a body systems approach with a strong emphasis on vocabulary and basic anatomy and physiology concepts as well as the basic mechanisms of disease and pathologic conditions associated with each body system. Readability and coverage reflect the appropriate level for first-time students' anatomy and physiology study.

Lifetime Health. Holt, Rinehart, and Winston. Grades 9–10.
> Promotes active exploration of health concepts, character building, and life skills by requiring students to apply what they learn within the context of the real world.

Macmillan/McGraw-Hill Health & Wellness. McGraw-Hill. Grades K–8.
> Provides students with accurate, standards-based health content. The program focuses on ten health life skills, including teaching students to make responsible decisions and to set health goals at each grade level.

Teen Health. Glencoe/McGraw-Hill. Grades 7 and 8.
> An integrated, activities-based health program written especially for middle school students. This sequential, three-course program provides the perfect combination of course material and interactive multimedia resources. *Teen Health* helps students understand that good health affects their school performance, their friendships, their looks, and their lives. It includes an edition that is modified for Texas adoption.

ANATOMY AND PHYSIOLOGY

Anthony's Textbook of Anatomy & Physiology. Mosby. Grades 9–12.
> A thorough introductory text on human form and function, this text presents a large, complex body of scientific knowledge in an easily understood, straightforward writing style. Focusing on concepts rather than descriptions, the text uses a big picture theme of body function and also explains the body's homeostatic regulation.

Body Structures and Functions. Cengage Learning, Inc./Delmar Learning. Book with multimedia (CD-ROM). Grades 9–12.
> Introduces the basics required for the study of the human body and how it functions in a clear and concise manner. Text is accompanied by a student workbook and a StudyWARE CD-ROM that offer additional practice through interactive quizzes and fun activities that correlate with each chapter in the text.

HEALTH OCCUPATIONS

Diversified Health Occupations. Delmar Learning Diversified Health Occupations. Grades 9–12.
> Provides the health occupations student with the basic entry-level knowledge required for a variety of health occupations. Provides updated information on CPR, standard precautions, and OBRA regulations as well as cultural diversity, technological advances, legal responsibilities, medical terminology, anatomy and physiology, communication skills, and professional standards and appearance.

Health Care Science Technology: Career Foundations. Glencoe/McGraw-Hill. Grades 9–12.
> Written to address the National Health Care Skills Standards. It covers general skills, such as teamwork and communication, as well as skills required for specific jobs within the career paths. This text helps your students build a solid foundation for success, no matter which health care career they choose.

Health Careers Today. Elsevier Science. Grades 9–12.

Covering more than 45 health careers, this book offers a practical overview to help students make an informed decision in choosing a profession. Not only does it discuss the roles and responsibilities of various occupations, but it also provides a solid foundation in the skills needed for all health careers.

Introduction to Health Occupations: Today's Health Care Worker. Prentice Hall. Grades 9–12.

This is an ideal resource for students preparing for entry-level health occupation positions. Features new to the sixth edition further strengthen instruction with exercises that include enhanced visual learning, team building, communication, multicultural competence, and familiarity with technology.

TERMINOLOGY

The Language of Medicine (text and E-book package). Elsevier Science. Grades 9–12.

This market-leading text helps readers understand and learn complex terms. Terminology and complex medical processes are described in an easy-to-understand manner, which is readily accessible to learners of all levels. The text brings medical terms to life with a text/workbook format organized by body systems.

Medical Terminology: A Programmed Learning Approach to the Language of Health Care (with CD-ROM). Wolters Kluwer (formerly Lippincott Williams & Wilkins). Grades 9–12.

This step-by-step, self-paced method to learning medical terminology provides the instruction needed to master the language of health care. The opening chapters lay a solid framework for understanding the prefixes, suffixes, and combining forms that structure medical terms and then lead you through the ins and outs of the medical record.

ONTARIO MINISTRY OF EDUCATION TEXTBOOKS

The Trillium List is published by the Ontario Ministry of Education, listing all the officially accepted textbooks approved for use in the schools under the ministry's authority.

Exercise Science: An Introduction to Health and Physical Education. Thompson Educational Publishing. Grade 12.

Exercise Science offers a unique blend of anatomy and physiology, combined with social and historical aspects of Canadian sport. Developed in association with the Ontario Physical and Health Education Association.

Foundations of Exercise Science. Sports Books Publisher. Grade 12. University Preparation.

A textbook designed for senior high school and introductory college programs in kinesiology and physical education. Explores the world of exercise science: the study of human movement and the body's response to exercise. Examines the systems, factors, and principles involved in human development within the context of society.

Healthy Active Living Education. First Canadian Edition. Thompson Education Publishing. Grades 9–10.

Promotes important educational values and goals, such as tolerance, understanding, excellence, and good health. These values are reinforced in other curriculum areas as well as in society itself. Parents, schools, health care agencies, peers, businesses, governments, and the media are all vital partners in helping promote these values to students.

The World of Recreation and Fitness Leadership. Sports Books Publisher. Grades 11 and 12 and college prep.

Developed specifically for the Ontario PLF4C course and introductory courses in recreation and fitness leadership. These resources were completed in collaboration with a select group of high school teachers and university professors to offer a student-friendly overview of the major areas of study.

Index

Aborigines (Australia), 138.
   See also First Nations;
   Native Americans
Access and searching for
   health information, 61–67.
   See also Electronic health
   information resources;
   Health literacy
Ackard, D. M., 58–59
Adolescents, health needs of,
   58–59. *See also* Children's
   health needs; Health literacy
Africa, 180. *See also*
   UNESCO and health care;
   Skilled-based health
   education
African-Americans, 138, 144
Agosto, Denise, and adolescent
   information needs, 57–58.
   See also Adolescents, health
   needs of
Agriculture and health
   education, 168. *See also*
   Instructional units for
   health; U.S. Department of
   Agriculture
AIDS (disease). *See* HIV/
   AIDS
Alcohol and alcoholism, 18,
   35, 82, 109, 100, 115, 138,

181. *See also* Drugs and
   drug uses; Instructional
   units for health; Resources
   for health education
American Association of
   School Librarians (AASL),
   3. *See also* School
   libraries; Standards, health
   and education
Anthropology and health, 49,
   130, 133, 139
Apples in folklore and
   mythology, 121. *See also*
   Instructional units for
   health
Art and health education, 99,
   115. *See also* Instructional
   units for health
Art research and health, 115
Artist and health education,
   100. *See also* Instructional
   units for health
Artists, 114–115. *See also*
   Instructional units for health
Arts, (Fine) and health
   education, 99. *See also*
   Instructional units for
   health
Assessments in health
   education, 35–36. *See also*

Standards, health and
   education
Athletes, 111–112. *See also*
   Dancers; Instructional
   units for health
Audiovisuals in health
   instruction, 25–28. *See also*
   Materials and resources for
   health education
Australia, 9, 84, 139, 154
Auto safety. *See* Traffic safety

Baldwin, Stephen C., and
   deaf education, 111. *See*
   Deaf, education for the
Baltimore County, Maryland
   Public Library, 62. *See*
   also Connections:
   Children, Youth & Family
   Resources
Bates, Marcia, 57–58. *See*
   also Electronic health
   information resources
BBC and health
   programming, 28
BBC and the British national
   health curriculum, 9
Beck, Charles, and physical
   education, 146
Behaviorism, 19

Berry Picking model for electronic searching, 58. *See also* Access and searching for health information; Bates, Marcia; Electronic health information resources

Biblioteca Américus, 194. *See also* South Texas Independent School District

Bicycle safety. *See* Traffic safety

Biography and health, 100, 105, 113–115. *See also* Instructional units for health

Blindness and health, 65, 66. *See also* Biography and health; Blindness and Helen Keller; Instructional units for health

Blindness and Helen Keller, 66. *See also Story of My Life* (Keller)

Blindness, education for. *See* Blindness and health

Book purchasing habits, 60. *See also* Publishers and health education

Books. *See* Health books in series

Boys and Girls Clubs (Philadelphia), 58

Brochures and pamphlets as health information, 96. *See also* Health books in series

Cable television. *See* Television and radio as health education

California Department of Education and textbooks, 39–40. *See also* Instructional units for health; Schools and health care; Textbooks and health education

California School Health Center Association, 22. *See also* Schools and health care

Canada, 9, 16, 59, 74, 82–83, 90, 96, 103, 111, 124–126, 138, 153–156, 170, 174

Celebrities and health. *See* Biographies and health

Cengage. *See* Gale (Company)

Center for Health Care in Schools, George Washington University, 22. *See also* Schools and health care

Centers for Disease Control and Prevention, U.S. (CDC). *See* U.S. Centers for Disease Control and Prevention

Chelton, Mary Kay, and Information literacy, 59–60. *See also* Information literacy

Children and health, 2, 6, 8–10, 15, 17, 23, 26–28, 67, 69–70, 100–101, 105. *See also* Africa; Children's health needs; Globalization; HIV/AIDS; Instructional units for health; UNESCO and health care

Children's health needs, 58–59. *See also* Adolescent's health needs of

Cholera, 138, 141

Climate change and health, 42, 139, 164–167, 171–173, 176, 180–181. *See also* Globalization; Instructional units for health; Weather and health

Cognition. *See* Cognitive theory

Cognitive theory, 19

Collaboration and curriculum, 18, 40–41, 156

Collection development and health resources, 156, 207–208

Commercial film companies, 95

Communication and medicine, 206–207

Community television and radio. *See* Television and radio as health instruction

Community outreach and planning, 191–202

Connections: Children, Youth & Family Resources, 62. *See also* Baltimore County, Maryland Public Library

Consultants and health education, 44–45. *See also* Health care workers; Instructional units for health

Coordinated School Health Program (CSHP), 2, 18. *See also* Instructional units for health

Council on Economic Education, national standards, 169

"Crippled children play on roof, Henry Street, ca. 1909" (historical illustration), 133. *See also* Disabilities

Crippled people. *See* Disabilities

CSHP. *See* Coordinated School Health Program (CSHP)

Curriculum and health, 4, 6, 15–19, 28, 49–50. *See also* Instructional units for health

Curriculum models, 15–18, 33. *See also* Curriculum and health; Curriculum and the future of health care; Curriculum themes and concepts; Instructional units for health

Curriculum themes and concepts, 6, 165–189. *See also* Teaching units for health

Curriculum, and the future of health care, 205

Dancers, 111–112. *See also* Athletes; Instruction units for health

Databases for health. *See* Electronic health information resources

David, H. T., 152

Davis, Kathryn, 151–152

Deaf, education for the, 110–111

Deaf, theater for the, 110–111

Deaf Side Story: Deaf Sharks, Hearing Jets, and a Classical American Musical (Rigney), 110

Demographics and health, 42, 140, 153, 186, 197, 208. *See also* Geography and health; Globalization; Instructional units and health

Demonstration programs and health, 20, 23. *See also* Travis County, Texas Negro Extension Service, ca. 1950 (historic illustration)

Dental health, 10, 22, 70, 89, 129, 141, 158–159. *See also* Toothbrush drill, New York City public schools, ca. 1913 (historic illustration)

Department of Agriculture, U.S. *See* U.S. Department of Agriculture

Department of Health and Aging (Australia), 83

Department of Health (United Kingdom), 83

Developmental curriculum, 17

Diabetes and health, 32, 43, 46, 71, 77, 87, 96, 97, 110, 121, 128, 141, 158. *See also* Obesity and health

Digitization and health instruction, 25–26

Disabilities, 87–88, 95, 132, 133. *See also* Instructional units for health

Discovery Health (Discovery Channel), 28

Disease and art. *See* Art and health education; Artists; Art research and health

Disease and biography. *See* Biography and health education

Disease and community. *See* Community outreach and planning

Disease and dance. *See* Dancers

Disease and drama. *See* Drama and health information

Disease and economics. *See* Economics education and health

Disease and etymology. *See* Etymology and health vocabulary

Disease and folklore and mythology. *See* Folklore, culture and health education

Disease and globalization. *See* Globalization

Disease and government. *See* Government and health care

Disease and hearing. *See* Hearing and health education

Disease and information. *See* Information, searching for health

Disease and languages. *See* Languages and health education

Disease and literature. *See* Literature and health education

Disease and mathematics. *See* Mathematics and health education

Disease and music. *See* Music and health education

Disease and performance activities. *See* Performance activities and health education

Disease and physical education. *See* Physical education and health

Disease and schools, 1–13, 19, 24. *See also* Community outreach and planning; Schools and Health care

Disease and sports. *See* Athletes

Disease and statistics. *See* Statistics and health education

Disease control and community outreach. *See* Community outreach and planning

Distance and online learning as health instruction, 27–28

Drama and health education, 100. *See also* Instructional units for health

Drinking, alcoholic consumption. *See* Alcohol and alcoholism

Driving safety. *See* Traffic safety

Drugs and drug uses, 8, 10, 17, 35, 59, 69–70, 178, 187–188. *See also* Alcohol and alcoholism; Instructional units for health; Resources for health education

Drugs, illicit. *See* Drugs and drug uses

EBSCO (Company), 61

Economics education and health, 168–169. *See also* Social sciences and health education

Ecosystems. *See* Environments and environmental health

Education curriculum, 16–18

E-Health Information, 84–90. *See also* Electronic health information resources; Materials and resources for health education

Electronic health information resources, 60–61, 67–71. *See also* Access and searching for health information; Health literary; Materials and resources for health education

Electronic transmission of information, history of, 74. *See also* Internet, history of; Instructional units for health

Ely, D. P., and educational technology, 20

English teachers (United Kingdom) and health education, 34

Environments and environmental health, 2, 5, 17, 20–22, 25–26, 31–34, 42–44, 52, 74, 87, 98, 102–103, 115–116, 132, 136, 139, 140, 142, 148, 157, 162, 164–165, 168, 172–173, 175–176, 181, 183–185, 187–189, 192, 198–199, 206–208. *See also* Instructional units for health

Etymology and health vocabulary, 127–128. *See also* Instructional units for health; Languages and health education; Medical terms

European Union. *See* Europe

Europe, 8, 138, 141, 147, 171, 179

Extension programs and health education, 20–21. *See also* Distance and online learning as health instruction; Online searching for health information

FDA. *See* U.S. Federal Drug Administration

Fiction, foreign languages, 123–125. *See also* Foreign languages health materials; Instructional units for health; Medical fiction, reading of

Field trips and visits as health education, 26. *See also* Instructional units for health

Film libraries, 95

First Nations, (Canada), 88, 111, 138. *See also*

Aborigines (Australia); Canada; Instructional units for health; Native Americans

Folklore, culture, and health education, 120. *See also* Instructional units for health

Folklore and mythology and health education, 120–123. *See also* Instructional units for health

Food and Drug Act, U.S. (1906), 8

Forecasting, theory of, 205–206

Foreign language fiction. *See* Fiction, foreign languages; Foreign languages and health education; Instructional units for health

Foreign language health materials, 96. *See also* Literature and health education; Materials and resources for health education

Foreign languages and health, 134

Foreign languages and health education, 118–128. *See also* Instructional units for health

4-H clubs, 9

Free Library of Philadelphia, 58

Future, predicting the, 205

Gale (Company) (Cengage Learning), 60–61

General Agreement on Tariffs and Trade (GATT), 187

Geography and health, 5, 49, 93, 130, 133, 134, 139–140, 162. *See also* Demographics and health; Globalization; Instruction units for health

GetHIP, 196, 198. *See also* Health literacy; Teacher Enrichment Initiatives

Globalization, 153–170, educational themes and, 165–189. *See also* Instructional units for health

Government and health care, 8–9, 134–137, 147, 153–154. *See also* Instructional units for health; Public Health

Government school lunch program (historic illustration), 135

Great Britain, 16, 28, 153, 192. *See also* United Kingdom

Greeks (ancient) and physical education, 145–146. *See also* Physical education and health

Guidelines for health education, 2, 4, 28, 34, 67–68

Hayden, Jerome D., 152

Health and illnesses in history, 4, 5, 7, 11, 12, 20, 41–42, 48–49, 101, 105–106, 117, 126, 128, 132, 134, 136, 137–138, 148–149, 159, 174. *See also* Instructional units for health

Health and science, curriculums in, 4, 34–35. *See also* Instructional units for health

Health books in series, 94. *See also* Materials and resources for health education

Health Canada, 9, 59. *See also* Canada

Health care, future of, 205

Health care, Schools, 1; *See also* Coordinated School Health Program (CSHP)

Health care workers, 1–2, 18, 118, 178, 179. *See also* Librarians and health, role of; Consultants and health education

Health care workers, postage stamp honoring (historic illustration), 1
Health films, 95
Health guidelines, 2. *See also* School library standards; Standards, health and education
Health Information for Youth: The Public Library and School Library Media Center Role (Lukenbill & Immroth), 90
Health in fictional literature. *See* Medical fiction, reading of
Health information, 2, 19, 57–67. *See also* Health literacy; Information literacy
Health Infoway (Canada), 83
Health libraries, 95. *See also* School libraries and curriculum implications
Health literacy, 3, 31–35, 57–60, 116. *See also* Health literacy research
Health literacy research, 57–58. *See also* Health literacy
Health management, 1, 3, 7, 20, 63, 109, 113–114, 134–35, 140, 156, 164, 169, 201. *See also* Health literacy; Health relationships, shared by musicians, athletes, and dancers; Instructional units for health
Health relationships, shared by musicians, athletes, and dancers, 111–112
Health rubrics and health education, 36. *See also* Instructional units for health
Health vocabulary. *See* Etymology and health vocabulary
Hearing and health education, 112–113. *See also* Instructional units for health

History and illnesses. *See* Health and illnesses in history
HIV/AIDS, 2, 11, 36, 59, 69, 114, 132, 137–138, 153, 154. *See also* Africa; UNISCO and health care
Holistic health education, 32–33, 71–76, 81. *See also* Instructional units for health
Home economics. *See* Human ecology
Howard, T., 152
Hughes-Hassell, Sandra, and adolescent information needs, 57–58. *See also* Adolescents, health needs of
Human ecology (Home economics), 69. *See also* Globalization; Instructional units for health

Idioms and proverbs, 121. *See also* Instructional units for health
Information literacy, 5
Illinois School for the Deaf, 110. *See also* Deal, education for the
Illnesses in history. *See* Health and illnesses in history
Information, searching for health. *See* Health literacy
Information skills and processes, 3; *See also* Access and searching for health information; Information literacy
Information technology and medicine, 206–207
Instructional approaches and designs, 19–28, 23–28, 31–32, 34, 42–43, 45–47, 50–51. *See also* Instructional units for health
Instructional strategies. *See* Instructional approaches and designs
Instructional subjects and contents, 48–50. *See also*

Curriculum and health; Instructional approaches and design; Instructional units for health
Instructional units for health: Anthropology, 139; Art and artists, 114; Athletics and sports, 111–14; Biases and stereotyping, 38–39; Biology and genetics, 150–151; Biography and government activism, 186; Climate and weather changes, 171–173; Community surveys, 133; Dance and dancers, 111–114; Diseases (and globalization), 176; Demographics and population studies, 153–154; Ecological changes, 173–174; Folklore and mythology, 120–123; Food and energy, 151; Food and water, 170–171; Foreign languages, 119–128, 138, 141, 142; Government and public policies, 136–37, 185; Geography, 139, 153–154; History and illnesses, 137–138; Information technology and communication technology, 179–180; Justice and litigation systems, 182–183; Labor and work, (includes child labor), 183–184; Listening skills, 133; Literature, 103–106; Maps, 133; Marketing, 186–189; Mathematics, 153–154; Measurements, 151–154; Medical biography, 138; Medical research, 138; Music and Musicians, 110; Musical theater, 110–111; Physical education and health, 157–159; Population and migrations, 174–175; Psychology, 140–141; Public health,

177–179; Science, 150–151; Scientific methodology, 149–151; Social life and responsibility, 141–142; Sociology, 139, 188; Travel and transportation (includes travel safety), 180–181

Interactive technology as health instruction, 25–26. *See also* Instructional units for health

Internet, history of, 74. *See also* Electronic transmission of information, history of

Keller, Helen and blindness, 66. *See also* Biography and health; Instructional units for health; *Story of My Life* (Keller)

Kinyoun, Joseph J., 148. *See also* U.S. Marine Hospital Service (USMHS), Laboratory of Hygiene and; Zeiss microscope (historic illustration), and cholera

Kuhlthau, Carol, 57–58. *See also* Information literacy

Languages, foreign. *See* Foreign languages and health education; Foreign languages, health materials

Languages and health education, 5, 118–128, 134. *See also* Etymology and health vocabulary; Instructional units for health; Medical terms

Lectures as health instruction, 23–24

Lewis, Dio, and physical education, 146. *See also* Physical education and health

Liberal education curriculum, 16

Librarians and health, role of, 2. *See also* School librarians

Library use skills. *See* Information literacy

Lincoln, Abraham and the U.S. Department of Agriculture, 8

Literary criticism, elements of, 101–104

Literature and health education, 99–105. *See also* Instructional units for health

Little Ice Age, 140. *See also* Climate change and health; Weather

Malaria, 7–8, 138, 140, 174, 177

Management, 2–3, 8–9, 16, 20, 33, 43, 50, 115, 132, 136, 168, 174, 177–178, 187. *See also* Policies and policy making

Materials and resources for health education, selection criteria for, 68, 83–84. *See also* Electronic health information resources; Health literacy; Professional reference guides for health care; Resources for health education

Maternal & Child Health Library, George Washington University, 96–97

Mathematics and health curriculum, 4, 148–149

Mathematics and health education, 148–54. *See also* Instructional units for health; Statistics and Health education

Mayer, Gloria, 3

Media That Matters Film Festival, 95. *See also* Materials for health education

Medical anthropology. *See* Anthropology and health

Medical fiction, reading of, 104–105. *See also* Foreign

languages fiction; Instructional units for health

Medical practices, participatory, 206

Medical sociology. *See* Sociology and health

Medical terms, 3, 42, 72, 111, 120, 123, 127, 178. *See also* Etymology and health vocabulary; Instructional units for health; Languages and health education

Medical vocabulary. *See* Medical terms

Medline, 69. *See also* Medline Plus; U.S. National Library of Medicine

MedlinePlus, 69. *See also* Medline; U.S, National Library of Medicine

Mental health, 4, 6, 9, 22, 27, 34–35, 44, 59, 60, 82, 85–86, 88–89, 95, 109, 144, 147, 157, 159, 162, 168, 178, 184. *See also* Instructional units for health

Military and health, 20, 117

Minneapolis public schools, 21–22. *See also* Schools and health care

Montana State University, health curriculums, 34–35. *See also* Curriculum and health; Health literacy

Morgan, Sylvia, 20

Motifs in folklore, 121. *See also* Folklore and mythology and health education; Instructional units for health

Musical theater and health, 103, 109–110. *See also* Instructional units for health; Opera and health

Music and health education, 100. *See also* Instructional units for health; Opera and health

Musicians, classical and health, 107–110. *See also* Instructional units for health

Musicians, popular and health, 110–111. *See also* Instructional units for health

Mythology and health education. *See* Folklore and mythology and health education; Instructional units for health education

Native Americans, 111–112, 114, 139. *See also* Instructional units for health

National Council of Social Studies outstanding trade books, 95

National Health Education Standards (National Cancer Society), 32–35, 38–39. *See also* Guidelines for health education; Standards, health education

National Health Service, (United Kingdom), 9

NLM (National Library of Medicine). *See* U.S. National Library of Medicine

National Public Radio (U.S.). *See* Television and radio as health instruction

National Science Teachers outstanding trade books, 94

National Standards for Foreign Language Education (NSFLE) guidelines, 134

National Theater for the Deaf, 111. *See also* Deaf, education for the

Networking, 207. *See also* Collaboration

Neumark-Sztainer, D., 58–59

New Jersey State Department of Education, 147

North Dakota Health Department, Technology Division, 82–83

North Dakota Standards and Benchmarks Content Standards: Foreign Language (North Dakota Department of Public Instruction), 119–128. *See also* Instructional units of health

Nutrition and health, 2–4, 8–9, 21, 35, 44, 76, 85, 90–91, 108–109, 113, 128, 139, 141, 148, 152, 154, 157, 164, 169, 174, 198–199, 208

Obesity and health, 164. *See also* Diabetes and health

Online learning. *See* Distance and online learning as health instruction

Online searching for health information, 62–66. *See also* Electronic health information resources; Health literacy; Materials and resources for health education, selection criteria for; Professional reference guides for health care; Resources for health education

Opera and health, 108–110. *See also* Biography and health; Instructional units for health; Music and health education

Outcome measures and health education, 36–38. *See also* Instructional units for health

Outreach to the community. *See* Community outreach and planning

Pamphlets. *See* Brochures and pamphlets as health information

Peart, Pamela, 151–152

Pedestrian safety. *See* Traffic safety

Performance activities and health education, 99, 106. *See also* Instructional units of health

Philadelphia Team Leadership program, 58. *See also* Agosto, Denise

Physical education and health, 145–148; Comprehensive programs and, 146–148; history of, 145–146; lesson plans for, 157–159

Pictures in the Air: The Story of the National Theater of the Deaf (Baldwin), 111

Planned Parenthood of America, 95. *See also* Sexual health and education

Policies and policy making, 4, 6–7, 16, 19, 34, 62, 67, 130, 139, 169, 176, 185–186, 196

Predicting the Future: An Introduction to the Theory of Forecasting (Rescher), 205. *See also* Future, predicting the

Professional reference guides for health care, 10–12. *See also* Materials for health care education

Public health, 7–8. *See also* Schools and health care

Publishers and health education, 44–45. *See also* Book purchasing habits

PubMed, 44, 69. *See also* Medline MedlinePlus; U.S. National Library of Medicine

Psychology and psychological health. *See* Mental health

Questioning as health instruction, 24–25

Rescher, Nicholas, 205

Resources for health education, 70–72, 84–90, 209–234. *See also* Electronic health information resources; Health literacy; Materials and resources for health education, selection criteria for; Professional reference guides for health care; Rigney, Mark, and deaf education, 110

Santa Clara County, California, 22. *See also* Schools and health care
School demonstration programs and health, 21–23; *See also* Schools and health care
School librarians, 6, 19, 32, 207. *See also* Librarians and health, role of; Schools and health care
School libraries and curriculum, implications for, 6–18, 45
School library facilities and health information, 207
School library standards, 41–42, 45. *See also* Guidelines for health education; *National Health Education Standards* (National Cancer Society); Standards, health education
Sociology and health, 4, 49, 130, 133–134, 139, 159, 161, 168. *See also* Anthropology and health; *Standards for the 21st Century Learner* (AASL); *Standards for the 21st Century Learning in Action* (AASL)
Schools and health care, 1–2
Scientific education curriculum, 15, 148–151. *See also* Instructional units for health
Scientific reasoning and health education, 150. *See also* Instructional units for health
Searching for health information. *See* Access and searching for health information

Service learning and health education, 36. *See also* Instructional units for health
Sex education. *See* Sexual health and education
Sexual health and education, 60, 148. *See also* Physical education and health (lesson plans); Planned Parenthood of America
Skill-based health education, 2, 4–5, 36, 131–133, 149, 164. *See also* Instructional units for health; UNESCO and health care
Smith, Mark, 15
Smoking and tobacco use, 11, 17–18, 33, 35, 39, 42–43, 59, 76, 89, 138–139, 158, 166–167, 177, 182, 200–201, 206, *See also* Drugs and drug uses; Instructional units for health
Social Sciences and health education, 130–142. *See also* Instructional units for health
Social studies and health curriculum, 5. *See also* Instructional units for health
Social themes, 135–136. *See also* Instructional units for health
Social/moral education curriculum, 17–18
Society and health, 41, 46, 48, 71, 88, 100–101, 103, 124, 128, 132–137, 139, 141–142, 144, 147–149, 156, 177, 184, 187–189. *See also* Instructional units for health; Sociology and health
Society for the Arts in Health Care, 115–116
Sociology and health, 4, 49, 128, 133–134, 139, 159, 162, 168. *See also* Instructional units for health; Society and health

Speaker programs as health instruction, 27. *See also* Instructional units for health
Special child and parents, health information for, 96–97
Spector, M., 20
Sports and health education, 99. *See also* Instructional units for health; Performance activities and health education
Sports medicine. *See* Athletes
South Texas Independent School District, 23, 24, 194. *See also* Schools and health care
Standards for the 21st Century Learner (AASL), 3. *See also* American Association of School Librarians
Standards for the 21st Century Learning in Action (AASL), 3. *See also* American Association of School Librarians
Standards, health education, 35–38. *See also* Guidelines for health education; *National Health Education Standards* (National Cancer Society); TEXSHARE, guidelines for databases
Starr, Lea K., 80–81
Statistics and health education, 151–154. *See also* Instructional units for health; Mathematics and health education
"Stereotype Bias," health education unit, 38–39. *See also* GetHIP; Instructional units for health; Teacher Enrichment and Initiatives; University of Texas Health Science Center, San Antonio, Texas
Story of My Life (Keller), 66. *See also* Biography and

health; Blindness and health; Instructional units for health

Students and health, 5. *See also* Schools and health care; Community outreach and planning

Summer of 1815 and climate changes, 140. *See also* Climate changes and health; Instructional units for health; Weather and health

Teacher Enrichment Initiatives, 38, 159. *See also* GetHIP; Health literacy; University of Texas Health Science Center, San Antonio

Teachers and health instruction, 32–35, 38

Teaching units for health, 38–39, 72–76. *See also* Curriculum models; Curriculum themes and concepts; Instructional units for health

Technology education and health, 168

Television and radio as health instruction, 28

Texas Health Department film library, 95. *See also* Film libraries; Health libraries; U.S. National Library of Medicine

TEXSHARE, guidelines for databases, 67–68

Texas School for the Deaf, 110. *See also* Deaf, education for the

Textbooks and health education, 39–40; adoption of, 155–156. *See also* Materials for health education

Textbooks for health education, 155–156, 231–234; publishers' content descriptions, 156

Themes in health curriculum. *See* Curriculum themes and concepts

Themes, teaching health, 131–133, 141–142. *See also* Instructional units in health

Tobacco, use of. *See* Smoking and tobacco use

Toothbrush drill, New York City public schools, ca. 1913 (historic illustration), 7. *See also* Dental Health

Traffic safety, 5, 33, 95, 119–120, 181–182, 200. *See also* Instructional units for health; Transportation and travel

Transportation and travel, 26, 123, 164, 166, 168, 175–176, 180–181, 196, 202. *See also* Globalization; Instructional units for health; Traffic safety

Travel. *See* Transportation and travel

Travis County, Texas Negro Extension Service, ca. 1950 (historic illustration), 22. *See also* Demonstration programs and health

TRIPS: Agreement on Trade-Related Aspects of Intellectual Property Rights, 187

"Uncle Sam Says 'Garden to Cut Food Cost,'" (historical illustration), 132

United Kingdom, 9, 34, 83. *See also* Great Britain

U.S. Army and health, 20–21

U.S. Centers for Disease Control and Presentation, 2, 8, 146, 147

U.S. Department of Agriculture (USDA), 8, 9, 20, 70, 120, 124, 133, 139, 153, 169, 179–180

U.S. Department of Health and Human Services, 70, 82, 178, 183

U.S. Federal Drug Administration, (FDA), 8, 70, 97

U.S. Marine Hospital Service (USMHS), Laboratory of Hygiene and, 148. *See also* National Institute of Health; Kinyoun, Joseph; Zeiss microscope (historic illustration), and cholera

U.S. National Institute of Health, 95, 148

U.S. National Library of Medicine, 8, 26, 44, 68, 88, 95–96, 120, 139, 197. *See also* Medline, Medline Plus, PubMed

Understanding Health Care Information (Robinson), 81. *See also* Health literacy

UNESCO and health care, 2, 4, 23, 28, 34–35, 131–134, 152–153. *See also* Africa; Skill-based health education

University of Texas at Austin, health courses, 34. *See also* Curriculum and health, Health literacy

University of Texas Health Science Center Library, San Antonio, Texas, 38, 158, 198. *See also* GetHip; Health Literacy; Teacher Enrichment Initiatives

Villaire, Michael, 3

Virtual field trips, 26. *See also* Digitization and health instruction; Field trips and visits

Voice and health, 112–113. *See also* Instruction units for health

Weather and health. 43, 166, 172–174. *See also* Climate change and health; Globalization; Instructional units for health; Little Ice Age; Summer of 1815 and climate changes

WHO. *See* World Health Organization

Women and health. *See* Globalization

World Diabetes Foundation. *See* Diabetes and health

World Health Organization, (WHO), 166, 177, 178. *See also* Africa; UNESCO and health care

Zeiss microscope (historic illustration), and cholera, 148. *See also* Kinyoun, Joseph J.; U.S. Marine Hospital Service (USMHS), Laboratory of Hygiene

About the Authors

W. Bernard Lukenbill is a professor emeritus in the School of Information at the University of Texas at Austin. He earned a Ph.D. from Indiana University. He did his undergraduate work at the University of North Texas. He has worked as a librarian at Seguin High School in Seguin, Texas, and as a references librarian at the Austin College Library, Sherman, Texas. In addition to his position at the University of Texas at Austin, he has served on the faculties at Louisiana Tech University and the University of Maryland, College Park. Dr. Lukenbill's research interests center on children's and adolescent literature, media, communication theory, popular culture, and the sociology of information. He is listed in *Who's Who in America*, the *Directory of American Scholars*, and *Contemporary Authors*. He has presented his research widely in both the United States and internationally.

Barbara Froling Immroth is a professor at the School of Information at the University of Texas at Austin. She earned her Ph.D. from the University of Pittsburgh. She is co-author of *Health Information for Youth* (Libraries Unlimited, 2007). She is the recipient of the Beta Phi Mu Award from the American Library Association and the Texas Library Association Lifetime Achievement Award.